Stewardship Studies

Stewardship

Studies

by ROY L. SMITH

ABINGDON   PRESS
New York • Nashville

STEWARDSHIP STUDIES

Copyright MCMLIV by Pierce & Washabaugh

Library of Congress Catalog Card Number: 54-8242

SET UP, PRINTED, AND BOUND BY THE
PARTHENON PRESS, AT NASHVILLE,
TENNESSEE, UNITED STATES OF AMERICA

Introduction

BISHOP WILLIAM C. MARTIN

*President of the National Council of the Churches of
Christ in the United States of America*

A GOOD BOOK, we say, comes from the mind and heart of an inspired author. This is true. But it is also true that a good book is the response—whether conscious or unconscious—to a need that is acutely felt by many people. Both of these elements were operative in the writing of this interpretation of Christian stewardship.

To Dr. Roy L. Smith, as to few people in this generation, has been given the ability to see through the written Word, as through a window, into the human situation out of which the Word came. When he searches into the deeper meaning of a phrase or a scene from the Scriptures, the reader finds himself constantly saying, "Strange that I did not recognize this truth before." In this volume especially the reader is likely to exclaim over the wealth of scriptural teaching about stewardship on which Dr. Smith is able to focus new light.

Yet continual discovery in the Bible of stewardship implications that lie beneath the surface should not be a matter of surprise when we recall the atmosphere out of which the entire Book comes to us. Its writers experienced such vital and sustained relationship between man and God that they assumed, without conscious effort or special awareness, the recognition of God's ownership and man's trust.

One of the answers to today's alarming threat of materialistic secularism lies in the recovered acknowledgment of that relationship. The author of this book does not believe the recovery will be made on the basis of a narrow legalism. His conviction is that it must be made in terms of a vital personal relationship which includes the whole area of man's outreach toward his fellow man and his upreach toward God.

During a memorable trip to Korea for sixteen days I preached in

5

army chapels and visited at mission stations. Crossing from one to the other I was impressed, and at times depressed, by the wide disparity in the resources available for them—the army maintained by taxation, and the mission work supported by voluntary gifts of church members. Though I begrudged no dollar spent to keep an American soldier warm and well-fed in the Korean winter, I kept asking myself, "Is there not some way the church can rouse itself to enter the wide-open doors of missionary opportunity in a confused and hungry world?"

And the urgent needs closer home must not be overlooked: new churches on the edges of rapidly growing cities, additional space in older churches to provide for the growing tide of children, increased support for our Christian institutions—colleges, hospitals, homes, and orphanages. How can all of these pressing demands be met?

The answer must be found in Christian stewardship. We cannot do everything. We can do something. In this crucial day the least any Christian can do, in good conscience, is to put into the Kingdom's treasury that portion of his income on which the approval of Scripture and the test of experience agree—the tithe. And, as has often happened, in finding the solution for an immediate problem he is sure to discover the answer to a profound and age-old question, "How can man's relation to his material possessions be a source of strength and joy rather than a problem and a pitfall?"

This needed book by a gifted author will prove a stimulating guide to thousands who are searching for new approaches to an established truth and for light to increase their own faith and help them convince others.

A Rewarding Christian Experience

As A COLLEGE student I came under the influence of a pastor who was a vigorous champion of the tithe, and, at his suggestion, I signed a tithing covenant card. But because of an irregular income, fluctuating economic pressure, and undisciplined financial practices, the agreement was kept with no better than a varying degree of fidelity.

A few days following our marriage my bride and I sat down to make our family financial plans. As a result of serious involvement in debt, due to the protracted illness of another member of the home, it was agreed that our income should be tithed but that no effort be made to make actual cash payments until some pressing debts could be liquidated. In the meantime a careful record was to be kept, and "God's account" credited with the tenths of the various sums that were received.

At the end of some months a startling discovery was made. We had accumulated one more creditor and one more debt. We were owing the Lord an amount large enough to give us some concern. Thereupon it was agreed that the plan must be altered. An amount equal to the unpaid tithe was dispatched to the mission board as a payment on a pledge made some weeks before, and from that time forward a tenth was taken out of each dollar before any expenditures from the nine tenths were planned.

In the years that followed it became my rule in five different pastorates to preach on the subject of tithing at least once a year, and sometimes oftener. A serious effort was made to enlist tithers, not for the sake of increasing their contributions to the work of the church, but in the confidence that the habit would produce large spiritual results in the lives of the stewards. From the pulpit, in private conversations, by the distribution of tracts, and in occasional study classes, the principle of the tithe was kept before the people. As a consequence some amazing instances of spiritual development were witnessed.

In 1943 at the invitation of Harry S. Myers, then executive

secretary of the United Stewardship Council (now a department of the National Council of Churches), I began writing a series of comments on the Sunday-school lessons in which the stewardship aspect of the scripture was emphasized. This material was furnished by the council to nearly two hundred writers whose responsibility it was to prepare comments on the Sunday-school lessons. They in turn were at liberty to incorporate the suggestions into their own material, or to publish it over the name of the author, if they preferred. In this way it has received wide currency.

With the completion of a decade of such service I was asked by the Joint Department of Stewardship and Benevolence of the National Council of Churches to make a compilation that could serve as a presentation of the subject of stewardship with a special emphasis on tithing. This necessitated a sifting of nearly six hundred articles, the elimination of duplications, and a rewriting of a majority of the comments to make them conform to an agreed-upon pattern.

Broadly interpreted, stewardship means "responsibility"; and the term is often used to describe much more than the simple principle of the tithe. In this collection of studies, however, the original root meaning of the word "economics" has been emphasized with the result that the tenth has been given conspicuous attention.

It will be noticed that the material falls into two general classes: that which deals directly and actually with scripture associated with the principle of the tithe, and that which can be interpreted legitimately in terms of economic implications. No attempt has been made to set forth a consecutive argument. The collection is designed instead as a series of studies, each one presenting some fragmentary aspect of the general principle.

Throughout our entire experience in the Christian ministry my wife and I have adhered to the principle of the tithe, not as a slavish obedience to a law but as a confident expression of faith. After an experience that has continued for more than forty years, we are prepared to bear our testimony to the fact that God honors the confidence men put in him when they accept his challenge to "prove me now herewith" (Mal. 3:10 K.J.V.) or, as the Revised Standard Version expresses it, "Put me to the test." No single religious exercise has contributed more to our spiritual life than the habit of laying by in store one tenth, as the Lord has prospered us. This book, then, is a preachment and a testimony, offered in the complete assurance that God will prove himself to any honest Christian who will accept the challenge.

Roy L. Smith

8

Contents

9

10

According to the astronomers the great telescope atop Mount Palomar in California has made it possible for man to look out into space for a distance of at least one billion light years. Whereas the ancients were familiar with a few thousand stars, today's scientist is within sight of millions. And out of that knowledge one amazing fact emerges. Nowhere in all the starry spaces is there another planet, so far as the astronomers can positively affirm, whereon there is to be found any living being. This earth of ours, one of the tiniest specks in all the universe, is the one place where we *know* there is anything like a personality.

This means that our earth is the only speck on which a song is ever heard, a poem written, a philosophy developed, a government formed, an ideal achieved, or God worshiped.

"Man is only the tiniest and most infinitesimal speck, astronomically speaking," a skeptic said contemptuously; to which a great scientist replied, "Astronomically speaking, man is the astronomer." As a personality he is more important than the constellations, the nebulae, or anything they contain. Jesus had this same fact in mind when he said that it was a stupid thing to give one's soul for even the whole world. To be made in the image of God is to be set apart and above any other thing in all creation, except another personality.

For any creature so endowed and so designed to live as a slave to things—to be the servant of possessions—is to be a victim of a terrible embezzlement of life.

For a man made in the image of God to spend all his days as the servant of a machine, as the owner of a farm, as the manager of a business, whose life and destiny are determined by his possessions, is high tragedy. One of the prime functions of good religion is to provide deliverance, and it is exactly at this point that the doctrine of stewardship demonstrates its value.

"I never really felt that I had risen above my possessions and was their master until I began tithing," said a layman whose religious experience was highly satisfactory. "For years I accepted dictation from my business. I was its servant. Then I declared my independence. I turned it over to God, accepted a stewardship, and have been its manager ever since. It gives me a feeling of freedom."

²⁶ *God said, ". . . Let them have dominion."*

THE WORLD into which man has been thrust by the act of creation
is an amazing one, pulsing with energy, infinite in its possibilities,
and almost incredibly varied in its potentialities. And he has been
given the authority to use the earth and make the most possible out
of the life it will support.

The revelations of the nuclear scientists make it plain that up to
this point in human history we have hardly been even toying with
the fringes of power that are resident in the earth. What a world
it can become, and what glorious possibilities await mankind, if the
doctrine of stewardship can be injected into the situation alongside
the infinite powers that are breaking through the seams.

Stewardship is the religious name we have applied to the doctrine
of dominion and responsibility, but the courts have applied the
philosophy through many centuries. The farmer is, in most states,
held responsible for the stock he allows to wander on the highway;
the factory is held responsible for the fumes generated in its labora-
tories; the housewife is held responsible for the disposal of her gar-
bage; the factory owner is held responsible for the safety of his workers; and in recent years the doctrine has developed that industry is
responsible for the old-age care of those workers who have given
their lives to its operation. Everywhere we turn, the doctrine emerges
in some form or other.

Tithing, as a method of computing one's stewardship, roots down
in something far more significant than the Sunday morning church
collection. It is, actually, a tangible acceptance of this doctrine of
dominion as it is applied to the strictly religious and philanthropic
responsibilities with which every man is confronted. The churchman,
no more than any other man, is responsible for the maintenance of
the spiritual life of the race. That individual who lives in a community, gets the benefit of all its cultural and religious activities and
values, and makes no contribution to them, is living off public charity
as surely as that one who is on relief.

All wealth, like all life, is a gift from God, and the gift of dominion
is perhaps the greatest gift of all. Tithing is not a device for raising
money, though it will accomplish that purpose. It is a solemn acceptance of a relationship with God which becomes of the most
intimate significance.

[17] *Of the tree of the knowledge of good and evil you shall not eat.*

BASIC IN the economic and religious philosophy of the ancient Hebrews was the thought that God is the owner of all things and that man acts as his agent in administering his property matters. As such he is responsible to God.

In the story of the garden of Eden this concept is set forth in unmistakable terms. According to the account in Genesis man was established in the midst of delectable circumstances with the privilege of using everything in sight *except the fruits of one tree.* No explanation is made as to why that particular restriction was made, but that some restriction was laid upon the race is central in the theme. Man's rights in the garden depended upon the faithfulness with which he observed the restriction.

Whether the story of the garden of Eden is accepted as sober history or as allegory, the lesson of the case is the same, and its moral and spiritual significance is identical. God is the owner of the property, man is the tenant, and the rules are laid down for him. As he keeps the faith, he keeps his privilege. God never abdicates his position as the proprietor of this earth.

In a certain city there was a worthy institution engaged in public service that was badly in need of a piece of valuable real estate. The owner was a man entirely sympathetic with the work that was being done, and the use to which his property was to be put. He was quite willing to contribute the land, but for purely personal reasons he did not want to make it as an outright gift. He therefore executed papers that conveyed the plot to the institution for a period of years on the condition that an annual rental of one dollar should be paid. He did not need the money, and the payment certainly was no hardship, but it maintained the fact of the donor's ownership.

By similar logic the tithe is the token that God expects from those who use the property he has furnished. The payment thereof is an acknowledgment of his ownership in perpetuity. We do not actually *give* to God when we make payments to those causes in which he has especial interest. We make payments which become, in effect, an acknowledgment of God's ownership of all we possess. The tenth can be called the "fruit of the tree of knowledge," to which we have never had any proprietary rights.

⁹ *Then the Lord said to Cain, "Where is Abel your brother?" He said, "I do not know; am I my brother's keeper?"*

THE MAJESTIC quality of those early chapters of Genesis does not arise from any historicity of the events they record, but from the profound significance of the moral and spiritual issues they raise. Nowhere else in all the field of literature does the human mind come to grips with so impressive a series of basic questions in such a brief compass.

The origin of the universe itself, the fact that all the earth is subject to a moral authority outside itself, the explanation for the appearance of the human race, the amazing diversity of the races, the problem of pain—these are but a few of the great questions with which the writer (or writers) wrestled in producing this amazing work.

The problem of the moral responsibility of the individual—his stewardship for society, if you prefer—is faced with complete candor and the judgment rendered. "Am I my brother's keeper?" the killer cries, and the answer is an unequivocal declaration of responsibility.

Again and again the scriptures declare, first in one phrasing and then in another, that no man lives unto himself and that every man is under a sacred responsibility to his fellows. The very fact that he is a member of society—an individual living in the midst of an organized state and the beneficiary of social institutions—involves him in a long series of responsibilities from which there can be no escape.

There are situations in which each of us holds the safety, property, comfort, and the very life of other individuals in our hands, just as there are other situations in which our happiness, success, peace, and privilege are dependent upon the decisions and judgments of others. The doctrine of stewardship which assigns responsibility in such cases is one of the principles which provide society with coherence. Without it no civilization would be possible.

It was not necessary for Cain to have struck his brother in order that he should become responsible for his death. Had he allowed him to die through neglect, his guilt would have been equally great. This means that in the eyes of God the blood of all those who cry to us from slave labor camps, concentration camps, refugee hostels, and orphanages becomes a charge against our account which cannot be dismissed with a smug denial of responsibility.

³ I will bless those who bless you, and him who curses you I will curse; and by you all the families of the earth will bless themselves.

Every Christian is absolutely essential to the cause of the kingdom of Heaven at some place and in some way. Each day we live there is at least some period during which we are the sole representative of Jesus Christ. If our Lord is to have any testimony in such a situation, we are the ones who must offer it.

An old gentleman was looking at a church that had stood on a prominent corner of the city for many years. Turning to a friend, he said, "I suppose it is a little silly, but years ago when I was a boy I made a pledge to the building of this church, and I paid it. The whole transaction made a very deep impression on me at the time, for I was only a youngster, and though the pledge was not a big one in terms of dollars, it was a big one to me, for it was the first time I had ever tried to help put up a church.

"Just because I invested fifteen dollars in this church as a boy I never get into this part of the state that I do not try to get over here and have a look at 'my church.' And I have sometimes tried to imagine that some of the bricks in that old wall are actually mine—that I paid for them and that at least a small section of the wall is my personal contribution to the building. It gives me a sense of importance. I like to think that the kingdom of God depended upon me at one time, and that there might have been a hole in this wall if I had not paid my pledge."

Who is to say that the old gentleman was wrong in his fancy? It is probably true that, if he had not given his fifteen dollars as a boy, someone else would have been found who could have supplied that much more. But he had a right to assure himself that a part of the wall was his. That is the glory of that kind of wall. It is made up of the bricks supplied by good stewards, each one furnishing his proportionate share.

Into the hands of each of us, as into the life of Abram, God has guided some measure of the good things of the earth, and from each of us, "as he may prosper" (I Cor. 16:2), is expected the gift which represents his stewardship. Let each gift be made, therefore, with the confidence that "out there somewhere on the long line" our contribution is helping hold the fortification.

²⁰ *And Abram gave him a tenth of everything.*

THE FIRST mention of the payment of tithes to be found in the Old Testament occurs in Gen. 14:17-21, in which the story of one of Abram's exploits is told. The story appears in a very sketchy form with no more than a few facts given; and because of serious doubts as to the historical accuracy of the account of the wars of the four kings (Gen. 14:17) it is dangerous to use the record as the basis for any major doctrine. That portion which introduces Melchizedek is of much value, however, in at least one particular: it establishes the fact that the custom of paying the tithe is of great antiquity.

The name Salem was an ancient form of the more modern name Jerusalem (see also Ps. 76:2). In the Tell el-Amarna tablets (dated around 1400 B.C.) the city is described as one of the most important towns of Canaan and is called Uru-salim, or "the city of the god Salim."

The root "Zedek" is to be found in the names of several of the ancient Salem (or Jerusalem) kings, and it seems reasonable to assume that Melchizedek was the chief or ruling priest of the local temple. The priests of Zadok who are met on numerous occasions in the Old Testament (II Sam. 8:17; 15:24, 25; 18:19; I Kings 1:8; 2:35; 4:4; I Chron. 6:8; 15:11; 24:3) were a distinct order, quite apart from the Levites, and the descendants of the original pagan cultists. They seem to have accepted the worship of Jehovah (or Yahweh) at the time of David's capture of the city, and because of the prestige they carried over from their pagan days, they enjoyed great favor at the hands of the people. Rivalry between them and the Levitical priests sometimes became very intense.

According to an ancient Babylonian custom it was expected that a king returning from a successful military adventure would present gifts at the shrine of Salem in token of his gratitude for the aid rendered him by the god, these gifts taking the form of tithes of the loot or other goods. As the ruling priest of the pagan temple in Uru-salim, Melchizedek was the one designated to receive the gifts from Abram. The blessing he pronounced on the patriarch is one which appears in several other Aramaic inscriptions of the same historical period.

The record that Abram paid tithes to Melchizedek establishes the fact that tithing was a religious custom which antedated the formation of the Hebrew kingdom by many centuries.

¹ *After these things the word of the Lord came to Abram in a vision,*
"Fear not, Abram, I am your shield; your reward shall be very great."

FROM THAT moment in which God revealed to Abram the unique
and thrilling destiny that attended him, the old patriarch was unable
to live like an ordinary person. He had been called and chosen. That
simple fact altered every decision he might have made from that
day onward.

Charles Leber, the secretary of the Presbyterian Board of Foreign
Missions, tells the story of an old black man he met in Africa who
seemed to be doing a strange thing. Now and again in the course
of his day's work the aged one would stop, lay his hand solemnly on
the top of his head, move his lips as though in prayer, and, this
completed, would proceed with his task.

"He has been a Christian for some years now," the missionary
explains, "and he carries in his memory a very vivid impression
which attended his baptism. It meant that from that moment on
he must live an entirely new and different type of life. Now,
when he finds himself confronted with some new responsibility,
temptation, or bewilderment, he stops, lays his right hand on his
head at the spot where the baptismal water was placed, and says to
himself, 'You are a baptized person.' That seems to steady him and
to open up for him the sources of power. And it is amazing how
the dear old saint has grown as a person and as a Christian."

God has called every Christian to be different. The simple
ceremony of baptism, if it has any meaning whatever, is a call—a
challenge, if you please—to each baptized person to be a new
creature.

The Christian will accept his standards and values from the
New Testament, rather than from his political party, his labor
union, his chamber of commerce, his college fraternity, or his social
classification.

The baptized person is under a sacred obligation to God to stop
in the presence of every bit of compensation or profit he receives
and say, "I have been baptized in the name of One who died on
the cross for me." Before we squander our resources, God calls us
to consider our stewardship of that which has been entrusted to our
care and keeping. Surely it is not asking too much of a Christian,
who has been redeemed by the sacrifice of Christ on the cross, to
suggest that he tithe his income for the spreading of the good news.

[25] *Far be it from thee to do such a thing, to slay the righteous with the wicked, so that the righteous fare as the wicked! Far be that from thee! Shall not the Judge of all the earth do right?*

HE WAS a junior executive in a giant business organization and had come to his pastor in a greatly troubled state of mind. A situation prevailed in his industry that outraged his sense of justice. "I cannot believe God is neutral in this case," he said very positively. "I know I cannot be, and surely God is as sensitive in such things as I am."

There was something of this same mood in the mind of Abraham when, in evaluating certain situations in the life of the ancient East, he said, "Shall not the Judge of all the earth do right?" Honorable men expect their God to measure up at least to as high standards as they maintain in their own thinking.

It can surely be said, therefore, that anything that outrages the moral sensibilities of a righteous man must have the same effect on the heart and conscience of the Almighty. If men loathe injustice, selfishness, and callousness, what must God's attitude be?

Jesus left the impression that the God whom he called "Father" was just such a deity. It is impossible to believe he would be neutral if a city's morals were being despoiled by avaricious landlords who were more concerned about rentals than they were about renters. It is equally impossible to believe that he would be neutral when strikers terrorized the families of other workers with whom they had a quarrel. Certainly no Christian can believe that God, the Father of our Lord, would have no concern for the fate of millions who starve in the wake of war, nor would he be complacent while those who have been spared from the ravages of the conflict feast sumptuously every day in the presence of their brethren who are in dire need.

If God cannot be neutral, is it possible for Christians to be indifferent? Can any Christian defend himself successfully against the charge of callousness if he hears the cries of the sufferers and makes no effort to relieve their sufferings in Jesus' name?

Wherever justice is endangered, there the Christian steward has his responsibility cut out for him. Wherever other Christians are starving, there we may expect to find our Lord calling from their midst.

22

⁹ How have I sinned against you, that you have brought on me and my kingdom a great sin? You have done to me things that ought not to be done.

ELBERT HUBBARD, the brilliant eccentric once printed on the front cover page of his magazine, *The Philistine,* this wholesome advice:

Remember the Weekday and Keep It Holy

This is to say that there is a sanctity about labor which is as real and as significant as any worship.

A clever young woman who possessed great skill as a private secretary left her employment in an insurance office and took a position as the confidential assistant to the manager of a distillery. When her pastor remonstrated with her on the matter, she replied, "But one has to make a living, you know, and this new job will pay me ten dollars a week more than the insurance office did."

A young college man with a magnificent voice was offered a position with a night club. The salary offered him was sufficient to pay all his school expenses and enable him to live in style. "I am preparing to serve mankind," he explained to a Christian friend, "and if the night club is willing to pay me well, why should I not take the money if I am to use it for a good cause." Thus did a young Christian misconceive his stewardship.

A man who had served as a Sunday-school superintendent, and who was one of the leaders of the church, came into the possession of a small estate quite unexpectedly. He had always worked on a modest salary. This was the first time in his life that he had ever attempted to invest money; and in his eagerness to invest wisely, he consulted his pastor, confessing his intention of investing in a certain enterprise that was at the moment paying a handsome dividend. "But they have the reputation for paying their girls the lowest wages offered in this city," the preacher warned him. "I am not going to be responsible for their labor policy," the Sunday-school superintendent said. "I am interested in dividends on my money." And that was the way he misconceived his stewardship of his inheritance.

If God holds us to a strict account for the way we cast our ballots, perform our daily tasks, meet our obligations at the grocer's and the butcher's, and keep our word, is it conceivable that he is not concerned with our stewardship of our labor?

²² *This stone, which I have set up for a pillar, shall be God's house; and of all that thou givest me I will give the tenth to thee.*

THE SECOND Old Testament mention of the tithe occurs in the story of Jacob's prayer at Bethel on the occasion when he saw the ladder stretching from earth to heaven and angels ascending and descending.

At the time the record was written, the Bethel shrine was very old. Numerous customs and traditions, including the payment of tithes to the officiating priests, had grown up around its services and observances. The story of Jacob's original experience on the spot was intended to be an explanation of the shrine's founding, and Jacob's vow was reported as the explanation of the custom of tithing there.

Quite apart from any question concerning the history of the shrine at Bethel, the story of Jacob's vow is extremely revealing. He is portrayed as a young man quite incapable of any moral magnificence or ethical distinction. His prayer is a contemptible effort to strike up a favorable bargain with God, the terms of which are to be fixed by the sinner. Whatever he may have become in later years, under the guidance of God, the youngster is made to appear as a cheap and vulgar character at Bethel.

Jacob had just deceived his father, defrauded his brother, connived with his mother in seeking an illegal and unfair advantage, and was now in full flight in an effort to escape the well-earned wrath of his father, Isaac. In his dream he has a tremendous vision of God; and quite without either reverence or repentance, but with an indecent effrontery, he offers the Almighty the terms upon the basis of which he is ready to serve him. He will do great things for God, but only after God has done greater things—ten times greater—for him.

We shall do well, however, if we are a bit cautious about heaping condemnation upon Jacob. The disposition to deal with God on a barter basis is also a modern attitude. It even happens sometimes that the tithe is preached as though it were a very advantageous way to bribe God. It sounds like good business to promise one tenth if we can be sure of a larger nine tenths, but it is very poor religion.

The Christian doctrine of tithing rests down upon the solid and reverent conviction that all property is God's and that man is only the divinely appointed administrator who pays his tithe as a token.

¹⁵ *The Lord said to Moses, "Why do you cry to me? Tell the people of Israel to go forward."*

A VERY great deal of the confusion that exists in the realm of religion is due to a misconception of what faith is. There are those who assume it to be nothing more than a blind acceptance of the incredible, the unreasonable, or the unproved. Others think it is a supine surrender to the inevitable. They say, very piously, "God's will must be done," but what they actually mean is, "We are helpless to do anything about it, and we must therefore suffer any burden God lays on us."

True faith, however, is an eager and enthusiastic acceptance of that which is believed to be the will of God, and a courageous acting upon the best judgment we can bring to bear on the situation. It is a confident performance of those duties to which God seems to have assigned us. As a small boy prayed one morning at the breakfast table, "Lord, help us to do today what we've got to do, and do it without squawkin'."

It is as if one were to say, "The will of God must be done for the sake of the good of all, and I propose to be the one who does it."

When Jesus prayed, "Not my will, but thine, be done" (Luke 22:42), he was not reluctantly accepting the inevitable or that from which there was no possible escape. Instead, he was confidently declaring his inflexible determination to *do* the thing which appeared to be the will of God. If he had accepted his assignment reluctantly or with any spirit of rebellion within his heart, he would never have become the world's Redeemer. His faith had a quality of confident joy about it that issued in forthright action.

The man of faith does not demand that God shall demonstrate himself, his power, or his approval. He lives as though God were dependable, and acts as though he were perfectly sure that God will not fail him but will meet him at the end of the trail and that the two of them will rejoice together.

That form of faith which proceeds fearfully, joylessly, cynically, or dismally, even though it proceeds dutifully, is not the kind of loyalty God seeks among his children. He who says reproachfully, "I guess it is the will of God, and I shall have to do it," is actually saying, "If I had my way in the matter, I certainly would not." And there is no joy in that.

Whether we give, apologize, make restitution, or repent, let it be done with joy, as though we were initiating a good work.

¹⁵ *You shall not steal.*

THERE WAS a time when stealing was a relatively simple matter. It consisted of taking property that belonged to another, probably by stealth. And that other person was someone within easy reach. This, of course, is still stealing.

As life has become more complicated, however, stealing has likewise. Today thieves steal from those who may live thousands of miles away. On the other hand, the thieves may be stealing from those who are members with them in the same church, lodge, neighborhood, or even from members of their own families.

There was a group of businessmen, for example, who arranged to float a bond issue to finance an industrial enterprise. By various devices the project was made to appear like an exceptionally good investment in spite of the fact that its promoters were well aware of its dubious character. Innocent people invested their funds, many of them having no knowledge concerning the identity of the promoters. When the crash came, few people knew that the projectors of the scheme had protected themselves by getting out before the crash. And they all attended the same church, met at dinner parties, and lived in the same neighborhood. In such a way sin is made to appear innocent and the sinner is completely disguised.

At this point the doctrine of stewardship enters into the consideration very intimately. The genuine steward will not only undertake to give as in the sight of God; he will also undertake to earn according to the same principle.

"No, I do not think I can afford to put any of my money into that proposition," one careful steward said. "You see, the money I invest is, after all, the Lord's. I am only his agent. And I do not think he would be very happy if he knew that I had put up some of his funds for that kind of business." And thus he decided the question of investing in a proposition that promised big returns from a questionable enterprise.

A great distance separates the investor from the board of managers of the corporation, and a great many Christian dollars are engaged in business enterprises of which the Lord Christ could not possibly approve. Whether by ignorance or by carelessness, however, the investor is responsible at least in part for any of the thievery of which such dollars are guilty. No more solemn obligation rests upon any Christian than this, that he manage his money properly when it goes out looking for interest.

¹⁷ *You shall not covet your neighbor's house; you shall not covet your neighbor's wife, or his manservant, or his maidservant, or his ox, or his ass, or anything that is your neighbor's.*

GREED is a disease to which no man, rich or poor, is ever immune until he has experienced a work of divine grace.

It is all too commonly assumed that greed is a malady peculiar to the rich, but such is not the case. It frequently appears in its most loathsome form among those who live from hand to mouth.

The spiritual disease called greed consists of a hardening of the heart, an insensitivity of the spirit, a paralysis of the generous emotions, and an atrophy of all the graces of friendliness and concern.

The greedy man does not hesitate to operate for profit a business that thrives on the weaknesses of his fellows; he will sabotage any honorable enterprise for the sake of his personal profit; he sleeps soundly the night following the day he robs another man of all his security.

Greed usually begins with a due and praiseworthy concern for the necessities of tomorrow, but it grows as fancy multiplies these necessities out of wants. In all the record of the race there is no instance of a greedy man being a happy man. There is something about the disease that destroys all joy, whether it be the joy of the greedy or the joy of his victim.

So far as the science of psychology knows, there is no cure for the disease, which is in itself a spiritual affliction, except an entirely new concept of the meaning and privilege of life—an experience that must be accompanied by a profound religious experience. A "conversion" that leaves a man's economic interests untouched can hardly be called a conversion.

It is one of the unfortunate but common facts of our modern life that the greedy always organize for the purpose of protecting their greedy designs. This makes it necessary for the generous also to organize. Restricting the covetous by law is one of the most serious problems of government. To keep the door of opportunity open for the generous and to lock it against the greedy calls for discretion and judgment of a superlative quality.

The doctrine of stewardship is the richest contribution religion makes to life at this point. Once the individual accepts the fact that God is the owner of everything and that man is his steward, responsible and dedicated, the way is cleared for the solution of many problems.

²⁹ *You shall not delay to offer from the fulness of your harvest and from the outflow of your presses.*

WHEN THE Children of Israel forced their way into the Promised Land, they overran an ancient and superior civilization without destroying it. Because they were untrained in the military science of the time, and because they were not equipped to break down the high stone walls that surrounded the cities, they were able to take possession of the farm lands but were relatively helpless against the fortified cities.

This meant that the Canaanites were bottled up inside their towns and behind their walls. In the course of time they contrived to make peace of a sort with the invaders by which they exchanged their knowledge of agriculture for a degree of freedom. Oddly enough, they actually became landlords and teachers in some instances.

Basic in the Canaanite religion was the principle of fertility, and their gods were saturated with the sex motif. Sex practices of all kinds, some of them actual perversions, were engaged in at the shrines with religious sanction. Inasmuch as the Hebrews had not yet arrived at any clear monotheistic concept, they tolerated and, in many instances, participated in these practices.

In the first years of their occupation of the land certain shrines were designated (Deut. 12:5) as the centers to which the people should come with their "first fruits" for the purpose of rendering their thanks and expressing their gratitude for the "increase" of their crops and the fecundity of their flocks. These festivities took on much of the spirit of that first Thanksgiving observed by the Pilgrim Fathers in the New World. They were occasions of hilarity, feasting, and rejoicing, festive in every respect.

The distinguishing characteristic of the Israelite observances was the religious significance attached to feasts and offerings. The presentation of the "first fruits" and the "firstlings" of the flocks was an acknowledgment that "the earth is the Lord's" (Ps. 24:1; 50:12; 89:11; I Cor. 10:26).

In connection with these feasts the people were expected to present their tithes, this being an indication that the offerings were a matter of strict regulation and not merely a question of individual generosity or inclination. This scripture, taken from the oldest textual material in the Bible, is highly significant.

*[11] But if he cannot afford two turtledoves or two young pigeons,
then he shall bring, as his offering for the sin which he has committed,
a tenth of an ephah of fine flour for a sin offering.*

ONE WILL search in vain in the Old Testament or the New for
an explanation as to why the "tenth" was chosen as the proportionate gift that would be acceptable unto God. Why it was not a
sixth, or a twelfth, or a seventeenth, no man knows. Among the
Hebrews the numeral seven had a holy significance. Just as we
speak of 100 per cent as being typical of perfection, so the Hebrew
spoke in terms of seven, like the "seventh son of the seventh son."
Those who came to Jesus asking him for a model of forgiveness
asked if they should forgive "seven times" (Matt. 18:21), suggesting thereby that such forgiveness would be perfect. It is a little
odd, therefore, that the seventh was not established as the rule of
giving. But it was not. Instead, time and the Law endorsed the
tenth.

Special consideration was given in the Hebrew Law in the case
of those who were very poor. In coming to the altar as penitents
they were permitted to bring a pair of pigeons (the most common
and least expensive birds) if the sacrifice were accompanied by
the spirit of penitence (Lev. 5:5-10), the gift being the material
evidence of the spiritual attitude of sorrow for sin. If the destitute
lacked the pigeons, they might substitute a tenth of an ephah of
fine flour (about one gallon); but none were entirely excused from
giving, it being assumed that every person should give something
as a sacrifice unto the Lord.

That there is much merit in proportional giving quite apart from
tithing goes without saying. If one gives a twentieth, or even a
fiftieth, of his income and does it methodically and faithfully, he
will gain a spiritual blessing greatly superior to that enjoyed by
the occasional or casual giver. But the tenth bears the imprint of
great antiquity. It is the standard that has served throughout all
Hebrew and Christian history, and is not to be discarded without
extremely good reason. And it should be said that no such sufficient,
sanctioned reason is to be found anywhere in the Scriptures.

If Christians hold themselves under an obligation to keep the
Sabbath because it is the day set apart by God for worship, then
there are equally convincing grounds for honoring the tradition of
giving the tenth as a standard of giving. One is as firmly embedded
in the Scriptures as the other.

²³ *The land shall not be sold in perpetuity, for the land is mine; for you are strangers and sojourners with me.*

MODERN agronomists, soil chemists, and conservationists may be using a new vocabulary and a different technique, but they are dealing with a very old problem as they try to conserve the values of the land. The Hebrew lawmakers of three thousand years ago knew at least something about the stewardship of the soil, and, with a philosophy thousands of years ahead of their times, they undertook to stand guard over the good earth.

Every living thing upon the face of this earth is dependent upon the maintenance of this infinitesimal veneer of fertility with which the hard core of the earth is covered. That which has been called "the planet's skin"—the top four inches of productive soil—contains all the vitamins and life-giving chemicals upon which all plants, animals, and human beings depend. To waste the soil, to allow it to wash down to the sea, is to commit racial suicide.

It may not be an explicit part of the responsibility of the Church to supervise the soil conservation program of the nation or of a community, but it is the duty of the Church to preach the doctrine of stewardship as applied to our natural resources. Rural pastors in particular live under a solemn charge at this point. To squander the productive earth is to plunder the unborn generations. In every community the Church of Jesus Christ should be among the best friends of those who are laboring to conserve the good things of the earth.

To preach the doctrine of stewardship to those who till the earth and cut the forests is a highly responsible ministry. Contour plowing, reforestation, scientific fertilizing, and reclamation projects have deeper theological implications than usually appear on the surface.

Conservation of natural resources is not merely a problem of legislation, in which one follows the pattern of his political party leaders, but a stewardship in which the humblest citizen must share. When we enter the balloting booth or put a plow into the soil, we may be dealing with the destiny of unborn generations. The way we administer our stewardship may mean the difference between plenty and want for those who come after us. Being a good Christian means, of course, being a good citizen. It is impossible to draw any line between good religion and a wise use of God's gracious gifts.

[30] *All the tithe of the land, whether of the seed of the land or of the fruit of the trees, is the Lord's; it is holy to the Lord.*

THE GREAT problem that the Jews of the Exile had to face was a very simple one: *Why had God allowed the Hebrew nation to be destroyed?* Were not the Children of Israel the chosen people? Had not God entered into a solemn covenant with their fathers at Sinai? Had he not agreed to guide, defend, and prosper them? What, then, was the meaning of the terrible catastrophe that had overtaken them when the Babylonians breached the walls of Jerusalem and led the thousands of captives across the desert sands to the valleys of the Tigris and Euphrates? Had Jehovah been overpowered by the Babylonian god, Marduk? If so, would it not be better for the Israelites to turn to the pagan deity and worship him? Certainly they wanted an ally that could be relied upon.

This problem engaged the bravest minds and the most stalwart faith of the people through a period of at least seventy years. The learned and devout among them gave their utmost care and most persistent thought to the matter, and in the process pored over the ancient codes and literature that had come down to them from their fathers.

Finally, as a result of the combined intellectual and spiritual efforts of their finest minds, it was agreed that the unhappy fate of the nation was due to the fact that their fathers had broken the laws of God, and that if ever there were to be a restoration of the nation it could be possible only as a result of the nation's obedience to the will of God. Therefore faithfulness to the Law became the test of every man's patriotism.

In order that no man might be left in ignorance of the Law, a great "Book of the Law" was compiled by the priests, scribes, doctors of the law, scholars, and devout citizens. This was a harmonization of all the ancient codes, organized into one complete whole designed to form the basis of the new government that would be set up when the nation was restored to the Land of Promise. Originally it was issued in one huge volume, but in our English Bible it appears as five books (Genesis, Exodus, Leviticus, Numbers, Deuteronomy) and is known as the Pentateuch.

One of the laws that had been ignored and, according to the scholars, would have to be restored was that of the tithe. It belonged to the Lord and could not be evaded.

> [3] *Why does the Lord bring us into this land, to fall by the sword?*
> *Our wives and our little ones will become a prey; would it not be*
> *better for us to go back to Egypt?*

THE WORD "security" has come to have an almost hypnotic fascination for our generation. Politicians, economists, psychologists, and demagogues all vie with one another in offering their particular brands of "peace of mind" to the public. Every month's list of best sellers includes at least one book that professes to describe the highway to the delectable "land of no concerns."

As the Children of Israel journeyed through the desert, they realized that back in Egypt they had enjoyed security—of a sort. The lush valley of the Nile had produced abundantly; the warm African sun had answered so many of the needs that now pressed them. The change of diet from the vegetables that grew in abundance in Egyptian patches had started a whole series of digestive disturbances. The wandering tribes of nomads that hovered along their flanks, constantly threatening them, appeared so very menacing. It is easy to understand how a people without political or military experience might succumb to terror and beg to be led back again to the comfort and the slavery of their taskmasters.

There are those in every generation and among all peoples who are ready to return to the lashes and the bondage of Egypt, rather than face the hardships and the privations that are a necessary and inseparable part of the Promised Land. This seems to be one of the basic principles of history: crises produce heroes, and prosperity produces paralysis. The greatest hours through which the Children of Israel ever lived were those that found them facing the most insuperable odds.

All the great promises of God are to those who go on with the struggle, who keep up the fight for righteousness, who suffer the wounds and undergo the privations that are incident to a great conflict against evil. It is to those who persevere, go on with their work, maintain their spiritual disciplines, continue to make heroic efforts, resist evil temptations, and suffer indignities for their faith that the assurances of victory are offered.

"I think I might have given up if it had not been for my lifelong habit of tithing," she said. "My salary had been cut three times, and I thought I had economized in every way possible. But I tithed as an act of faith, and every time I gave a dollar to some good cause, it aroused my hope. I trusted in God afresh, and at last I came through. My tithing did it."

[21] To the Levites I have given every tithe in Israel for an inheritance, in return for their service which they serve, their service in the tent of meeting.

THE CAREFUL student experiences no little difficulty in unraveling the various strands of Hebrew history because the records contradict themselves frequently. The historian who tries to trace the origins of the Levites is in a particularly embarrassing position.

We know that Moses, the founder of the Hebrew state, and the architect of its religious system, was a member of the tribe of Levi (Exod. 32:26-29), if it can actually be said that there was such a tribe in the original community. With the establishment of Aaron, Moses' brother, as the priestly head of the nation, it was perfectly natural that other members of the tribe should be recruited to assist him in administering the divine oracle, offering incense, supervising the sacrifices, and instructing the people (Num. 18:2).

When the tribes forced their way into the Promised Land, the heads of families were allotted tracts of land, and the tribes were given their specific boundaries. This was not so in the case of the Levites, who were left landless and scattered throughout the nation to serve as priests wherever their services might be required (Judg. 17:7-9). Even one of Moses' grandsons was so employed (Judg. 18:30).

The position of the Levites as spiritual ministers to the people is clearly defined, as is also the provision for their support. They were to receive a tithe of the agricultural produce of the land (Num. 18:21, 27), though at least one mention is made of the tithe of animals (Lev. 27:30-33) that was to be paid to the Lord. This means, if we are to accept the statistics of the book of Numbers, that 22,000 priests (Levites) were supported by 600,000 citizens.

According to another scripture (Deut. 14:22-29), the tithe payer ate his tithe in the course of a family feast to which the Levite was invited as an honored guest two years out of each three, the total tithe going to the Levite on the third year. But it is perfectly clear that the tithe was for the support of a priestly class that served no civil function. Their services were strictly religious or ecclesiastical, and the tithing system was devised for the support of the nation's religious system. This consecration of the tenth to spiritual purposes is the essential fact in the whole consideration.

26 When you take from the people of Israel the tithe which I have given you from them for your inheritance, then you shall present an offering from it to the Lord, a tithe of the tithe.

THE SPIRIT of democracy is conspicuous in the history of the Hebrew people. There was a spirit of equality and fraternity among them that was to be found in no other race of antiquity. They had their royal families, but there was no "ruling class" or aristocracy of the blood. In a remarkable degree all men stood on an equal footing.

The Levites were set apart from the beginning as a priestly class, and their status and support were closely guarded, but their unique function as ministers to the spiritual life of the people did not exempt them from the principle of the tithe. They were specifically required to offer a "heave offering"—a tithe of the tithe paid to them —unto the Lord (Num. 18:26).

Five young couples, all theological students, were discussing their personal plans for their school years. "We do not feel under any obligation to tithe," one of the young men said. "We are giving our lives to the church, our income is almost negligible during these school years, and what little we earn we are investing in our preparation. That is all that should be asked of us." Three of the other couples agreed with him, and during the three years these four couples did not tithe.

The fifth couple took an entirely different view of the matter. "The ancient Levites were expected to tithe," the young wife said, "and we cannot find anything in the Scriptures that promises us any special privilege or exemption. If we ask our people to tithe their income when times are hard, we can scarcely expect to be excused when our own income is small. However, we think of tithing as an expression of our faith in the good promises of God, and these seem to us to be as valid in bad times as in prosperous days. If God cannot be trusted during the dark days, then he is not very reliable for bright days. We therefore expect to continue our program of tithing, and we feel perfectly sure God will honor our faith."

Three years later, about the time they were graduating, these same five couples came together again and compared notes. It was discovered that, in spite of the fact that all had had about the same incomes and outlays, the tithers were the only ones out of debt. The system had worked.

²² *After that you shall return and be free of obligation to the Lord and to Israel; and this land shall be your possession before the Lord.*

JUST AS the crucifixion and resurrection of Jesus are the great basic facts underlying the Christian religion, so the exodus of the Children of Israel from Egypt, with all its attendant miraculous circumstances, is the great basic fact of the Hebrew faith. Throughout all their history it had been agreed by the prophets, priests, and psalmists that the very existence of the nation and its residence in the Land of Promise were acts of God.

This concept of Israel as the recipient of divine favors from Jehovah colored all the economic thought of the people. It resulted in a distinctive philosophy concerning land that set the Hebrews apart from their pagan neighbors as a peculiar people (cf. comment on page 53). It resulted in a devotion to "the land of the fathers" that has been one of the distinguishing characteristics of the Jew even down to the present day. In a way altogether unique the descendants of Abraham are associated with the little land of Palestine by ties far deeper and more significant than mere sentiment.

Hebrew teachers and thinkers, however, drew a sharp line of distinction between ownership and possession. The nation, they said, held the land as a trust. When the trust was betrayed, their possession was jeopardized because God's ownership was never to be questioned. This was one of the major points upon which the spiritual leaders insisted during the Babylonian exile. Israel had lost the land, they said, because the nation had not kept the faith.

This distinction between ownership and possession is the essence of the doctrine of stewardship. He who accepts his possessions as though they were the property of God entrusted to him for purposes of administration acknowledges not only that he is accountable to the Divine for returning the tenth, or the tithe, but that he is also responsible to God for the conduct of all the relationships of the possession. That means he is under a stewardship for the nine tenths as he is also for the one tenth.

To return one tenth for the promotion of God's causes and then to administer the nine tenths with a complete indifference to God's preferences is to betray one's stewardship. It is by such logic that the acknowledgment of one's stewardship has the effect of spiritualizing all of life's decisions.

[37] *He loved your fathers and chose their descendants after them, and brought you out of Egypt with his own presence, by his great power.*

No MAN was ever born free. Every person now living came into life as an heir to the sacrifices, savings, and achievements of the past. These things constitute a body of obligations from which we can never free ourselves.

Before we arrived at the first moment of self-consciousness, we began accumulating these obligations. First we became indebted to home and parents, then to the community that provided us with schooling and opportunity, then to the nation that preserved for us our social and political rights as citizens. The more carefully we study history, the greater that obligation appears to be.

No man has ever lived who was at liberty to do as he pleased. All of us represent too much of the investment the past has made. We can never escape the duties we owe to the generations that preceded us.

Much effort has been expended on the subject of human rights, and much still remains to be done in that field before all men's rights have been made safe. But we dare not lose sight of the fact that every right is matched by a responsibility and that our privileges all come to us on a cash-and-carry basis. They must be paid for in service to the generation of which we are a part.

If we are not to live as parasites, we must repay the world for the benefits it has conferred upon us. To consume more than we produce is to live at other's men's expense—at least, that is what the economists say. To take more from life than we put into it is to be an object of charity, to be supported at the expense of other people (the living or the dead).

To be born of a good family and not to contribute to the good name of that family is to betray it. To be born into a just world and not at least to maintain the world's stock of justice is to fail as a citizen. To be born the beneficiary of the past and make no sacrifices for the future is to be a consumer and not a producer.

Upon the basis of such reasoning the community has a right to expect that any man who claims the title of "good citizen" shall contribute his proportionate share to those institutions that maintain the spiritual and moral health of society. From this there is no honorable escape.

> [7] You shall teach them diligently to your children, and shall talk of
> them when you sit in your house, and when you walk by the way, and
> when you lie down, and when you rise.

As a TINY little lad John Yates watched with something like awe
as his mother made laborious entries in an old brown account book.
If the hens laid fifteen eggs one day, she noted the fact in the evening, and then in a special column she wrote down, "One and a
half eggs." If she was fortunate and sold thirty cents' worth of
garden truck out of her little "patch," she entered that fact in the
book and in the special column very solemnly put down the figure 3.
"That's the Lord's," she explained to her son. "Everything we have
we owe to him, and we return one tenth to him because we are
grateful."

The family was numbered among the poorest of Georgia's poor,
but their names were on the roll of a little neighborhood church,
and John's mother had a reputation for being very devout. In her
quiet way she was a great influence among the humble people with
whom she associated. To her growing son she was a saint, whose
judgments were infallible.

As a youngster of fourteen John secured his first regular employment; and when on Saturday night he was paid a dollar and a half
for his week's work, he carefully counted it out, set aside fifteen
cents, and on Monday went down to the bank and opened an
account in the name of "John W. Yates and Company." In that
account he deposited the fifteen cents.

"Who's the Company, John?" the banker asked, just a little amused.
"That's God," the fourteen-year-old replied. "We're in business
together, and that's his share of the week's profits." That was the
beginning of a lifelong habit.

John Yates is today one of the most successful insurance executives on the West Coast, and his reputation as a tither has gone
across the nation among his business associates. Many of them,
while calling upon him in his big private office, have seen the old
brown account book, and have read the ancient penciled entries
written in a cramped hand. Alongside the book is a New Testament.

It is not the amount of money that John Yates has been able to
contribute to various good causes that makes his mother's example
so significant, though his giving has been very generous and very
wisely placed. What is important is the influence of that godly
mother's example on the entire business career of one of America's
business leaders. "She sits in on every conference I hold," John
Yates has said.

HUMBLE ORIGINS NO INDICTMENT   Deut. 12:10-11

*¹¹ Thither you shall bring all that I command you: your burnt offer-
ings and your sacrifices, your tithes and the offering that you present,
and all your votive offerings which you vow to the Lord.*

THERE HAVE been those who have declined to accept the doctrine
of stewardship and the practice of tithing because, as they say, "The
whole thing originated in the mind of a primitive man who was
driven by a fear of the gods and sought some escape from divine
wrath, or sought some divine favor." And it must be admitted that
the earliest records of the payment of the tithe suggest some very
primitive thinking.

But the humble origins of a doctrine should not be used as arguments against its validity, for all our great major beliefs, both
political and religious, developed from humble beginnings. If we
are to bypass tithing because it began as a result of primitive concepts, then we must by the same logic abandon all culture and
scholarship.

The first music, for example, was produced when some primeval
man discovered that he could produce a pleasant sound by blowing
across the end of a hollow reed, or that he could produce an exalted
mood by pounding rhythmically on a hollow log. But we do not
disband a symphony orchestra because its progenitors were a simple
flute and a forest tom-tom.

The first art came into existence when some primitive man discovered that he could scratch characters on the soft sandstone and
leave images that suggested the form of other creatures. But we do
not dismantle the Louvre or the Vatican Gallery because the beginnings of paintings and sculpture were humble.

Through many long centuries all pictures, even those produced by
the greatest masters, were strictly two dimensional. Then some
inspired genius discovered the principle of perspective and thus
revolutionized the entire field of art. But we do not lock up our
galleries today because the first artists were ignorant of this great
principle.

It is true, of course, that the first tithes were offered to the gods
in the hope that the petty deities might be flattered by men's gifts
and thus persuaded to increase the crops and the herds. But that
has not been the end. By linking philanthropy to religion there has
been let loose upon the world a tide of healing that has revolutionized human relations throughout the earth. Even nations go to
the rescue of unfortunate or stricken peoples, taxing their own
citizens for the purpose of providing relief for the sufferers. It is not
the beginning, but the end that forms the basis for final judgments.

²² You shall tithe all the yield of your seed, which comes forth from the field year by year.

A GREAT many people who admit the advantages of tithing as a method of giving refuse to accept it as their personal plan "because it represents Old Testament legalism."

As though to live under the grace promised in the New Testament relieved us of responsibilities plainly stated in the law of the Old Testament! As though there were more and better reasons for the ancient Jew to live under a stewardship than for the modern Christian to accept the status of a responsible administrator of God's goods!

"All I have belongs to God," one good man said in reply to his pastor's urging. "I spend every dollar as though God were watching, but I do not believe in tithing for that puts the whole matter on a legalistic basis."

Yet that same Christian home kept the Sabbath with great fidelity. The wife was on an allowance out of which she was expected to pay the household expenses, and once a month there was a study of the accounts to see that she had kept inside the "quotas." The rent was paid regularly to the landlord on a legalistic basis. And once a year the head of the house paid his income tax as required by law.

The good man paid his club dues regularly. Had he not done so, he would have been dropped. The finance committee might have been lenient, and he might have postponed the day of reckoning a short time, but in the end the dues would have to be paid. That was the law of the club, and a just law at that. He faced the same situation in relation to his lodge dues. His daughter was in college, and her tuition was likewise placed on a legalistic basis.

But in dealing with God this good man took the position that his giving must rest on an altogether different basis. In getting away from "legalism" he degenerated into haphazard giving, with each gift taking on the coloration of a gratuity offered to the Lord out of whatever surplus happened to be on hand at the moment. If there was nothing left after the necessary bills had been paid, then he excused himself from all giving by saying, "I just don't have the money." This, of course, ignored the fact that he once had the money—the Lord's money—but had spent it for other purposes. This meant that God must stand aside for the landlord, the club treasurer, and the tax collector.

²³ You shall eat the tithe of your grain, of your wine, and of your
oil, and the firstlings of your herd and flock.

ANY EFFORT to trace the history of tithing back to its origins in the
Old Testament is certain to end in disappointment, for a great deal
of confusion surrounds the subject. Comparing the text of this
study with Num. 18:24-28 indicates the wide variance of viewpoint
and practices that prevailed. It is therefore extremely difficult to
find uniformity in the observances during the first five hundred
years of Hebrew history.

At first the tithes were presented at the shrines and consumed
during the great feasts. These were occasions of great rejoicing,
hilarity, and merrymaking. Such events had religious significance,
of course, but they could hardly have been called worship services
(Deut. 14:22-23), at least in the modern meaning of the word. If
any man lived too far away from the central sanctuary, he was
permitted to sell his sacrifices and buy other animals at the scene
of the feast.

Some time later the law stipulated that the tithe of each third
year should be set apart for the support of the Levites and the poor
(Deut. 14:29; 26:12), this being the first instance in which religion
and benevolence were linked as religious acts.

Still later it became the law (Num. 18:24-28) that the tithe
should provide the support for the Levites who, in turn, were to
serve as ministrants at the altars and shrines. This marked the beginning of a professionally religious class supported at the expense
of the people, the tithes being dedicated to this purpose.

According to the beliefs of the Canaanites, who occupied the
Promised Land prior to the Hebrew invasion, every field and valley
had its own god who provided it with fertility and the flocks with
fecundity. When the Children of Israel came in from the desert,
untrained in agriculture, their enemies were the only ones who
could teach them how to plant and harvest crops. In thus instructing
them they taught the Israelites idolatry, and every farm had its
shrine where offerings were presented.

In the middle of the seventh century B.C., after King Josiah, in
a vast reform movement, ordered all these "high places" destroyed
and the nation's worship transferred to the Temple, the payment of
the tithes was more carefully regulated.

During the period of the Exile the religious services of the Jews
passed through numerous refinements, and in the case of the tithe
a strict procedure was set up.

²⁹ *The Levite, because he has no portion or inheritance with you,*
and the sojourner, the fatherless, and the widow, who are within your
towns, shall come and eat and be filled.

WHAT CAUSES have a legitimate claim on my tithe?

Finding a satisfactory answer to this question has given many
Christian people no little trouble. In fact, some denominations insist
that no giving can be considered tithing except that which is done
directly through the Church.

However, in the case of the scripture involved in this study, we
have a perfectly clear case. According to the Deuteronomic code
the tithe of the produce of each third year was dedicated to the
support of the Levites, the orphans, widows, and sojourners.

In the course of the Exodus Moses assigned special functions to
"the sons of Levi" (Exod. 32:25-29), and in time they became the
ministers at the altars and shrines of the nation (Judg. 17) with a
peculiar religious standing in the nation's life (Deut. 33:8-11). In
New Testament times no small part of the Temple revenues
was expended in caring for the small army of priests recruited from
the Levites.

It is inevitable that a certain number of orphans and widows are
to be found among any people. In a large number of cases they
are entirely dependent upon the community for their care, and each
society makes such provisions as may seem just and fair. The device
employed by the Hebrews in designating the tithe of each third
year's produce indicates that their numbers among the Children
of Israel may not have been large, but even the few were not
neglected.

In the provision that makes the "sojourner" share in the benefits
of the tithe, we have one of the most remarkable illustrations of the
advanced social thinking of the Hebrews. Among all the other
nations of the ancient East justice and concern were expressed on
the basis of a man's importance in the community. In this regulation
we find that the individual's need is the index used in determining
the responsibility of the nation.

The sojourner was an alien, a stranger, and one who was outside
the community. Yet if he were in need, he was to be considered a
legitimate claimant on the generosity of the public. From this
apparently simple stipulation one can draw an extended series of
social inferences.

Certainly this scripture is abundant warrant for the tither's assigning some portion of his tithe to works of charity and benevolence.

*⁵ No man shall be able to stand before you all the days of your
life; as I was with Moses, so I will be with you; I will not fail you or
forsake you.*

IT IS relatively easy for average Christians to believe that God was
with Moses, David, Isaiah, and Jeremiah; but to believe that the
Almighty will be with us is an entirely different matter.

The problems and difficulties we face seem so new because they
are new to us; they seem so difficult because they baffle us so
completely; they seem insoluble because we find it so hard to take
the long look at them. It is not easy to see that the solicitous God
who guided the Children of Israel in their flight from Egypt is the
same deity who is guiding our modern world through the intricacies
and terrors of the atomic age. Everywhere men are in the paralyzing
grip of a deep-seated anxiety that is producing a series of nervous
disorders of the utmost seriousness, and as a consequence the mental
wards of our hospitals are filled.

There may have been times when Joshua, Moses' successor,
had the feeling that he was going it alone. The Hebrews were not
an easy people to lead, and the desert was a parsimonious land in
which to live. All about were the enemies of the refugees, ready
to war upon them on the slightest pretext or if there should be
presented the slightest hope of profitable loot. No one need envy
Joshua; he did not have an easy time of it. But the one fixed point
to which he returned again and again was the promise of this
scripture: "As I was with Moses, so I will be with you." If any man
grows discouraged over the Church, let him consider the long list
of crises it has survived under God's guidance.

God is no novice in our world. He knows the laws by which
life operates, for he ordained them, he trusts them, he governs
by them. Let any man discover a law—a principle that has proved
itself—and he is in touch with eternity.

It is for this reason that the preacher urges his people to tithe.
Down through the centuries devout men have demonstrated the fact
that the tenth given to God as an act of faith, and in token of our
heavenly Father's ownership of everything, results in an inner
strength and peace that can be achieved in no other way. Thousands
of tithers testify to the fact that their experience of serenity and certainty began with their acceptance of God's challenge, "Put me to the
test" (Mal. 3:10). It seems so fair. God is still dependable.

[14] They lifted up their voices and wept again; and Orpah kissed her mother-in-law, but Ruth clung to her.

THE WRITER of the book of Ruth drew a fine line of distinction between the two daughters-in-law of Naomi when he said of them, "Orpah kissed her mother-in-law, but Ruth clung to her." In that single sentence we have the difference between a formal loyalty and a great devotion.

As old Naomi turned back to the land of her birth, there was nothing about Orpah's conduct that she could criticize. The girl had been a good wife to Naomi's son; she had fulfilled her filial duty; and there never had been any hard feelings. When the two women parted, each was entirely friendly toward the other, and "Orpah kissed her."

The glory of Ruth lay in the fact that she exceeded expectations and revealed herself as a woman who was capable of a devotion that included everything she had and was. She vowed herself to the old mother when the future looked black and when it was very certain that the oath would cost her heavily.

The remaining chapters of the story portray Ruth as a faithful daughter who found herself and her future as she did her duty. Life is like that; one of the basic laws of life comes to the surface as the tale goes on. The best and the worst always come to those who are able to live with abandon. Those who live righteously and to the limit always collect a magnificent dividend. Those who live with abandon in behalf of evil also collect to the limit, and always a terrible limit.

The Church of God is full of Orphas—people who believe in goodness and in God, who have a generally favorable opinion concerning the Church, and who want to be listed among the "good people." But they never have enlisted for an all-out devotion to the cause of the kingdom of Heaven on earth. They give, but all too many times they give reluctantly for the simple reason that they are afraid to commit all their economic affairs to the management of God. They enlist for service but always with certain reservations. They declare their faith in Christian doctrines, but they seldom take the trouble to know precisely what they believe.

No man can be said to have really lived who has not lived to the limit. To hug the shore, to hedge, and to be afraid of making a complete consecration may mean that we live in security, but it seldom means that we live gloriously. The Christian steward draws no line this side of the absolute limit.

²⁸ *I have lent him to the Lord; as long as he lives, he is lent to the Lord.*

WE SHOULD probably have more Samuels if we had more mothers like Hannah.

At the edge of a small southern town there lived a little family, the mother being a widow and desperately poor. But every Sunday morning she gathered her tiny brood about her, put a penny into each youngster's hand, and then hustled them all off to Sunday school and church, for she was one of those godly women who believed that even a young child would get something out of the service if he saw his mother giving reverent attention.

In one respect she was a woman of great wealth, for she had a great faith. She believed, as surely as she believed there was a North Star, that God would see the family through any desperate circumstance if they all kept their consciences clear and their records clean.

Under the preaching of a pastor early in her married life she had become convinced of the reasonableness of tithing as a method of giving, and she kept her accounts with a strictness that would have reflected credit upon a government treasurer.

The day she presented her young son at the altar of the church for Christian baptism, she spent a half hour with him, both before and after the service, making the significance of the sacrament clear to him—as clear, at least, as it could be made to a five-year-old. She had already begun teaching him the principle of the tithe.

When at the age of eight the lad expressed a desire to unite with the church, she treated the matter seriously, discussed it with him at some length, and then the following Sunday morning went forward to the altar and stood at his side while he took the solemn vows.

The evening he came home from his first regular job, brandishing his pay check with great pride, she sat down with him and helped him start his tithing account in a little book he cherishes to this day. When he had accumulated the first five dollars in his "God's Account," she sat with him for much of an entire evening, planning the investment of the money so that it might produce the largest dividends.

And thus did one Hannah train one Samuel in a small American village so that he became in time one of the great laymen of his denomination.

> [1] The men of Kiriathjearim came and took up the ark of the Lord, and brought it to the house of Abinadab on the hill; and they consecrated his son, Eleazar, to have charge of the ark of the Lord.

OCCASIONALLY there are individuals who seem to assume that because they give a tithe of their income to the Lord's work, they have thereby discharged their obligations to Christ and his Church. The author of this scripture probably had no thought of doing so, but he has described quite accurately the attitude of some churchmen when he says, "They consecrated his son, Eleazar, to have charge of the ark of the Lord." As if to say that safeguarding the holy shrine were one man's responsibility!

No man's stewardship has been discharged by the simple act of making a cash contribution. That there is a financial obligation resting upon every churchman goes without saying. But just as it is true that "man shall not live by bread alone," so it is also true that no church can survive on money alone.

It is not enough to provide a beautiful educational unit for the use of the church school. There are classes of boys waiting for men, and classes of girls waiting for women, who are willing to take the training that will equip them to teach the great truths of God and faith in such an effective fashion that they will work a transformation of young life. Certainly if teachers are required to train for the teaching of the facts of history, they can hardly be expected to teach the great spiritual laws of life without training.

Keeping the ark, in the case of the modern church, is more than any one man can do, no matter how personable he may be, and no matter how attractive he may be as a preacher of the Word. When the organ has been installed, there is still need for a choir. When the money has been raised, there is still need for the services of a faithful finance committee that will serve as stewards of the Lord's funds. When the poor come knocking at the church door, there is a desperate need for kindly hearts to receive them in the name of Christ and to help them find some solution for their terrifying problems.

If the work of the Church is to be done, some very big men may have to assume responsibility for some very small tasks. It sometimes happens that a clumsy usher defeats a brilliant preacher in the pulpit, or that an inconsiderate worshiper who whispers during the "preliminaries" makes it impossible for a sensitive soul to cultivate the sense of the presence of the Divine. A comprehensive concept of stewardship includes all of one's life attitudes toward God and one's fellows.

PUT AWAY THE FOREIGN GODS

I Sam. 7:3-4

Put away the foreign gods and the Ashtaroth from among you, and direct your heart to the Lord, and serve him only.

It is difficult for the modern man to understand how the shabby little gods of the Canaanites could hold such a fascination for the ancient Hebrews, but this is because we cannot comprehend the social and the economic conditions under which men lived in that primitive age.

Where there was no scientific agriculture, everything was left to accident and chance. The cumulus clouds that came drifting in from the Mediterranean might shed showers on one man's land and leave another's acres completely dry. It was quite natural for the man whose field was watered to believe he had somehow won the favor of the gods, and for the man with the parched fields to believe that he had somehow offended them.

Coming in from the wilderness, having lived all their lives in the desert, the men of Israel had to learn all their agriculture from the Canaanites whom they had not driven out of the land, which is another reason why we cannot compromise with any of the vestiges of evil. But the Canaanites assured the Hebrews that there would be no crops if they did not worship the little divinities that were enshrined in the fields. This maintained idolatry for several hundred years. It was an economic problem, not merely a theological question. It took a stouthearted believer to risk his crops by refusing to pray to some little mud image on a shrine.

This temptation of crops and prosperity continues with us. It takes a stouthearted Christian to stand out against the allurement of a few more bushels, a few more pounds, a few more per cent, and a few more dollars.

The crux of the entire situation is precisely at this point. The kingdom of Heaven to which every Christian is committed is put forward by those who can say no to their understandable ambition to prosper when prosperity asks too high a price.

When young men enter the armed services of the nation, they are carefully instructed that they are putting behind them all their civilian interests in everything economic, and that from the day of their enlistment onward their first responsibility is to the government whose uniform they wear. That is what Christian baptism ought to mean to the baptized. From that hour on, he is to put away all foreign gods. And this includes our possessions.

¹² *Samuel took a stone and set it up between Mizpah and Jeshanah, and called its name Ebenezer; for he said, "Hitherto the Lord has helped us."*

IT MIGHT be a wholesome thing if in the midst of every community a monument were raised whereon was engraved the single word "Ebenezer."

The Children of Israel had undertaken one of the most hazardous enterprises in all the annals of the East, and there were times almost without number when it appeared that someone would have to work a miracle or all would be lost. Under such circumstances the old prophet Samuel turned to the stone he had raised, and said to himself, "Up to this moment the Lord has helped us. He will not fail us now."

Nothing could have appeared more hopeless that dreadful Sabbath when Jesus lay in the tomb of Joseph than the cause of Christ that had come to such an inglorious end the night before. The wrath of Caesar was so relentless; the power of Annas, the crafty high priest, was so complete; the number of disciples, even after three amazing years of preaching, was so small—perhaps 150 in all.

Nothing could have appeared more futile than the paper nailed to the cathedral door in Wittenburg by an inconspicuous monk—a nobody. The spiritual authority of the pope was so dominant. By holding the keys of heaven in his hands and having the power—at least, so someone said—to open or close the doors of heaven, he seemed all-powerful. Who dared defy him? But somehow that word "hitherto" burned its way into Martin Luther's soul.

At every junction of history there has been someone who has been ready to go forward with confidence in the hitherto, and another hitherto has been added to the long list.

A young medical student had come to the end of his rope. Profoundly convinced that he was obeying the will of God, he had enrolled in the medical school without sufficient funds to see him through even the first semester. "But my mother has taught me that God always comes to the rescue of the man who is doing his duty, if he persists in doing it," he said in describing his situation to his pastor. "And although my experience is very brief, I have found it to be true thus far." And with that assurance of the hitherto, he went over to the school to take his semester examinations, not knowing how he would be able to pay his next semester's tuition. But the problem was solved in a perfectly honorable fashion, and the gospel of the hitherto was again vindicated. It never fails.

A VISITOR FROM MARS I Sam. 16:6-7

⁷ The Lord said to Samuel, ". . . The Lord sees not as man sees; man looks on the outward appearance, but the Lord looks on the heart."

IT IS EXTREMELY sobering, albeit rather reassuring, to be warned that God penetrates through all subterfuge and pretense—even our self-deceptions—and looks squarely upon our naked hearts, our inner purposes, and our secret and unconfessed desires. Having seen exactly what our motives and purposes are, and being completely undeceived concerning our motives, he judges us. It is an impartial and strictly accurate judgment that admits all the evidence both pro and con. From his verdict neither justice nor mercy can make an appeal.

Suppose that some space ship should bring to this planet an inquiring reporter representing some newspaper published on the planet Mars, and suppose this keen investigator should undertake to evaluate the contemporary scene as he viewed it from the vantage point of complete detachment. What might we expect his reports to be?

What would he write, for example, concerning the way we license the sale of a beverage that always unmans the drinker? What might we expect his judgment to be of the way we are handling the problem of alcoholism?

What would he be apt to say about the sometimes-fascist ways we have of dealing with national problems? And what would he be apt to decide was our actual interest in the questions of individual freedom and liberty as they are actually practiced in our democracy?

Suppose this Martian journalist were to attend one of our Christian churches some Sunday morning and hear a sermon on foreign missions, in which the preacher warned his people of their solemn obligation to "go into all the world and preach the gospel" and afterward went back into the treasurer's office with the finance committee and helped count the collection.

Suppose he were to be told that it was the avowed purpose of the Church to take this world captive for Jesus Christ and then discovered that the average congregation numbered less than 30 per cent of the total church membership on any one Sunday and that the cosmetic and tobacco bills of the worshipers exceeded all their contributions to the world enterprise of the Church.

What might we expect his report to his managing editor to be after making such discoveries concerning us? Would we be justified in objecting if he were a bit cynical?

²⁴ I will not offer burnt offerings to the Lord my God which cost me nothing.

NOTHING ADDS to the beauty and the value of a gift as does the sacrifice of the giver. King David had come to a shrine to offer sacrifices to God in the hope that he might thereby stay the plague that was decimating the nation. When the owner of the threshing floor where David proposed to burn his offering discovered that it was the king who sought the privilege, he offered it without cost and urged that his own oxen be burned and that his sledge used in threshing be the fuel. All this the young monarch refused, using one of the most sublime statements with which he has been credited anywhere in the Old Testament. "I will not offer burnt offerings to the Lord . . . which cost me nothing."

A businessman, whose income would have made it possible for him to buy anything in the way of clothes that might strike his fancy, was displaying a new shirt to his friends at the lunch club. "This is the finest shirt I have ever had on," he said. "My daughter made it for me. She and her husband are trying to finish his work at the university, and they are having it pretty rugged. So she made this shirt for me with her own hands, and I have never had anything in all my life that has pleased me so much."

Perhaps God feels the same way about the sacrificial gifts we make to him. "The gift without the giver is bare," is the opinion of the poet, and he seems to have sensed something of the heart of God when he wrote the line. "Give until you are sure you have made God very happy," said the pastor as he took a Christmas offering for the benefit of the poor who lived in the immediate neighborhood of the church.

"I never look at this envelope that I do not have a guilty feeling," the treasurer said. "The old lady who put it into the collection lives in an old people's home. She does not have a living relative, so far as anyone knows. Her income is derived from an old-time friend who sends her five dollars a month for spending money. But every Sunday her envelope with three pennies in it is to be found on the collection plate; and when we are taking a special collection, there is always an extra nickel along with those three pennies. When I compare her three cents with my three dollars, I am very sure that she has made God much happier than I have, for she has given what has cost her a real sacrifice. I have given only something out of my surplus. And God knows the difference."

[27] Those officers supplied provisions for King Solomon, and for all who came to King Solomon's table, each one in his month; they let nothing be lacking.

THE COLLAPSE of Solomon's kingdom was not the result of any attack by an enemy from the outside, but the inevitable outcome of structural weaknesses within that were produced by indulgence, extravagance, impiety, moral laxity, and conceit.

The sentimentalists have called Solomon "the wisest man in history," but the facts in no way justify the characterization. As a matter of fact, few individuals more stupid or shortsighted ever occupied the Hebrew throne.

The little land over which he reigned was never designed to be the homeland of a great empire. Nowhere within its borders were there any mineral deposits, great forests, precious stones, quarries, or broad productive plains. The program of elaborate public works instituted for the purpose of gratifying the king's vanity so far exceeded the ability of the people to pay that toward the close of his reign Solomon was under the necessity of assigning twenty cities to the king of Tyre to satisfy a mortgage. His son, Rehoboam, came to the throne of a bankrupt nation, torn by conflict, undermined and weakened by intrigue, and spiritually vitiated. The entire tragedy was the result of false idealism enthroned within.

The tinsel and the gaiety with which Solomon deluded himself during the last decade of his clumsy rule are not entirely lacking in today's world. We are in danger of assuming that night clubs, television, atomic explosions, four-color advertising, deep-freeze units, and sulfa drugs have some miraculous power to save us from our secularism, superficiality, cynicism, and lack of idealism.

The things that might have saved Solomon's kingdom—caution, self-discipline, righteousness, temperance, stewardship, and the willingness to live inside our income for the sake of our children's security—are precisely the things that could save our generation.

We have perfected the television instruments and now wait for someone to say something that will justify the enormous expenditure and be worthy of an audience of millions. We have crowded our lives without filling them; we have forced ourselves to live on the run without getting anywhere; we have never talked so much and expressed so few ideas. We are sophisticated but we lack stability; we are noisy but we are not happy. And the pity is, no one has forced us into this condition. It's an inside job.

I Kings 11:6, 9-11 STEWARDSHIP THAT MADE HISTORY

[11] *Since this has been your mind and you have not kept my covenant and my statutes which I have commanded you, I will surely tear the kingdom from you and will give it to your servant.*

IT IS ONE of the most impressive facts of Hebrew history that during those periods in the nation's life when the people were most faithful in observing their religious vows and in maintaining their ancestral worship, they were also most prosperous and safest from attack from outside enemies.

The scripture that says "righteousness exalts a nation" is more than a merely pious phrase. History has demonstrated that it is a sound political principle as well as a beautiful bit of scripture. As a matter of fact, the principle holds true of even pagan nations. Just as the Roman Empire, for example, began its headlong plunge into the religious chaos about the time of Christ, so also it went tumbling into political decline. There is a close association between political disaster and religious backsliding.

When the little kingdom of Judah fell under the hammer blows of Babylonia and the devout leaders began searching for some explanation of the tragedy, they made the discovery that there had been one period of nearly fifty years during which no Sabbath had been observed. They also discovered that there had been a marked laxity in the matter of paying tithes.

National immorality had followed as an inevitable consequence. At one time it was discovered that a considerable number of "holy women" (sacred prostitutes) had actually been housed in the Temple in Jerusalem as a concession to the pagan cultists who had shared the worship there. It was all done in the name of liberalism, of course, and there had been those who had insisted that the nation must concede something to paganism for the sake of commercial advantage.

It was when Judah turned back to her ancestral faith and re-established the old disciplines, inaugurating the observance of the Sabbath, the tithe, and the altar sacrifices, that the land began to regain its strength. It was during the years when Greece was young and clean that she reached her greatest heights, and it was during the time that Rome was in the vigor and chastity of her youth that she produced her greatest characters.

Tithing, as a part of our religious culture, is certainly no guarantee of political security, but any nation that becomes careless in its support of its religious institutions will soon be confronted with the word "finis." The prophets of every generation have warned us against our backslidings.

51

EASY RELIGION IS FATAL   I Kings 12:25-28

²⁸ You have gone up to Jerusalem long enough. Behold your gods, O Israel, who brought you up out of the land of Egypt.

AT THE VERY outset of their experience as an independent nation the people of Israel were led astray by a king who undertook to make their religion easy. It was a mistake from which the nation never recovered.

During the chaotic days that followed Israel's repudiation of the house of David and the young King Rehoboam, a refugee named Jereboam was called back from Egypt to take the throne of the new kingdom. He had been a fugitive from Solomon's court and during his sojourn in Egypt had learned much about the national worship of the Nile country where the cow was regarded as sacred.

Fearing that the annual visits of the people to the great Temple in Jerusalem might result in a continued loyalty to the house of David, Jereboam undertook to overcome the natural trend by erecting two gilded calves at the two great popular shrines—Dan and Bethel—in Israel. Then, as though greatly solicitous in his people's behalf, he said, "You have gone up to Jerusalem long enough. Behold your gods, O Israel." And throughout all the remaining history of the northern kingdom, Jereboam was referred to as "he who made Israel to sin."

In all the history of the races of men there is no record of any nation that has ever survived the loss of its religious faith. When we set out to make religion easy, we undermine the foundations of public morals, the basic loyalties of the people, and the national character upon which true greatness depends.

Explain it as you may, there is some mysterious power in the difficult that makes an enormous contribution to the soul and life of that individual who attempts it courageously and determinedly.

It is perhaps at this point that tithing makes one of its most vital contributions to the life and character of the tither. The very fact that it has the appearance of being difficult has the effect of frightening the timid and the uncertain. But let any man accept the challenge of the tithe, and let him maintain the pledge of the tenth for one year in the face of difficulty and unexpected obstacles, and he will discover that a virility has been introduced into his faith and into his religious experience just a little different from anything he had ever known before. There are times when the difficulty of tithing becomes its greatest asset to the tither.

³ Naboth said to Ahab, "The Lord forbid that I should give you the inheritance of my fathers."

DURING THEIR forty years' wandering in the wilderness the Hebrews developed a philosophy of land that marked them as a peculiar people for a thousand years.

Inasmuch as every man's life depended upon his having free access to land and water, the people came to believe that these two elements of life were gifts divinely bestowed. Living about the little springs and wells that dotted the desert, and subsisting as nomads, they moved about from one oasis to another in search of food for themselves and scanty pasturage for their herds. They never stayed long enough in one spot to plant vineyards, develop orchards, or harvest crops. Just as we say that something is "as free as the air you breathe," so the Hebrews thought of land and water as something essential to life and therefore not to be bartered or sold.

Once they had forced their way into the Promised Land, they adapted their desert philosophy of land to the new circumstances. Under Joshua and Caleb the Land of Promise was parceled out to the heads of families, each family or clan being assigned its holdings, these to be held in perpetuity. For a man to sell his patrimony was, in the estimation of a devout Hebrew, as serious a sin as if a man had denied his own parentage.

Ahab, the king, did not attempt to rob Naboth, the landowner, of his field. According to the philosophy of Baal he made a perfectly honorable proposition. He would trade the farmer a better piece of land or, if he preferred, he would buy the field outright at a good price. Economically the peasant would not have suffered by the transaction.

Naboth's refusal to consider the proposal rooted down in this ancient land philosophy. According to the way he had been trained to think, he held the land as a trust from his father, who had, in turn, received it as a trust from his. The stewardship ran clear back to the days of Joshua and Caleb when the founder of the family had been ceded the land as a trust from Jehovah. A long list of progenitors had kept the faith, and to Naboth it was inconceivable that he should betray the trust after so many generations of faithfulness.

It is highly significant that in defense of this ancient philosophy of land stewardship the prophet Elijah came out of the mountains of Gilead to be the first of the long succession of Hebrew preachers of social justice. It began with stewardship.

⁸ The king of Israel said to Jehoshaphat, "There is yet one man by whom we may inquire of the Lord, Micaiah the son of Imlah; but I hate him, for he never prophesies good concerning me, but evil."

IT IS SAID that when Lorenzo de Medici lay dying in his Florentine palace, he turned to one of his staff and, with one of his last breaths, said, "Send for the honest priest." In the most critical hour of his life, the corrupt old monarch was asking for Savonarola, who had been the victim of his hatred so many times.

The test of good preaching is not the applause it elicits nor the popularity that accrues to the preacher. It often happens that some Jehoshaphat mutters, "I hate him"; but if the preacher is true to his trust, the spirit of eternity is in his message. He will be called back.

It is extremely unfortunate that only on the rarest of occasions does a preacher speak frankly and courageously to his people on the subject of money. Yet the circumstances of modern life make it absolutely necessary that he do so, if he is to discharge his spiritual obligations to his people, for there is no other subject upon which plain speaking is so badly needed and, perhaps, no other subject upon which plain speech is so unwelcome.

There is good precedent for plain speech on money, however, for at least one third of Jesus' parables revolved about this theme, and the Master spoke repeatedly on the subject even when he made no reference to thievery, theology, or some of the gross sins of mankind.

There come times when the eternal salvation of individuals and congregations depends upon whatever chance they have to hear the question of money discussed candidly and frankly. Plain speech on the subject is extremely rare because the preacher is sensitive to the charge that he is "always talking about money."

The skill of the physician is not to be measured by the pleasant way in which he deals with his patient. Often he is able to cure a fatal malady only by using the most drastic remedies. The teacher is only doing his duty by his pupils when he assigns difficult lessons and insists upon their mastering their subjects.

Just as the hearer welcomes the assurance of peace and power which the preacher brings on the Sabbath day, so he should welcome the sincere word of warning if it is offered with the same sincerity.

It often happens that the sinner resents the preaching of the same things his conscience is telling him in private. "The reason it made me so angry when my preacher talked about tithing was that I knew he was right," said one layman.

[17] Elisha prayed, . . . "O Lord, I pray thee, open his eyes that he may see."

I DO NOT know how our people can possibly build the kind of plant we really need," said the chairman of the finance committee. "Our people are not rich, as everyone knows. We are all salaried people with fixed incomes and no extras coming in from dividends or investments. But we are devoted, and I know we will do our best. But I also know something more than all this. I know God expects us to do something really significant in this community. He has put us here in the presence of a great opportunity; and if he expects us to do the impossible, he will provide us with the unexpected ability to meet the situation. For this reason I am in favor of this building program that will require us to raise twice as much money as I think we can. If God has thrust us into this, I have faith that he will see us through. If each of us will do what he can, this church will do what it must. The biggest fact in the situation, as I see it, is not our small ability, but God's great confidence in us. And as for me, I do not intend to disappoint him."

It was a heroic speech, and everyone in the meeting knew that the chairman of the finance committee could be relied upon to follow his words through with action. In the long run the impossible was achieved, but it took that kind of realism to bring it about.

The pessimists have monopolized the word "realism" all too long. For the Christian there is no realism that leaves the fact of God out of the picture.

Those who seek the heartening facts of life are as surely realists as those who search for the disheartening and disagreeable facts.

Elisha did not deny that the Syrians had closed in upon him. No one knew that any better than he did; but he also knew something else and something very much more important. God was also closing in upon him, and for him the Syrians were no match. The young man had not seen the whole picture until he had seen God in it.

The Christian steward is one who sees all the bills that have to be paid, all the difficulties that have to be met, all the dire things that can happen. But he also sees God alongside every problem, every financial threat, and every difficulty that seems insoluble.

There is a mild form of atheism in that declaration of faith that says, "I believe in God the Father Almighty," and which then hedges about doing one's plain duty.

[13] The Lord warned Israel and Judah by every prophet and every seer, saying, "Turn from your evil ways and keep my commandments."

THE BREAK-UP of the little kingdom of Israel is one of the greatest tragedies recorded in the Old Testament. The defenders of Samaria, the capital city, were brave almost beyond belief; the invading Assyrians en route to Egypt in quest of loot were held up for almost two years. The Israelites withstood the terrible might of the empire to the last ounce of their blood and the last quiver of their nerves, but it was to no avail. The kingdom was destroyed.

But the tragedy did not come without warning. It is a fact, of course, that the Old Testament contains but one book of sermons coming from a prophet of Israel of that time (Hosea), but there were many godly men who cried out their protests against the evils which brought the nation down to its doom. Year after year, and from one generation to another, devout men had pointed out the inevitable doom that must surely await the state that transgresses the laws of God. But no one took the trouble to listen.

Our own generation has been similarly warned. Long before Pearl Harbor courageous voices were lifted, warning the United States and Canada against the folly of shipping gasoline and scrap iron to Japan. "It will come back to us in the form of shells and submarines as surely as the sun sets in the west," one West Coast preacher cried out from his pulpit week after week. And as a consequence he was branded as a "red" by some, as a "radical" by others, and as a "communist" by a few.

Forty years before the outbreak of World War II the Christian missionaries in the Far East were pleading for help with all the powers at their command. The missionaries in Japan, for example, declared that their forces needed quadrupling "before it is too late." "This pagan doctrine of the divinity of the emperor will some day bathe the world in blood," one veteran missionary declared with prophetic insight. And Pearl Harbor was the proof.

Some proof of the wisdom of the missionaries' appeal appears in the fact that the 300,000 Christians of Japan, Protestant and Catholic, became the peace party of the empire. If they had been double this strength, they might have been able to stop the headlong rush of the war lords. But the United States and Canada had been warned!

Rare indeed is the case of the individual who finds himself plunged into disaster without warning. Most of us go every day kicking against the goads.

² *The Lord is with you, while you are with him.*

THE TRUE scientist starts out from the proposition that the conditions are already laid down. It is his responsibility to find them and, finding them, to conform to them.

The chemist sets out to discover what laws operate among the atoms and molecules. Once he has discovered a law, he is in a position to reduce at least one small area of the laboratory to order. Every law he proves to be true enlarges the area under his control. The same principle holds in every field into which science has entered. There can be no management of any of the forces of nature until we know the laws which operate among them.

The prophet performed a truly scientific service for the young king when he laid down in unmistakable language the conditions which he must follow for success as a monarch. "The Lord is with you, while you are with him." God does not humor the whims of a young and inexperienced king. He must conform to the laws of God or his reign will collapse.

It is here that the law of proportional giving renders its vital service to the Christian. The man who has determined to give one tenth, one twentieth, or even one hundredth of his income to God's causes, and insists upon doing it faithfully and conscientiously, soon discovers that he has moved over into the immediate and intimate company of God. Every dollar that comes into his possession is a vivid reminder of his personal relationship to God. As he views the needs of the world and considers his own ability to make a contribution to them, something holy enters into his life. In time this has the effect of sanctifying all his business relationships and his personal attitudes.

"This habit of tithing has changed so many of my attitudes toward so much of life," said a young engineer. "It may be that I take a childlike position, but I trust God to help me handle my business affairs just as I would trust my dad to help me if I took him into my confidence in the same way. The result is that I have lost much of the irritability that once characterized me. Tithing has taught me to trust, and it has had the effect of relieving my mind. Never before in my life have I had the same feeling that I had the endorsement of God. Trusting God in money matters has taught me to trust in everything else."

The serenity that stewardship is capable of injecting into one's life is worth much more than the financial cost of the tithing system.

¹⁰ *All the princes and all the people rejoiced and brought their tax and dropped it into the chest until they had finished.*

In Mexico, just across the border from a great American city, a bull fight was staged with four matadors from the United States killing bulls for the entertainment of the public. The admission fees for that Sunday afternoon were going to a fund for erecting a small chapel that was to bear the name of Jesus Christ.

One wonders just how happy the Lord Christ was, and how much satisfaction he may have taken in that kind of financing. Suppose, for example, that those same matadors had put on the same exhibition for the purpose of raising money with which to buy gifts for their mothers.

There are no statistics to prove the case, of course, but there can be little doubt that the low esteem in which the church is held in some communities is a result of the cheap and tawdry—the irreverent—methods it has used on many occasions for raising funds with which to carry on God's work. An institution that is compelled to resort to begging, lotteries (which are illegal in most states), carnivals, and similar devices can hardly complain if the community does not take it seriously.

Government is maintained by the dignified process of taxation; and though many a scandal is connected with the misuse of public funds, no one is suggesting that municipalities undertake to finance their public improvements with street-carnival fees. No self-respecting American city would stoop to side-show levels to maintain its police department. How, then, can men and women who have announced their devotion to the Lord Christ consent to degrading methods for financing the most holy institution in their lives?

There is a spiritual value in good entertainment, and the church owes a definite stewardship to serve its people in the area of recreation. But when entertainment is employed for the purpose of relieving Christians of their stewardship for the house and worship of God, then a positive spiritual damage has been inflicted upon the people and upon the Church.

The glory of Joash's chest lay in the fact that it was filled with freewill gifts, and the people found enormous joy and spiritual inspiration in giving because it represented their acceptance of a partnership with the Most High in a holy enterprise. It always works that way.

⁵ *He set himself to seek God in the days of Zechariah, who instructed him in the fear of God; and as long as he sought the Lord, God made him prosper.*

THERE IS an extremely pathetic note in this scripture. King Uzziah was, in many ways, a rather remarkable ruler. In the early years of his reign he was faithful, devout, and just. Then came prosperity and secularism. The Chronicler says, with keen insight, "As long as he sought the Lord, God made him prosper."

It was not that the little nation became destitute during Uzziah's reign. As a matter of fact, public finances were never in better condition. The internal defenses of the nation were strengthened, an abundance of stores was accumulated, and, according to all economic standards of measurement, matters went well. But something went out of the soul of the nation.

The poor were exploited, the widows and the defenseless found themselves victims of a myriad of injustices, the fine old democratic morality began to disintegrate, and the people became retrograde.

Within the experience of many pastors there are those instances of young couples who were, at the time of their marriage, devout, purposeful, and splendid. Then have come prosperity, membership in fashionable clubs, and sophistication, all of which has resulted in a breakdown of moral character and the loss of all spiritual integrity.

Some philosopher once said, "The worst thing about money is that it costs so much." And it has happened so many times that men have paid for their fortunes with every good thing in their lives.

The phone beside a preacher's bed rang about two o'clock in the morning, and a young man at the other end of the line pleaded, "Please come over to the hospital and pray for my baby." The minister went and did all he could, of course, and at a little after six o'clock, when the crisis seemed to be passed, the young father followed him to the door of the hospital and said, "It's a terrible thing, isn't it? Just four years ago I was the head of the youth organization of our church, and this morning I have to beg you to come to pray for my own baby. All because I have so far forsaken the Lord."

In those four years he had handled large sums of money and saved a tidy sum, but it was poor consolation when his baby was struggling for breath and he could not pray!

⁹ They came to Hilkiah the high priest and delivered the money that had been brought in to the house of God.

ONE OF THE economic, as well as spiritual, miracles of the years has been the amount of good works the Church of Jesus Christ has been able to encompass with the limited funds that have been placed at its disposal. No small part of this commendable success is due to the painstaking care with which the average church treasurer handles the funds that have been entrusted to him.

There are those individuals, of course, very rare in the history of any church, who have proved to be unworthy of the trust imposed in them. Only on the rarest of occasions is it true that moneys have been misappropriated. In view of the millions of dollars that pass through the hands of church treasurers, on both the denominational and the local level, the moral integrity of those officials who have been made the stewards of other men's sacred funds is one of the greatest proofs of the divine character of the Church.

"I have a strange feeling when I am counting the collection," said one finance committee chairman. "I look at the envelopes, I know the circumstances of many of the people, and when I consider the fact that these people trust me with administering the most holy money they ever handle, it makes me feel as though I were somehow a partner with God himself. I am very sure that, as I disburse the funds, I use more care than I would if the money were mine. My obligation to the people and my obligation to God invest my office with a sanctity that leaves me very serious."

Hundreds of thousands of treasurers of religious groups handle tens of millions of God's dollars every year—money that has been taken out of slender incomes in many instances—without bond and, in many cases, without an official audit of any kind. The security of the givers rests down upon the solid base of Christian character. Except in the case of those who serve as treasurers of great benevolent boards, these same treasurers and finance chairmen serve without compensation and give of their financial skills as though it were their ministry in the name of the Lord Christ.

Shaphan, Maaseiah, and Joash have been succeeded by a great army of those who have been true to their trust, and the spirit of devotion they have exhibited is one of the finest jewels in the diadem of the Church.

Ezra 1:1-4   GOD LOVES AN ADVENTUROUS STEWARD

³ Whoever is among you of all his people, may his God be with him, and let him go up to Jerusalem, which is in Judah, and rebuild the house of the Lord, the God of Israel.

Living was lush along the gently flowing waters in the Babylonian canals. Any Hebrew who considered returning to the narrow valleys and tawny hills of Palestine must therefore have been moved by some profound conviction. The Jews of the Exile ate more, were better clothed, and enjoyed a larger measure of the good things of life than had any of their forefathers. Moreover, they were far better provided for than were the inhabitants of the land out of which their fathers had been driven into Babylonian captivity. Viewed from a material standpoint, they had been greatly the gainers by the political misfortunes that had uprooted them from their homeland.

But there are values in life that far exceed food, clothing, and shelter. Moved by a passionate patriotism a few thousand Hebrew exiles were determined to return to Judea, pick up the broken threads of their national life, and bring alive again the nation that was God's chosen. It was a beautiful dream, a great faith, and a compelling destiny.

The number of those who returned to Judea was a relatively small proportion of the total Jewish population of Babylon, but destiny and history rode with them. The average Christian of today is quite unaware of the fact that for a thousand years the Jews of Babylonia constituted a mighty segment in that nation's life. Indeed, in Jesus' day, they outnumbered the Palestinian Jews in numbers. The Jewish university in Babylon was in every respect the equal of the great Jewish school in Alexandria, which took rank as one of the towering educational institutions of the ancient world.

Again and again it has happened that history has been determined by a small group of adventurous souls who have been supremely dedicated to a great ideal. The fifty-five Founding Fathers who gathered in Philadelphia to draft the Constitution for the infant American republic, and the small company of nobles who wrested Magna Charta from unwilling King John, influenced the history of mankind more profoundly than great marching hosts tramping across the field of battle.

In every Christian congregation the little group of tithers, probably unorganized, are influencing the life of the congregation far out of proportion to their numbers or their financial ability. It is in fulfillment of God's promise to the faithful.

[1] All the people gathered as one man into the square before the Water Gate; and they told Ezra the scribe to bring the book of the law of Moses which the Lord had given to Israel.

THE BOOK of Nehemiah chronicles one of the most dramatic episodes in all the strange history of the Hebrew people—the story of the first recorded every-member canvass.

A few thousand exiles had worked their way back from Babylon to Judea to begin life again in the Promised Land, but their obstacles were so great, their poverty so terrible, and their numbers so few that little progress was made. Then came the day when Ezra, a devout scribe and scholar, obtained permission to return with more exiles, and more treasure, to make a new effort.

The really great treasure he brought with him was the mammoth Book of the Law, which had been compiled from the various legal codes and historical books of the Hebrew nation by the patriotic scribes and scholars in Babylonian captivity. By a clever bit of stratagem he kept the contents of the book a secret and fanned the curiosity of the people, so much so that the first reading of the book brought all the people together before the Water Gate of Jerusalem.

From Nehemiah's description of the occasion it must have been a spectacular scene. For hours upon hours the people stood until the last word had been read in their hearing. Then, by a great popular vote which was unanimous, they agreed to make the Book of the Law their official code, their "constitution," and their final spiritual and civil authority.

Then something occurred that is altogether unique in human history, so far as the historical records of mankind show. By a unanimous and enthusiastic vote *the people agreed to tax themselves in perpetuity* for the support of their Temple, their priesthood, and their religious worship.

It is true, of course, that some civil functions were performed by the priests in connection with their services at the Temple altars, and to that extent the payments may have been said to represent what we would today call taxes. But the total income, democratically assessed and accepted, was primarily religious and was so esteemed by the people.

Throughout all the years that followed, until the destruction of the Temple by the Romans in A.D. 70, this tax upon all Jews continued in force and was paid as a religious rite. In Jesus' time it is said that upwards of ten million Jews scattered throughout the Roman Empire paid this Temple assessment.

²⁹ *Enter into a curse and an oath to walk in God's law which was*
given by Moses.

IN THE MIDST of the Babylonian exile the Hebrew people came under
a great conviction of sin. Their neglect of the law of God, they
believed, was the direct cause of their decline as a nation. Only by
a restoration of the Law as the governing principle of their national
life could they hope to be restored.

When Ezra and Nehemiah arrived in Judea with the great Book
of the Law, they came challenging the people to cut themselves off
from the surrounding paganism in a manner that would be absolutely uncompromising. The result was that they set up a series of
prohibitions under which they proposed to live and which were
both stern and puritanical. From that day forward the religion of
Israel tended to become a stifling thing of complex regulations,
inflexible law, and monotonous ceremonies.

Conspicuous in the Jewish system was the rule of the tithe. Giving
a tenth was a common religious practice among the ancients, but
the Jews invested it with an authority quite unique. The result was
that among strict Pharisees it actually became a rule that one must
count the grains of pepper or other spice before seasoning food, to
make sure that one had tithed his income accurately. This type of
legalism Jesus held in fine contempt.

But the fact that tithing has sometimes taken on an aspect of
legalism does not mean of necessity that it must be purely legalistic.
Rightly observed, the principle of the tithe can be a great spiritual
restorer, as thousands will testify.

At least three distinct benefits will appear as the individual tithes
his income with a glad heart and a thankful spirit. First, he will
have a heightened and intensified sense of the presence of God as
he takes out the tenth from each bit of income when it comes in.
Second, the tither soon discovers a new feeling of order and responsibility in his financial dealings, each one being invested with a
new sanctity. This inevitably produces a heightened sense of the
presence of God. Third, one comes to a sense of the daily companionship of the Father as each day's work is dedicated to the
cause of the Kingdom with the tithe. "I date the beginning of a
new spiritual experience from the first Saturday night that I sat
down to figure out my tithe," said one Christian.

² *Who is this that darkens counsel*
by words without knowledge?

WE HAVE made much sport of the old adage "Be good and you'll be happy," as though it had proved to be a mirage and a deception. The cynics have pointed us to the good people who have been defeated, disappointed, and betrayed, as though goodness were a mistake.

It is a fact, however, that goodness pays the good in a coinage all its own. Malcolm B——— was a tither, a faithful attendant upon divine worship, a good family man, and a young businessman struggling to get a small jewelry store on its feet. He paid his tenth with exact care, maintained a family altar, and taught a boys' class in the church school with great fidelity. Then business difficulties arose, the sheriff arrived at his door with a padlock, and he was listed as a bankrupt.

For a few weeks he was terribly confused. "Why did this thing have to happen to me?" he asked his pastor, and there was deep pain in his voice as though God had failed him—as though his whole program of righteous living had been a mistaken policy. The very earth was shaking under his feet, and he was in desperate need of something to which to tie.

Thirty years went by, and one Sunday morning in a distant city he sat again under the preaching of the pastor of his youth. At the close of the service he sought out the preacher, introduced himself, and said, "Do you remember the time I went bankrupt in the jewelry business in the little town where you were preaching? And do you remember the way I questioned the wisdom and goodness of God? Well, I want you to know that I found the answer, and I thank you for steadying me during those blinding days. Circumstances forced me out of the business for which I was badly fitted, and thrust me into another line in which I have developed considerable skill. My debts were paid off within the space of a few years, and I have enjoyed a prosperity since that I supposed would never be mine. I think the victory came when I determined to go on tithing, maintaining my family altar, teaching my Sunday-school class, and doing all the other godly things I had been accustomed to doing. I am very sure that God guided me when I trusted him. I am comfortable, though I have never become rich. But I am sure if I had ceased tithing I should have suffered irreparably within my own soul."

¹ *The earth is the Lord's and the fulness thereof,*
the world and those who dwell therein.

IN BASIC variance with all the ancient paganism the Hebrews began their religious faith with the proposition that God is the owner of all creation. This doctrine they placed at the masthead of the Old Testament (Gen. 1:1) and then reiterated the claim in the words of prophets and psalmists again and again (Job 38:4; Pss. 8:3; 50:10; Isa. 45:6, 9).

When the Beloved Disciple, said by many to be the most profound thinker the early Christian Church produced, undertook to write a statement of the new Christian faith in the hope of converting the learned Greeks of Ephesus to Christ, he began with the same principle stated in almost identical terms—"In the beginning was the Word" (John 1:1)—and continued with the sweeping declaration that "without him was not anything made that was made" (1:3). When the apostle Paul had his one chance to preach to the scholarly Athenians, he declared the doctrine of God's ownership of all created things in the plainest possible language (Acts 17:23-25, 28).

William Blackstone, the immortal commentator on English law, began his philosophy of ownership of property at this same point. "This is the only true and solid foundation of man's dominion over external things," he said, "whatever airy metaphysical notions may have been started by fanciful writers on this subject. The earth therefore, and all things therein, are the general property of all mankind . . . from the immediate gift of the Creator."

When the ancient Hebrews gathered at their altars to worship and offer their sacrifices, they sang jubilantly and acknowledged freely that all their goods had come to them from God (I Chr. 24:19), and in Christian congregations today the choir chants this ancient song of stewardship and acknowledges that the title to all goods still rests in God's hands. There is probably no single musical line so universally sung as the one that exhorts us to "praise God from whom all blessings flow." This line from the Doxology is a reflection of the doctrine of stewardship.

We live in a world that was created for us. It is impossible for a man, by taking thought, to add one element to the long list of the components of this earth. We can arrange, manipulate, analyze, employ, and combine the earth's constituents. But we cannot create; neither can we own. God holds the title.

' He who has clean hands and a pure heart,
who does not lift up his soul to what is false,
and does not swear deceitfully.

WE ARE IN great danger of overlooking the fact that the ancient Hebrews were actually a very devout people. Their religious system was ritualistic, mechanical, and legalistic, and their prophets accused them of great sinning with monotonous regularity. But the psalms bear evidence of the fact that there were many gracious spirits among them, and that they lived above the level of the paganism that surrounded them as the mountain towers above the plain.

The singer who first sang the twenty-fourth psalm must have been eminently just, high-minded, clean of spirit, and with an exalted concept of God. Quite evidently he had thought clearly on the subject of man's relationship to the Creator, and had managed to escape the prevailing legalism of his time.

A young man who had but recently lost his father, a humble man of great piety, stood holding a well-worn purse in his hands. "It was my father's," he said, "and it is one of my most inspiring possessions. I know it was seldom filled, and never stuffed. But it never held an unearned dollar as long as my father carried it, and it never contained a dollar that represented anything with the slightest taint of injustice on it."

The arts and graces of life seem to be distributed rather unevenly among men. Those who are gifted as painters, musicians, or scientists are relatively rare. There is a vast amount of talent in the world and no little cleverness, as well as much clumsiness. There are some skills that can be achieved only by the few. But any person has the right to aspire to the distinction of having clean hands. Any man determined to stand guard over the sanctity of his own life can hope to live inside the hallowed circle of those who "stand in his holy place."

To do so, however, each individual must declare his own independence of things. He must divest himself of the tyranny of his possessions; he must rise above the level of materialism; he dare not bow down and worship anything made by the hands of men; he must save his own soul from the seductions of secularism; he must master his property or be mastered by it; he must discipline everything he possesses and compel it to serve the highest purposes of his life; he must be prepared to find his satisfactions in ideas, ideals, and faith rather than in sensations, thrills, and an overstuffed stomach.

⁵ *I acknowledged my sin to thee,*
and I did not hide my iniquity;
I said, "I will confess my transgressions to the Lord."

CONFESSING ONE's sins is extremely serious business. It calls for the strictest honesty and the utmost of moral courage.

In the psalms of Israel we get a glimpse into the hearts of the ancient Hebrews, for all the psalms have come down to us because they struck a responsive chord within the souls of the people, somewhat as the Negro spirituals have come down to us from the cabins and the camp meetings of the black Christians who first sang them out of their experience.

One of the conspicuous qualities of the psalms is that they make candid confession of so many sins, but it is also significant that they never mention one of the most common sins—stinginess. For that matter, modern Christians do not either.

"In my career as a minister through a period of almost half a century I have had every sin in the catalog confessed to me," said a preacher who had served at the heart of three great American cities. "Every sin, that is, except one. Never that I can remember has any man ever come to me saying, 'I am a stingy man. Will you please pray for me that I may overcome this terrible thing within me that prevents me from sharing my plenty with those in need?'"

It is one of the strange perversities of the stingy man that he usually contrives to persuade himself that he is actually generous. He usually persuades himself that he has "done more than his share." Not that he is pretending; in most cases he is entirely sincere in believing his twisted reasoning.

Again and again a man stricken with remorse has asked for the prayers of his fellow Christians. Usually one who has been apprehended in one of the grosser sins is overcome with shame and pleads with God and his friends for mercy. But the stingy man will rise up and defend his stinginess as though it were a virtue. He prides himself on his niggardliness in the belief that he is only prudent or, perhaps, "conservative."

In every congregation there are those who will never make further spiritual progress until they have come to a new attitude on the subject of money. Just as it is the business of the preacher to warn the lecherous against their lechery, so it is the minister's responsibility to warn the stingy man.

⁵ *Commit your way to the Lord;*
trust in him, and he will act.

BISHOP ARTHUR J. Moore of the Methodist Church tells the story
of a conscientious old farmer who had become greatly troubled over
the question of tithing as a result of some straight preaching he had
heard from his pastor. The matter seemed to prey on his mind until
it became a conflict within his own soul. His preacher had convinced
him that the tenth belonged to the Lord, but the dear old man
could not quite bring himself to make the commitment.

Finally on one memorable Sunday afternoon he sat down at his
desk and wrote out a deed to the farm and bill of sale for all his
stock, by which instruments he turned his property over to the
Lord and agreed to give ten per cent of the income from the entire
establishment in token of God's ownership. That done, he experienced
a sense of spiritual peace he had not known for two or three years.

Three weeks afterward grasshoppers settled down on the farm and
began devouring everything. Within the space of hours the fields
were bare and even the trees were stripped of their leaves, and a
season's work was gone.

A few days later the farmer was in town and happened to meet
a neighbor, who immediately began commiserating with him. "The
'hoppers have just about cleaned you out, haven't they?" he asked.

"Yes, I reckon I'm lucky to have the barbs left on the wire fences
by this time," the farmer replied.

"You don't seem to be much worried. I'd be most crazy if it was
me," the neighbor exclaimed, with a bit of bewilderment in his
voice.

"No, I ain't worried," the old farmer replied. "You see, three
weeks ago Sunday I deeded that farm and all those hogs and horses
and cattle over to the Lord. They're his, and that farm is his, and
everything is his. And those 'hoppers are his, too, and if he wants to
pasture his own grasshoppers on his own land, then it's all right with
me."

One may smile at the picturesque way in which the good man
faced his problem, but one cannot dismiss easily the faith that such
a commitment inspires. The Psalmist must have had something of
that in his mind when he said:

> Commit your way to the Lord;
>   trust in him, and he will act.
> He will bring forth your vindication as the light,
>   and your right as the noonday.

⁴ For thou, O Lord, hast made me glad by thy work;
at the works of thy hands I sing for joy.

RAYMOND I. Lindquist, one of the nation's leading Presbyterian preachers, preached a Thanksgiving sermon on the text contained in the first verse of this scripture and to it gave the title "The Attitude of Gratitude." It was a plea for the recovery of the spirit of thanksgiving in our daily lives.

Modern life is very hard on the spirit of reverence. When our grandfathers went tramping through the woods and came upon a stream or a spring, they stretched out upon the bank, drank the refreshing draught, and gave thanks to the God who taught the little stream to flow as it did in the cool places. But the modern man, thirsty and spent, goes to the faucet and turns on the water without a thought of the Almighty. There is little about modern plumbing to inspire reverence.

So many gadgets obtrude themselves upon us, shutting out the revelation of God. The modern man turns on an electric current and air-conditions his home; a tank car delivers the winter's supply of fuel oil so that he does not so much as soil his hands; from one winter's end to another he is independent of nature, even though he may be at the mercy of a labor union or an employer's association. It all means that he never meets the God of nature.

A faithful practice of the doctrine of stewardship will have the effect of rescuing us from such a materialistic tyranny. It may call for a more active imagination than was necessary in the case of the spring or the little woodland stream, but the man who thinks of all his possessions as being the property of God—that God is the actual owner and he is the steward—will find his heavenly Father in sulfa drugs, industrial chemistry, and nuclear fission.

The God who packed energy into the atom is just as real as the God who started the little stream flowing down the valley between the rocks and trees. The man who looks for God among the electrons will be as sure to find him as the one who looked for him in the rain clouds over the dry land.

The attitude of gratitude will have the effect of redeeming life from its sordidness, its monotony, and its secularism. The doctrine of stewardship that produces the spirit of gratitude can result in the redemption of even the most drab and uninspiring experiences. We preach stewardship not for the sake of raising money, but for the purpose of uplifting life.

GRATITUDE PAYS DIVIDENDS

Ps. 104:1-6

¹ Bless the Lord, O my soul!
O Lord my God, thou art very great!
Thou art clothed with honor and majesty.

THAT PERSON who never learns to express his gratitude inflicts positive damage upon his own personality. Not only do we owe words of thanks to friends who have served us well, but an expression of the spirit of gratitude provides us with what the psychologists call "an emotional release," which is of very great value.

It is quite possible to crowd feelings, impulses, desires, and urges down into the subconscious with unhappy results. To repress the spirit of thanksgiving—to fail to offer thanks—is to produce a spiritual condition that acts like a poison inside the soul of man.

One does not need to look widely about him to discover that those who are first to express their thanksgiving are the happiest. To fail to say or do the kindly thing, to ignore appeals for assistance that we are able to render, to shut our hearts up against all needs outside ourselves, is to provide a breeding ground for spiritual distempers that are capable of wrecking all our happiness and peace of mind.

The father of a considerable family of splendid sons came to the conclusion that if he complimented his boys he would make egotists of them. As a consequence he bottled up within himself all natural expressions of appreciation with the result that in the course of the years he became a stern man, unhappy and unsatisfied. The young men survived their father's taciturnity, but the aging man grew progessively hard. His churlishness affected his own outlook so that he ceased to see the world in any true perspective.

His pastor said of him, "He never really laughs heartily. He seems to smile grudgingly. As a consequence he is missing many of the deepest joys of life."

The apostle Paul, commenting on this same type of soul, said, "God loves a cheerful giver" (II Cor. 9:7), as though generosity in itself is not enough. For the giver to get the joy of giving he must bestow his gifts with a certain hilarity of soul. The reluctant philanthropist is only a few degrees removed from actual stinginess. The psalmist in the scripture of this text caught the spirit of pure joy and impregnated his song with the hilarity that comes with an outpouring heart. Giving without praise is almost as barren as praise without giving.

70

¹ Out of the depths I cry to thee, O Lord!

I HAVE suffered much and have lost heavily. I have given to good causes with some liberality and have watched my profits go down at a terrifying rate. But because I have been faithful to every trust imposed in me, according to the best of my ability, I believe that God will some day strike a balance on my books and I shall be satisfied. Because God is what Jesus said he was, I am going to trust him and not fear. Moreover, I am going to go on giving to the causes that I think have his endorsement and to have the satisfaction of knowing that I am a worker together with him."

This was the testimony of a man who was tragically familiar with the depths—one who had cried out to the Lord again and again. It was also the testimony of a man who had experienced the help of the Lord in the hour of his emergency. He could not point to any instance in which his fortunes had been saved by some divine interposition, but he did know that in the face of every disaster he had been able to maintain something like calm. As someone once said of him, "He never seemed to lose his head just when he needed it most."

The believer and the unbeliever share many of the same experiences of life. Sickness, pain, frustration, disappointment, and even death come to both. But the believer has a confidence whereas the unbeliever has nothing more than a vague hope to sustain him.

In the background of the believer's mind there is a consciousness that, through the years, he has made at least some effort to do the will of God. Just as the chemist trusts the laws that operate in the laboratory, and as the engineer relies upon the laws of gravity and tensility, so the believer puts his confidence in the moral and spiritual laws upon which the universe rests.

The unbeliever, on the other hand, has no such confidence. He has always tried to do the "right thing," but it has been no conscious effort to do the will of God. He has contributed to charities and other good causes as the whim suggested, but it has been without any sense of spiritual responsibility. He has regarded his possessions as being his own quite without any sense of stewardship. He therefore has no sense of security concerning the nature of God, and no faith because of his lack of relationship to him. The depths out of which he cries are different.

[1] Hear, O sons, a father's instruction,
and be attentive, that you may gain insight.

IN OUR DEEP concern for the welfare of our children, we undertake to provide them with educational opportunities in the fields of science, art, music, literature, and economics; but no parent has discharged his obligation to his child until he has taught him at least the rudiments of the fine art of Christian giving.

Here is the story of a big industrialist whose business amounts to many millions of dollars every year, and whose benefactions run into the hundreds of thousands of dollars.

"It began," he says, "when I was a little boy. My father was a tither, and when I was still a tiny little fellow, he sat down with me and explained the system with great care. He made it seem like a privilege, some kind of partnership with Almighty God.

"My weekly allowance in those days was a dime a week, and getting that dime changed into pennies so that I could set aside one of them for Sunday school became a religious ritual with me. When I started off for college, my father handed me a check for $300; and as soon as I arrived at the college town, I deposited $30 in a separate account at the bank and proceeded to draw upon it for my contributions.

"When I graduated from college and landed my first job, I went into conference with my father and with his help figured out what my tenth would be. Thereupon I dedicated it and made it a rule thereafter to set aside my tithe, keeping it quite apart from all my other funds. When I first went into business for myself, I set up a tithing account, entirely aside from my other business operations, and paid all my 'contributions' out of that. I did it on my father's advice, for he has always been my counselor in this matter, and it has been the best single piece of guidance he has given me."

On the fifteenth of each December his chief accountant comes in with the record of the giving of the year and together the two of them plan the program for the year ahead. When all causes have been considered, and the probable funds available have been estimated, a budget is set up with the same care that would be used in the case of plant expansion, labor costs, or advertising. Toward the last of each month the record is scanned to determine how nearly the account is "on schedule." Thus has giving been made a fine art.

²⁸ *He who trusts in his riches will wither,*
   but the righteous will flourish like a green leaf.

THERE IS a whimsical story of an eccentric countryman who dug a new well every New Year's Day on the theory that he was beginning life all over again with the first of every January. As though one had to dig a new well to begin a new life!

Some wells do not need to be dug again; they may need dredging, curbing, or deepening, but not redigging. There are values that have endured the ravages of time without depreciating. Certain habits pay dividends in every generation and under all circumstances. The author of the proverb "He who trusts in his riches will wither" had lived with his eyes open and his mind clear. Jesus' warning about the moth and rust that consume (Matt. 6:19-20) is as modern as this morning's headlines. Time has not altered it in the least.

The human race has been at this business of living for a great many generations, and in the course of the centuries it has learned some things the hard way—truths that cannot be changed by the turning of the calendar. He who abandons the judgments of the centuries is not wise, nor is he very clever. We do not need a new alphabet, a new octave, or a new spectrum. Neither do we need a new set of Ten Commandments, new beatitudes, a new Sermon on the Mount, nor a new thirteenth chapter of First Corinthians.

In the course of the centuries the race has experimented with every form of sex relationship and has come to the conclusion that there is but one solution for the sex problem—monogamy, or the love of one good man for one good woman.

Christians have experimented with every form of giving, but no other system has demonstrated so many advantages, produced so much spiritual good, raised so much money for holy causes with so little secular effort, or nurtured so many souls in a triumphant faith as has that one which is called tithing. Rare indeed is the tither who having given the method an honest and faithful trial ever abandons it afterward.

The Protestant churches commend tithing as a solution of the money problem in the life of the individual as well as the program of the church but, except for a few denominations, do not require it. Tithing commends itself in the contribution it makes to the spiritual life of the individual who practices it.

³ *What does man gain by all the toil
at which he toils under the sun?*

THE CYNICAL old soul, whoever he may have been, who wrote the book of Ecclesiastes, asked a searching question at the very outset of his book when he inquired:

What does man gain by all the toil
at which he toils under the sun?

It sounds just a little like Jesus' saying, "What does it profit a man, to gain the whole world and forfeit his life?" (Mark 8:36.)

Possessions are so powerful and at the same time so impotent; they can become such useful servants and such imperious masters; they open such heavy doors and close up the sources of so much inspiration; they will work so many wonders and embalm so many high ideals; they will tell so many horrid things about us or go to the ends of the earth to minister to the needy and unfortunate in our name; they can produce so much light and becloud so many minds; they can heal so many wounds and inflict so many injuries.

We can reduce them to subjection or march as their captives; it is all a matter of choice. The right to decide resides with us. This is one of the strange aspects of the image of God in which we were created.

One of the chief reasons for Jesus' residence with us was his desire to teach one simple truth—a principle he enunciated at the hour of his temptation. "Man shall not live by bread alone." (Matt. 4:4.) This he elaborated a little later in his ministry when he said, "A man's life does not consist in the abundance of his possessions" (Luke 12:15). Unless some kind of mastery can be established over the day's work, life is reduced to only a little better than chaos. It was for this reason that so much of Jesus' preaching was concerned with questions of money, goods, ownership, wages, talents, and stewardship.

It is only as a craftsman makes himself the master of his machine that he becomes a skilled worker; only as the student develops mastery over his instrument that he becomes a musician; only as an astronomer learns how to use the amazing possibilities of the telescope that he becomes a great scientist so that he can unravel the mysteries of the skies over his head.

Similarly, goods and possessions are the tools which a man must master if he is ever to achieve his true destiny as a being made in the image of God. Otherwise he becomes their slave and victim.

*[12] For who knows what is good for man while he lives the few days
of his vain life, which he passes like a shadow?*

IF WE WERE to have the privilege of meeting the author of Ecclesiastes in some modern setting, we should probably find him
to be a very polished gentleman, well versed in the ways of the
world, urbane and perhaps a little bitter, rather interesting but
entirely cynical. He would doubtless describe himself as "an enlightened liberal" who hated all pretense and insisted upon accepting
life as he found it—a realist.

With much of his cleverness we might be amused, and with his
intolerance of pretense we would be in entire agreement, though
there may be some merit in the pretense that gives a sheen of love-
liness to many of the stern realities. But the man with a vivid religious faith would have an answer for his question, "Who knows
what is good for man?"

Bishop Gerald Kennedy once remarked, "Every man's job is his
chief characteristic. If he is really a Christian, his Christianity must
eventually get down on the economic level and redeem it also."
And that is precisely the service that the doctrine of stewardship
renders to the man who accepts it and undertakes to be guided by it.

Unless something "good for man" can be found in economics,
the case for Christianity breaks up completely. There have been
those who, in an effort to shake themselves loose from economic
terrorism, have "vowed themselves to poverty" and esteemed all
possessions to be a hindrance to real spirituality. This, however,
is salvation by retreat. He alone has worked out his salvation who
has brought his economic interests under subjection and harnessed
them to the central purpose of doing the will of God.

This means that all of one's economic interests must be brought
into harmony with the will of God, as that will has been revealed
by Jesus Christ. What any man undertakes to make with his hands,
what he proposes to sell to his neighbor, what he proposes to buy,
the payment he demands and receives for his labor, the skills he
cultivates and the services he renders—all these must merit the
approval of the kind of God Jesus described the Father as being.

It is not good for a man, for example, to sell goods that debauch
his brother, to become the servant of the thing he makes, or to
own the thing that possesses him eventually.

BLOODY HANDS

[15] *Your hands are full of blood.*

IT WAS THE custom among the ancient Hebrews when they stood to pray to extend their hands upward, palms opened to heaven, and present their petitions.

In this scripture the prophet alludes to the posture and warns the nation that God will not listen when they pray because, as he looks down upon them at their prayers, the first thing he sees is their bloody hands.

We sing "God Bless America" with something like hilarious abandon, utterly indifferent to, or unconscious of, those sins of the nation that make the blessings of God almost impossible.

How clean are the hands we upraise to God when they have only recently marked a ballot in favor of the liquor interests?

How clean are the hands of a nation that spends millions of dollars a year for dog racing, prize fights, and burlesque shows, but neglects churches, schools, Community Chests, and orphanages?

How clean are the hands of a nation that squanders money on luxuries but ignores the starving and suffering who have been left bleeding and half dead in the wake of war?

How clean are the hands of a nation that fattens on its war industries but seeks to retreat from its world responsibilities?

How clean are the hands of that nation which reckons its foreign policy entirely on the basis of its trade balances and economic power, with never a thought of the world's great hungers?

It sometimes happens that our hands speak much louder than our voices, and God cannot hear the prayers we intone because of the raucous cries of our industrial struggles.

The Christian steward thinks of his whole life, in all its interests and activities, his earning and his spending, as a prayer—the expression of the dominant desire of his heart.

There is nothing in all of life more intimate than the money we handle. It represents our labor, our investment of talent and skill, our choice of life's purposes. The way we spend represents the inner desires of our heart, the secret motives by which we are guided. How often our treasure rises in judgment against us, accusing us of divided loyalties and unconsecrated passions.

David Lloyd George, Britain's prime minister during World War I, said, when that tragic conflict was over, that England had suffered a greater defeat when she tolerated a slum than when her soldiers were beaten on the field of battle. This is true of any nation.

[1] *"Woe to the rebellious children,"* says the Lord,
"who carry out a plan, but not mine."

THROUGHOUT his entire career as a prophet Isaiah was engaged in an effort to persuade the nation to put its trust in God. Its peculiar geographical location alongside the great trade routes over which the commerce of the ancient world flowed in a constant stream, exposed it to every international intrigue. All politics were world politics for the little nation.

Thoroughly versed in the world affairs of his day, Isaiah knew that no reliance could be placed on the promises of Pharaoh. He knew also that Judah was no match for the crushing might of the Assyrians. So far as he could see, there was no dependable ally to be found anywhere. Therefore he preached the doctrine of isolationism and of complete dependence upon God. But the kings and governments with which he had to deal during the half century that he preached to the nation, were all determined on "entangling alliances."

Faith in God means much more than an intellectual assent to the fact of God. It means a complete confidence in the wisdom of the will of God and a complete acceptance of the way of God in all the affairs of life.

It is probably true that tens of thousands of Christians are intellectually convinced that stewardship is a reasonable Christian doctrine, and that tithing is an admirable method of giving; but they have not been able to bring themselves to the point where they are willing to make the actual decision to give the tenth, because they cannot see in advance how it is going to come out for them. They listen with respect to the related experiences of others, and they applaud. But they have a vague fear. Their case, they think, is different. They are pressed by obligations and harassed by unpaid bills, and "there is never a dollar left over at the end of the month. How can we take out one tenth when the ten tenths are not enough?"

That is the miracle of it. Thousands of tithers testify to the fact that their bills are somehow met, their obligations fulfilled, and their whole economic program reduced to order in the process of adjusting to the tithing system. Having put their faith in God, and launching out on the method as an expression of faith, they experience an entirely new spiritual victory, which is accompanied by a new economic certainty.

Back of the tithing system stands the Creator of the universe, challenging us to put it to the test.

¹ *In the thirtieth year, in the fourth month, on the fifth day of the month, as I was among the exiles by the river Chebar, the heavens were opened, and I saw visions of God.*

POLITICALLY speaking, the case of the Hebrew exiles was hopeless. They had been uprooted from their homeland and transported across the desert to be dropped down alongside the canals of Babylon, where they had to begin life all over again without capital, experience, citizenship, or social standing. There is something very terrifying about the words of Ezekiel: "I was among the exiles by the river Chebar." It was as if he were saying, "I had come to the end of the road."

Someone, sometime, is going to make an extremely interesting and valuable study of the redemption that has come to this world by means of minorities. No small part of today's world is the result of small groups who have held out in favor of great ideals in the face of the mass pressures of all civilization.

Most of us have given little thought to the narrow bottleneck through which the great facts and bases of our faith have come down to us. No more than a few thousand Hebrews were deported to Babylon following the fall of Jerusalem, but they were the bravest souls, the finest minds, and the most devout spirits among the people. To them we owe every important moral and spiritual contribution the Children of Israel have made to civilization.

No more than a few million of the world's population have come to the New World, but those who came during a period of more than a century were lovers of liberty, apostles of freedom, and earnest souls who came in the hope of realizing a great dream.

It has been the tiny minority of the faithful who have kept the torch burning, and to whom we owe our Christian heritage. If they had failed, God would have had to raise up another Israel and prepare for another Messiah. No one could have guessed, back there in the year 450 B.C., that destiny walked the narrow streets of Babylon in the persons of such souls as Ezekiel, Ezra, and Nehemiah.

The hard core of the givers in practically any Christian congregation consists of that little group of unorganized stewards who take their stewardship seriously and dedicate the tenth of their income to the furthering of the cause of the kingdom of God among men. If the total number of tithers in Protestantism could be doubled, they would shake this world.

²⁶ *A new heart I will give you, and a new spirit I will put within you; and I will take out of your flesh the heart of stone and give you a heart of flesh.*

UNTIL THE time of Jeremiah the entire emphasis in Hebrew religion and faith had been placed on the nation. With the great prophet of the last days the emphasis upon the individual began to appear. In the Exile, with the nation in ruins and the Temple destroyed, the mantle of responsibility fell upon solitary men and women, here and there, who gravitated into posts of strategic importance. It was to strengthen and increase the faith of some of these individuals that Ezekiel preached some of his strongest sermons, this scripture being an excerpt from such an address.

In the motion picture of many years ago entitled "Baron Rothchild," there was an extremely moving scene to which was added a single comment of enormous power. The most dangerous hour in the life of the English people had come, and the great capitalist was about to throw his entire fortune into the breach in the hope of saving the nation. Just at that juncture some timid soul said, "But, Baron, one man can't save England." To which the great old patriot replied, *"But one man can try."*

Rarely can one man save a generation, but any man can save his own life from being overwhelmed by the debris of things, and the one life he saves may be the one life upon which God and the Church must depend in some critical situation.

One man can maintain a family altar inside his own home; one man can give a tenth of his income and by so doing make Christ the complete master over at least one income and one man's possessions.

God limits each man's stewardship to those things over which he has final authority. He holds no man responsible for those things which lie outside his control or his influence. As we establish control over our own lives, however, our influence lengthens; and as we accept the full stewardship over our own possessions, life takes on a meaning and a radius far greater than before.

No man can tithe another man's income, but he can assume the mastery over his own. He cannot fill a church on the Sabbath, but he can occupy a seat in a pew. He may not be able to stem the tide of godlessness that threatens to engulf a community, but he can stand out consistently against the immorality that rises up within his own soul.

THE CHRISTIAN STEWARD AND ISOLATIONISM
Dan. 7:13-14

*¹⁴ All peoples, nations, and languages
should serve him.*

ISOLATIONISM is more than a political opinion; it is a philosophy of life, and one in which no genuine Christian steward is ever able to share.

When Jesus said "Go into all the world" (Mark 16:15), he broke through all barriers of race, class, color, and station, and claimed the world as his rightful Kingdom. In that daring declaration he carried the banners of the Kingdom out into the open country and called to all men everywhere to join the movement for a new world of righteousness.

It was here that he became involved in his controversies with the Jewish authorities, who resented the extension of the Kingdom to the Gentiles. It was also here that the apostle Paul fought his bitterest fight in behalf of emancipation—the freeing of the gospel from restricting rules and ceremonies of the Jews. Except for the fact that he won in that struggle, we of the Gentile world should never have known the story of the gospel of Christ, for Christianity would have degenerated into some minor sect of Judaism.

There is a sense in which it must be said that there is no such thing as "foreign missions," for such a concept is alien to the basic concept of the kingdom of God as a social order designed for all humanity. The Christian who does not believe in preaching the gospel of the good news of Christ to the ends of the earth, does not believe in the whole Christian message.

Three things constitute the rock base of our stewardship of the gospel of redemption: knowledge of Christ, the power to spread the good news, and the opportunity to share the message. If we can testify to the fact that the incoming of Christ has made a difference in our life, if we have any income from which a tenth can be taken with which to help finance the cause of evangelism, and if we have the opportunity to help spread the gospel anywhere on earth, then these things constitute our stewardship.

Every unchristianized area of the world is a charge against us as Christians. Every struggling mission field and every undermanned institution are challenges to us. Money invested in luxuries will rise up to testify against us in that last day. Extravagances that take precedence over our tithe will destroy the very fiber of our soul. The Christian who looks out on this world through the eyes of Christ sees no color lines.

⁴ Bring your sacrifices every morning,
your tithes every three days.

As SCIENTISTS have pointed out on many occasions, no creature
has ever been betrayed by its instincts. The geese fly south with
the approach of winter, the salmon return to the stream in which
they were spawned, the swallows make their appearance at San
Juan Capistrano with clocklike regularity, and the species survives
as a consequence.

Psychologists and sociologists have seemingly taken genuine
delight in digging up evidence that many modern habits of man
are survivals of earlier modes of life and action. The anthropologists
assert that they can detect many traits in the behavior of the
civilized man that are the direct results of the struggles of the
primeval man.

The shrines of Bethel and Gilgal, to which the prophet Amos
referred, were very old gathering places where men came to offer
their sacrifices and pay their tithes. Their origins were shrouded
in the deep mists of the past. Long before the Hebrews dedicated
them for religious use, they were used by the Canaanites and
Sumerians for religious worship. No one can estimate how many
hundreds of years the heads of families had been coming to these
hoary shrines, there to offer their tithes and burn their sacrifices.

The payment of a tenth to the gods was a fixed rule among the
Babylonians, Assyrians, Egyptians, and Sumerians hundreds, and
probably thousands, of years before Malachi accused the Hebrews
of robbing God when they withheld their tithes (Mal. 3:8). Aris-
totle, Xenophon, Herodotus, Pliny, and Cicero all mention the
payment of the tithe as being a very old custom amounting to a
law in their day and among their people. It is almost as though
the payment of the tenth were instinctive as is the impulse to
self-preservation.

Among the pagans, of course, the payment of the tenth often
took on the form of a bribe offered to the gods in the hope that
they would bestow their benefactions as a consequence. Among
the Hebrews the custom was lifted to a higher level, and the
payment of the tenth represented the worshiper's acknowledgment
of his obligations to Jehovah, the creator and patron of the nation.

The payment of the tithe, therefore, did not originate with the
Hebrews but seems to have been a common expression of religious
loyalty and devotion common to all mankind.

MAKING WORSHIP SINCERE   Amos 5:7, 14-15, 23-24

*⁷ O you who turn justice to wormwood,
and cast down righteousness to the earth!*

IT IS EXTREMELY unfortunate that the prophet Amos is so little known to the laity of the twentieth-century Christian Church, for he was such a modern man. Preaching at a time when life was going to pieces in Israel, and when a terrible and impending doom was gathering on the horizon, he uttered words that have profound significance for our generation.

Laymen are interested in the prophet Amos, once they come to know him, because he himself was a layman, entirely without professional religious training or standing. When challenged to show his right to speak, he declared that he had his call directly from God (7:14). Interestingly enough, the written record of his preaching at the Bethel shrine constitutes the oldest complete book we have in the Old Testament—a layman's book.

Nothing in the gilded and guilty civilization against which he inveighed deceived him; he knew a mirage when he saw one. He was quick to recognize hypocrisy even when it disguised itself in professionalism and official authority. The crowds that thronged the shrines left him unimpressed, but the suffering poor, the exploited widows, the callous rich, and the graft-ridden courts moved him to an indignation that shook the earth.

Nothing could make the elaborate worship and colorful ceremonies of the shrines beautiful in his sight as long as the liquor business debauched the people and prostitution flourished unrebuked. If the hearts of men were unclean, their offerings at the altars of God were unacceptable, the prophet declared. In all the long history of religion he was the first, so far as we can discover, who linked good religion and social justice in a living faith.

As an employer Amos would have held himself responsible for the welfare of his workers, in addition to paying them wages. As an employee Amos would have held himself responsible for the welfare of his employer, in addition to drawing his wages. As a judge Amos would have held himself responsible for administering justice quite independently of the social status of the litigants. As a landlord he would have held himself responsible for the personal welfare of his tenants and their children as surely as he would have collected the rents. As a preacher he would have declared the judgments of God, whether they were comfortable or not. He was that kind of steward.

‘ Woe to those who lie upon beds of ivory,
and stretch themselves upon their couches.

THE LITTLE kingdom of Israel was suffering from delusions induced by its sudden prosperity. The vast tide of commerce that
flowed across the land paid handsome revenues into the national
treasury in the form of customs duties, with the result that unprecedented amounts of money were in circulation—with all the
attendant evils of inflation. The great monarchs of Egypt and
Assyria courted the favor of the Israelite court because the tiny
state lay athwart the trade routes that carried the world's commerce
and was therefore in a position to levy taxes against all traffic.
Luxury goods spilled off the long caravans and seeped out into
Hebrew life, persuading the upper classes that they were somehow
especially favored by Jehovah.

At the same time the courts of Israel became corrupt, being
subject to bribery in all its most loathsome forms. The Israelites,
normally a very temperate people, were becoming drunken and
besotted. Hard pressed farmers, caught in the grip of inflation
and high taxes, were being crowded off their farms, and a numerous
class of unemployed was appearing in the life of the nation.

Into this situation the farmer-herdsman-prophet from Tekoa
found himself thrust, and being unable to restrain his indignation
in the face of the general deterioration of life among the plain
people, he created a furore with his demands for justice. In this
scripture he paints a vivid picture of a generation that has been
blinded to the fundamental decencies by luxuries easily obtained.

It was not that the nation was either irreligious or unreligious.
Quite the contrary. The altars were piled high with sacrifices, and
the priests were supported generously. But it was a religion without a conscience.

Amos assumed a position commonly accepted now but revolutionary then. He said, in effect, that the privileged were responsible to
God and the nation for the way they employed all their resources.
It was not a question of paying the tithes. They were being paid.
But the residue of the great fortunes was being employed quite
without regard for the welfare of the state, and this, according to
Amos, was as much a sin against God as though the leaders were
forcibly plundering the people. They "are not grieved over the ruin
of Joseph!" he said.

THE GOOD STEWARD MUST PROTEST   Amos 7:10-17

[15] The Lord took me from following the flock, and the Lord said to me, "Go, prophesy to my people Israel."

To A FEW choice souls in every generation God seems to assign a stewardship of protest. It may be a John the Baptist in one generation, an Elizabeth Fry in another, a Francis E. Willard in another, or a Cardinal Mercier in another. Sometimes the protest must be made in the field of politics, sometimes in the field of economics, and sometimes in the ecclesiastical affairs of a people. It happens many times, however, that the protestors arise from ranks entirely outside those of organized religion. But whenever human rights are being flouted and simple justice is ignored, God seems to find a courageous individual who is willing to accept the challenge and defy the powers of iniquity.

The prophet Amos was in no sense of the word a "churchman" in his own generation. He had no professional training either as a priest or as a functionary in the Temple or at the shrines. He made no boast of knowing anything about the sacred magic or ritual usually associated with the offices of religion. He was not even one of a wandering band of dervishes who lived by their prophecies and were known as "sons of the prophets." Instead, he was a shepherd whose soul had taken fire at the sight of the injustices that prevailed in the life of Israel.

It has always been very difficult to silence the man who believes that he has been commissioned by the Divine. Amaziah, the presiding priest of the shrine in Bethel, probably congratulated himself at the close of the day, assuming that he had the matter all safely settled. Amos had been driven out of the city; order had been restored; the king had been reassured of the loyalty of the shrine officials; and the altars were piled high with the sacrifices. But the sermon the prophet Amos preached that day has aroused the souls of devout men through more than twenty-five centuries, and the only reason we even know the name of the proper old priest is because he opposed the prophet.

One of the saddest chapters in the history of the Christian Church is that one in which are recorded the martyrdoms it has imposed upon good stewards who have protested against social injustices. All too often godly men have been driven from its fellowship because of their denunciations of evil.

² Arise, go to Nineveh, that great city, and cry against it; for their wickedness has come up before me.

It is probably true that no portion of the Scripture has suffered more at the hands of its friends than the book of Jonah. In the first place, it is the story *of* a prophet but not *by* a prophet. In the second place, it aims to make one lesson plain, but a detail in the story has captured all the attention.

The book was produced at a time when the Jews were most exclusive. In the belief that they had been chosen of God for a unique purpose, they turned introvert, and forbade all contact, intermarriage, and missionary work with the outside world. The solace of their religion was reserved for the "chosen people," and only those who were willing to become Jews by way of circumcision and ceremony were to be countenanced.

Somewhere in the nation there was a great soul who believed that the mercy and salvation of God were also designed for the non-Jews if they were willing to repent, and as a device for preaching that doctrine he told the story of Jonah.

The point of the story is not whether God could make a fish big enough to swallow a man, but whether the mercy of God is big enough to include the whole world of sinful men. The author believed it was. The modern Christian believes the same thing. And the book of Jonah is the oldest "foreign missionary" tract known to the world. It is too bad it has been lost among the fish scales. It deserves a much better fate.

The author of this book *about* Jonah, whoever he may have been, was a profound believer in the destiny of his nation. He was convinced that the Jews were responsible for telling to the world the story of a God of mercy. Long before any Christian missionary sermon was ever preached, and long before Jesus said "Go into all the world and preach the gospel," this pamphleteer was voicing the same theme.

The modern Christian has one advantage over the ancient Jew. By means of our modern missionary organizations, it is possible for us to go to the foreign field in the form of our money. It will work, as our invested personality, among those who know not our Christ while we continue to work on the field at home. Jonah was called to work in Nineveh. We are called only to support some Jonah who has been called and is eager to go with the good news.

A NOBODY BECAME A PROPHET

Mic. 2:1-2

*² They covet fields, and seize them;
and houses, and take them away;
they oppress a man and his house.*

ACCORDING TO the accepted standards of those times, Micah was a nobody. Had he been a member of the landed gentry, or a son of one of the old families, his father's name would have been mentioned somewhere in his book; but it was not.

One of the glories of the Hebrew race, however, is that such a man could command respect and get a hearing. It was a part of the philosophy handed down from Moses that every man in the nation had rights that even the kings and the state were bound to respect, and this doctrine made it possible for an inconspicuous farmer from one of the obscure rural districts to call the government to account.

That Micah wielded an influence in the life of the nation is attested by the fact that when Jeremiah, the prophet of the last days, was on trial before the king and the high court, something Micah had said more than a hundred years earlier was quoted as though it were authoritative; and on the basis of the principle that the "nobody" had laid down, the great prophet was exonerated and liberated.

Every one of the great line of prophets in the Old Testament united in the declaration that there was a moral authority in this world to which all states and kings are eventually subject. This was a revolutionary doctrine for the time, for all other nations accepted their kings as the highest moral and political authorities, not to be disputed or defied.

Since the days of the conquest of the land the moneylenders, landlords, and "economic royalists" of the land had lived in Jerusalem. By a devious system they had contrived to build up huge landed estates and in the process had confiscated the holdings of widows, orphans, and the defenseless. By corrupting the courts they managed to sanctify their depredations; but humble men like Micah had seen families of substance destroyed or reduced to beggary, and as a consequence the prophet blamed all the woes of the land upon the big city—somewhat as many today ascribe all our economic ills to Wall Street.

Burning with indignation over what he believed to be a betrayal of the nation's honor and of the confidence of God, Micah lashed out at all the injustices of the times, pleading with the nation to deal justly with the poor. Ritualism and sacrifice, he declared, were no substitutes for mercy, honor, and fair dealings. It sounds so simple, and yet it was so revolutionary!

⁶ *A son honors his father, and a servant his master. If then I am a father, where is my honor? And if I am a master, where is my fear? says the Lord of hosts to you, O priests, who despise my name.*

SOMETIME ABOUT the year 450 B.C. life for the Jews was becoming vagabond. A series of agricultural misfortunes had overwhelmed the people, and there was a general feeling that God had dealt shabbily with them (Matt. 3:7 ff.). Those who were indifferent religiously seemed to get along about as well as those who were devout (2:17; 3:15). Earlier prophets, such as Zechariah and the Second Isaiah, had assured them that the divine wrath had been turned aside, and that they might expect better days; but their woes continued and their troubles multiplied. The people were bewildered.

Into the midst of the confusion came Malachi with a terrible indictment. The Temple services, he said, were a disgrace. The people were selling the fat rams and marketable sheep, and offering the sick, the lame, and the blind on God's altars. The priests, afraid of the people, were permitting the sacrilege to go on.

Speaking in God's behalf, the prophet cried out, "I am a great King, says the Lord of hosts, and my name is feared among the nations" (1:14). But "where is my honor?" (1:6.)

This is a doctrine that needs to be preached with all earnestness in every generation, especially ours. Our God can be very charitable, but he is no object of charity!

A God who owns all the earth cannot be treated like some underling at a hotel or some lackey at a club. It may be all perfectly proper to drop a quarter into the itching palm of a porter (if, indeed, it is possible to justify the tipping system under any circumstances), but *a great God is not to be tipped.*

Isaiah, Micah, Hosea, Amos, and a long list of other prophets preached with all the powers of their vast personalities against the social injustices of their times that were robbing the plain people of their rights. But Malachi made no mention of such matters. Instead, he charged the people with the gross sin of irreverence.

You would not treat a governor so—not even a cheap politician— he said, and yet you treat the Lord God of Hosts as though he were a mendicant or an object of charity (see 3:9 ff.; 1:7). Their ritual was ineffectual because there was no spirit of reverence in it. Above all, the whole nation was withholding its tithes as though it were dealing with some beggar on the street corner. It was all very shameful!

¹⁰ Bring the full tithes into the storehouse, that there may be food in my house; and thereby put me to the test, says the Lord of hosts.

THE PROPHET Malachi was so sure of his principle that he was willing to risk his whole case on a simple experiment. He dared the people to put God to the test!

For a period of many years life among the Children of Israel had been deteriorating. Public morals were sagging, the Temple services were neglected, and the foreign policy of the nation had been going from bad to worse. At the moment the prophet preached, the people were confronted by a real crisis in their affairs, and in that situation the preacher challenged the people to prove the whole matter by a single action. They were to test the way of God—honestly, sincerely, exactly—and he was willing to let the results speak for themselves.

Much of life must be accepted on faith. Our vision is so limited, our understanding so imperfect, and our experience so narrow that it is difficult to reason our way through some of life's difficulties and problems. Under such circumstances it becomes necessary to accept the guidance of those whose minds have been divinely illuminated. But there are those occasions in which God offers to prove his case. It was in the midst of such a situation that Malachi preached the doctrine of the tithe.

One does not need to be convinced of the merit of the tithe as a method of giving. It is easy to see what generous results can be achieved if all members of the Church contribute their tenth to its work. But it seems unreasonable to believe that the nine tenths can be made to go as far as the ten tenths did originally. Why, even the ten tenths were not enough! How can nine tenths accomplish what ten tenths could not?

Let any man who doubts the reasonableness of the plan try it—faithfully, honestly, precisely as an act of faith—for a period of three months. Let him dedicate his entire income to God and then subtract one tenth, giving it to various phases of the Lord's work as an expression of faith. Then let him judge the results that have appeared within his own spiritual life.

Giving which is the result of compulsion is never rewarding. He who makes a contribution because he is compelled to give always suffers from the resentment that builds up within his own soul. Perhaps the greatest reward that comes from tithing is that which issues from the sense of stewardship, in which one gives as an expression of real gratitude to the God who has made us his managers.

¹⁹ *Her husband Joseph, being a just man and unwilling to put her to shame, resolved to divorce her quietly.*

IT WAS SAID of Joseph, the head of the Nazareth household and the proprietor of the carpenter shop of the town, that he was a "just" man. The word as it was used in that time meant much more than merely to say that he was fair in all his dealings. It described him as a righteous man who maintained a high degree of religious loyalty in his own life and trained his household in the faith with all faithfulness.

There was a considerable amount of religious literature in circulation among the Jews during the period in which Jesus carried on his public ministry, and some scholars profess to find evidences in his preaching of an intimate familiarity with some of the better known books. It is possible that Joseph actually may have owned a small library to which the boy Jesus had access.

In the village of Nazareth the tourist will be shown an ancient room wherein, according to tradition that is entitled to great respect, Jesus sat as a schoolboy. But a very large part of his education came from Joseph and Mary. According to the Jewish law the head of the household was held responsible for the training of his children, and Joseph, being a "just" man, must have been judged faithful in this respect by his neighbors and by the rulers of the local synagogue.

Modern parents are, for the most part, scrupulously careful about the education of their children in most matters, but strangely enough the average child is allowed to grow up almost completely ignorant of the fine art of giving. This grace, which can be one of the most rewarding experiences of life, is pitifully neglected in even the average Christian home.

"I cannot remember ever having heard either my father or my mother discuss the question of giving," a young layman said in discussing his own benevolent program with his pastor. "I know they gave to the church and to other good causes, and I suppose they were at least decently generous. They trained me to be unselfish, but neither ever gave me any advice on the question of giving. They never inquired as to whether or not any part of my allowance was destined for religious or charitable purposes. The result is that I have no understanding of this aspect of my Christian life except that which I have picked up out of stray conversations with friends or have heard from my preacher on Sunday morning. I have missed something."

[11] Going into the house they saw the child with Mary his mother, and they fell down and worshiped him.

THE LATIN-AMERICAN countries have an extremely interesting custom of celebrating "All Kings' Day," instead of Christmas, in connection with the birth of Jesus.

On that day special gifts are presented to friends; special observances are planned for little children; and for three days previous to the holiday (eight days following Christmas) storekeepers are permitted to take their merchandise out on the streets and sell it from gaily decorated booths.

It is all intended to commemorate the visit of the Wise Men—three kings from the East—who came seeking the infant Jesus and bringing gifts with which to honor him.

Here is a custom some of the rest of the world might well imitate. What an occasion it would make throughout Christendom if, eight days after Christmas, we all assembled in our churches and brought gifts for the spreading of the good news of the gospel of Christ! What a setting for a missionary sermon! What an opportunity to instruct our children!

The visit of the kings was an occasion of such joy that even the most extravagant gifts were not considered a burden. No one worried about a "quota" or about "doing one's share." Imagine, if you can, what a sordid thing the visit would have been if the three kings had stopped to calculate their respective responsibilities and made it all a matter of careful bookkeeping. Instead, each one prepared his gift as the outpouring of his heart.

Christian giving has been made a burden because we have treated it as such. We have assumed that our giving would be reluctant, and as a consequence we have resorted to cajolery, competition, apportionments, and equitable distribution of the "load." The result has been a joylessness that is positively pathetic. We have tried to raise money for God's work by means which have attempted to disguise the fact that we were giving. We have sold tickets, arranged dinners, bought goods we did not want, asked our wives to work for returns that averaged no better than a few cents an hour for their labor, and otherwise persuaded ourselves that we were supporting God's work.

There is much to be said for an observance of All Kings' Day as an observance of the ancient rite of giving gifts in honor of the Christ who poured out his life for all men.

¹¹ *Opening their treasures, they offered him gifts, gold and frankincense and myrrh.*

THE CUSTOM of giving gifts at Christmas time is a very beautiful one and one to be encouraged, provided it is done with a sense of stewardship.

Unfortunately, the custom has become dyed with commercialism, so much so that our Christmas shopping frequently degenerates into Christmas swapping. Sometimes it is only a little way removed from clever merchandising. We give with the expectation of getting, and we cease giving when we are dissatisfied with our getting.

Too many gifts are given to those who need them least, and too few gifts are given to those who need them most. Mixed into every man's Christmas list there should be at least a few remembrances for those who will be able to give nothing in return beyond their gratitude.

Around the world there is a need for the necessities of life so pressing that it can almost be said that by their gifts you shall know them. There is something sinful about that form of giving which ignores need and thinks only in terms of flattery, prestige, or tradition.

The Christian who gives without praying is ignoring one of the sweetest accompaniments of his gifts.

Efficient giving calls for as careful thought and as balanced judgment as do intelligent investments. It is so easy to give unprofitable gifts to improvident recipients, in which cases the spiritual damage can be very great and very severe.

There are those gifts which are actually nothing more than a transfer of ownership titles. There is no bestowal of affection, no love to express, and no kindliness of heart with which to invest the gift with sanctity.

The good steward will give, not for his own personal satisfaction, not for the achievement of any feeling of superiority, not for any gratification of pride or vanity, and not as any cover for jealousy or spite.

There is something very tragic, if not actually blasphemous, about the gift that betrays the whole purpose of Christ. The good steward of the gospel of Christ cannot conceive of a Christmas spirit saturated with alcohol, or debauched by that which enslaves and unmans the one who is made in the image of God. At no point are we subjected to a more serious scrutiny than when we give ostensibly in Jesus' name.

⁸ *The devil took him to a very high mountain, and showed him all the kingdoms of the world and the glory of them.*

JOHN R. MOTT, one of the greatest Christian statesmen Protestantism has ever produced, one time said that "the will of God was Jesus' North Star." Like a mariner he reckoned all his directions and decisions by that one fixed point.

The report of Jesus' temptations in the wilderness that we have in the New Testament is of necessity brief and sketchy. Moreover, all we know about the experience through which our Lord passed has come down to us as that which the disciples remembered out of what he must have told them. Certainly no other person was present to observe and make a record. Jesus' habit of simplification in speaking and teaching is to be seen here in one of its most vivid instances.

It is impossible to believe that the spiritual struggle through which the Master passed consisted of brief encounters and simple decisions. The preaching of John the Baptist had aroused vast longings in the soul of the Carpenter of Nazareth in which the destiny of all the race and the whole world was involved. That phrase "the kingdom of heaven," which was so often on the lips of John was an extremely expansive term. The startling aspects of his baptismal experience (Matt. 3:13-17) could not have failed to move Jesus profoundly, and he needed time and opportunity to think his way through. It was for that purpose that he hurried off into the dessert.

There he was compelled to face the delicate and complex implications of his baptism and decide upon those attitudes that might enable him to do the will of God in the unprecedented situation that was opening up before him.

It is of the utmost importance that we note the simple fact that Jesus was offered "all the kingdoms of the world and the glory of them." But this world cannot be saved by power and prestige, no matter how attractive they may seem. If this were possible, salvation would have come long ago, for history tells the story of a long sucession of world conquerors who had all men at their feet because they were strong.

There is a weakness about possessions that Jesus recognized at the outset of his ministry. He seems to have discovered that a man's purse is not his best friend, but that instead it is extremely fickle and quite incapable of furnishing him with anything more than creature comforts. "Man shall not live by bread alone," he said. He needs bread, of course, but also something more.

¹⁶ *Let your light so shine before men, that they may see your good works and give glory to your Father who is in heaven.*

ONE CANNOT go far into the New Testament without coming to the conclusion that Christians are expected to be different. In this scripture Jesus says very distinctly that they are to stand out from the crowd, provide the saving element for society, and be lights in dark places.

The Beloved Disciple, in preaching to the pagans of Ephesus, said that any who would believe on the name of the Lord would be given the "power to become children of God" (John 1:12). The inescapable meaning of this is that a devoted follower of Jesus is one who has within him something in addition to the humanity of other men.

Again and again Jesus discussed the question of money in such a way as to make it plain that a Christian will look at his possessions from an entirely different angle. He will esteem his property as being one of the tools with which he is equipped to do the will of God and establish the kingdom of Heaven. This means, quite naturally, that the Christian who rents property will be a different type of landlord. If he owns an apartment house, he is charged with a stewardship which requires that he hold himself in some part responsible for the family life that is lived inside his building. It is inconceivable, for example, that a Christian who has become a child of God should be indifferent to the fire hazards or the health conditions existing in the property he offers for rent. It may be possible for other men to ignore their responsibilities to society, but not for one who is called to be salt, a light on a hill, or a child of God.

Anyone who has entertained the Holy Spirit as a guest in his heart will look upon his economic interests and activities as though they were his spiritual opportunities. He will not prey upon the passions or weaknesses of his fellows in order to provide himself or his family with luxuries. He will accept a stewardship for his investments which is as strict as his responsibility for his habits.

Salt changes the flavor of food, and the grace of God changes the flavor of a man's life. If we lack the flavor of salt, we are not salty; and if we lack the flavor of God, we are not children of God. Nowhere is the difference more quickly detected than in our economic activities. The Christian is one who is a bit different.

> [17] Think not that I have come to abolish the law and the prophets; I have come not to abolish them but to fulfil them.

IT IS QUITE regrettable that no record has been preserved for us by which we could know something of the early boyhood and youth of Jesus. Aside from the single instance of his visit to the Temple at the age of twelve (Luke 2:41-51) no story of any kind has come down to us that can in any way be trusted as historical evidence. For everything we know of the years previous to his baptism at the hands of John, we must depend upon general information concerning the period and the town of Nazareth.

There is a tradition, quite generally accepted, to the effect that Joseph, the head of the Nazareth household, died when Jesus was about fifteen or sixteen years of age. The youth was accepted by that time as a man and as a citizen in the community. In modern terms we would say that he had "come of age."

It is known to be a fact that there were other children in the family (Matt. 13:55). The Roman Catholic Church, without any historical information to back up the position, believes that these were offspring of Joseph by a previous marriage. In general it may be said that Protestants believe they were younger children, sons and daughters of Mary.

As the oldest son in the family Jesus would have succeeded to the responsibility of managing the Nazareth carpenter shop which must have been a public post of some responsibility. As its proprietor he would have been under the necessity of paying the taxes levied by the local publicans on behalf of the Roman government. In addition, he would have been responsible for the payment of the tax to the Temple in Jerusalem and the tithes and offerings which normally went to the local synagogue.

It is highly significant that when his life was being combed with the most searching care at the time of his trial, no one came forward to declare he was delinquent in his Temple dues. Nor did anyone testify that he had failed to pay his taxes to Caesar, and such testimony would have been very damaging evidence in Pilate's court if it could have been produced.

In nothing he ever said or did could it be said that he ever raised any objection whatever to the payment of the customary tithes. He did say some things were weightier matters (Matt. 23:23), but in all instances he supported the law of the tithe.

²⁸ *If you are offering your gift at the altar, and there remember that your brother has something against you. . . .*

JESUS WAS warning his disciples against the danger of trying to pray against a blockade of refusal to do the will of God. There come times in our Christian experience when prayer is futile unless we are willing to take a moral stand against some evil within our lives that makes it impossible for God to answer our prayers.

"There was something just a little strange about it," the old man said as he laid a check on the preacher's desk. "I had been praying for the success of our evangelistic program and the prosperity of the Church, and then it occurred to me that I had not done what I could in these matters myself. I have had a rather good business this fall, and have been able to collect some old bills, so that my affairs are in good shape. But I haven't paid anything on my missionary pledge. Right then I knew there was no use praying any longer until I had done something to answer my own prayers. So there's my check."

There is no more solemn obligation resting upon any Christian than the duty of praying for his Church and its far flung missionary enterprise, but there comes times when our prayers bounce back upon our own hearts for the simple reason that they strike the wall of our own inaction. There is something hypocritical about praying for the cause we are not supporting, for the Sunday-school class we have refused to teach, for the preacher we desert on Sunday morning, and for the heroes whose hands we are not helping to hold up.

Two Roman Catholic sisters were calling upon a businessman, soliciting his assistance in a certain good cause. They were trying to sell him some tickets to a concert, the profits of which were to go to the support of a work among children. "I'm sorry, sister," the executive said, with an expansive smile and a gesture of friendliness, "but I will not be in town that night. You are doing a good work and I am with you. I'll be away, but I'll be with you in spirit."

"That's wonderful," said the nun in reply, with a beautiful smile on her lovely face. "Now here is the ticket for your spirit. Just where do you want it to sit?"

It is a little difficult to say with any truth that we are supporting a cause in spirit if we are not paying for some spot upon which that orphaned spirit can sit. There is a form of hypocrisy in the support that exhausts itself in promises.

" Love your enemies and pray for those who persecute you.

THE WORLD into which Jesus was born was far from being a loveless one. The family life of the Jews was the finest type of its kind to be found in all the East. There was a devotion to the Temple and the Law unlike anything to be witnessed among any other people. There was an almost fanatical devotion to the civil and religious institutions of the Jews. But the Jews were a narrow, bigoted, and stern people because their love was inadequate and confined.

Jesus undertook to redeem that world by appealing to men to extend the radius of their love. If they would do so, he declared, they would redeem their own lives.

Ezra and Nehemiah, in an effort to preserve the life of the nation and the purity of the race, had laid upon them a strict prohibition of marriage with any peoples outside Jewry, and this had produced an extremely narrow nationalism. The religious ceremonialism under which they lived had held them aloof and above the common immoralities of the pagan world about them, but it had also given them a most obnoxious type of racial superiority complex. With this, in its extreme form, Jesus broke completely, and insisted that his followers must love all men everywhere.

In this scripture Jesus insists upon this same process of extending the radius of one's love, as though it were one of the first duties of a Christian. If a genuine spirit of Christian love—what Harry Emerson Fosdick calls "inextinguishable good will"—can be thrust into this world's life, it will be the best form of civilization insurance that can be devised.

Retaliation, force, military might, compulsion, revenge—all these may be demanded by those who hold to other faiths; but for the Christian there is a plain and simple program: "You shall love your neighbor as yourself" (Matt. 19:19). This, Jesus said, is the addition to the Jewish Law that must be made. It is Christianity's most significant contribution to the world's life.

Christians must find a way of stretching their love so that it may include those of other races, other economic groups, other social classes. They must love those they have never seen, the people who are admittedly unlovely, and even those who do not want to be loved.

This is the religious basis of the missionary movement, and this is the fundamental argument for giving to missions. Our money can express that love when nothing else can, for money talks.

³ *When you give alms, sound no trumpet before you, as the hypocrites do in the synagogues and in the streets, that they may be praised by men.*

MUCH EMPHASIS was laid on benevolence in the religion of the Pharisees. One of the Apocryphal books (Tobit 12:8-9) says that "Good is prayer with fasting and alms and righteousness . . . for alms rescue from death and it will cleanse from all sin." Even Jesus with his great compassion for the poor did not lay greater insistence upon charity than did some of the rabbis of his time.

The chief difference, however, was the humility Jesus urged upon his disciples. "Don't blow your horn when you bestow your alms," he said in effect. "Don't even let your left hand know what your right hand is doing in the way of giving."

A church finance committee had come to the point where something had to be done, and seven of the better-to-do members were having lunch together. "I will match any man's gift," said one of the company. "I have never allowed anyone to outdo me in giving to this church." And he appeared to feel very generous as he invited the others to join him in a charitable marathon that completely ignored their individual abilities to give. When their total gifts were added up, it was a tidy sum, but only because they matched one another, not because any man had reverently considered an honest stewardship and his proportional ability to give.

"I am chairman of the committee and I suppose I have to lead off, or the rest of them will not follow along." And with this type of reasoning another committee was cajoled into giving without any devout or due regard for their actual stewardship.

"I will give $5,000 to this new building project, but only on the condition that they build on the site I have picked out." Thus spoke another man of means, and the trumpet he sounded had a particularly brassy tone. He never seemed to realize that he was really saying, "I will pay $5,000 to have my own way."

"I think I will cut my pledge this year. I have just discovered that I am giving more now than my brother-in-law is, and he is able to give much more than I because he has so much less expense." It may not have been a trumpet we heard, but it was poor music in the ears of the Lord, at least.

It is said that money talks, but much of the time it does not need to speak a word. We condemn ourselves with our own boasting.

¹⁰ Thy kingdom come,
Thy will be done,
On earth as it is in heaven.

THE TEACHING of the New Testament is perfectly clear on this point: Jesus Christ came into the world to make it over and make it new.

John the Baptist came declaring that "the kingdom of heaven is at hand" (Matt. 3:2); and when Jesus volunteered to be a member of John's movement, he likewise caught up and echoed the cry. When his disciples asked him to teach them to pray, the first petition he introduced into his prayer was a plea that the will of God might be done on earth as it was in heaven.

A large percentage of his parables have the kingdom of Heaven at their center and a surprisingly large number of them refer to the problem of money and its relationship to the "Kingdom" that Jesus proposed to establish.

There may be differences of opinion among scholars equally reputable as interpreters of the Scripture, but all are agreed that Jesus represented God as a moral Being who had distinct and definite preferences in moral situations. It is inconceivable, for example, that a God of mercy could be neutral in any case where children were being debauched or women degraded.

It is not within the province of the Church to labor for the election of candidates because of their political party sponsorship, but it is the solemn duty of the Church to lay pressure upon all political parties in an effort to persuade them to adopt policies that the Christian conscience can endorse. It may be necessary, as when the issue of liquor or social vice may be concerned, for the Church to take sides, but the strength of its influence will always rest upon its independence.

If the Church surrenders to the economic pressure of the party in power, it forfeits its right to pose as the representative of Jesus Christ. If it remains silent in the presence of injustice, or inactive in the face of militant immorality, it has no right to pray our Lord's prayer without first praying the publican's prayer, "God, be merciful to me a sinner!"

There is a stewardship for contemporary life that the Church of Jesus Christ cannot evade and still keep its own soul. There is a silence that is cowardice and not "golden." There is an impartiality that is craven and not judicial. There is a parsimony that is both suicidal and morally indefensible.

²⁶ Every one who hears these words of mine and does not do them will be like a foolish man who built his house upon the sand.

THERE IS A principle firmly fixed in our legal system that knowledge of the law involves responsibility. Thousands of individuals have been convicted of criminal negligence on the basis of the fact that they *knew* of a dangerous condition *and did nothing about it.*

A very definite hazard is involved when a Christian listens to a missionary sermon that provides him with disturbing facts concerning the world's need. To know, for example, that the amount of money spent for a season ticket to the football games would provide food for a Korean orphan for six months, constitutes a responsibility for deciding whether we will gratify our interest in entertainment or feed the hungry. Having made our decision, we must be prepared to defend it in the presence of that one who died upon a cross for our redemption.

The essential argument in the story of the good Samaritan is that all three of those who passed the wounded man on the bloody road were equally responsible. The stranger (for such the Samaritan was in Judean territory) did no more than the other two were expected to do. All three were expected to exhibit a brotherly concern.

It is highly dangerous for a great nation like the United States to be rich and strong in the midst of a world that wallows in misery. The stricken of the earth may lose their lives as a result of the war, but the American people can very easily lose their souls as a result of the unprecedented prosperity that has come to them subsequent to the war. It is as dangerous to be the victor as to be the vanquished.

To read in our morning newspapers about the suffering of the world is to become responsible for relieving that suffering up to the limit of our ability as stewards. This is what Jesus meant when he reminded his hearers of the fact that they had not visited those who had been jailed, though they knew of the misfortune that had befallen the poor wretches (Matt. 25:36, 43). And James, the preacher, declared that the very essence of religion is to visit the fatherless and the widows in their affliction (Jas. 1:17).

The ignorant may excuse himself from some part of his stewardship on the basis of his ignorance, but the man who knows is obligated to discharge his responsibilities.

²⁷ The rain fell, and the floods came, and the winds blew and beat against that house, and it fell; and great was the fall of it.

WHETHER THIS parable is read in Matthew's Gospel or in Luke's (6:46-49), its essential teaching is the same. In building his life every man owes it to himself to take the long look.

Looking at a map of Palestine one might think that it is a land of many streams, for little wadis are drawn as though they were watercourses, whereas they run full only a few days, or weeks at most, in the spring. Through the rest of the year they are empty and dusty, so that many a shepherd has built up a mud hut at some sheltered spot only to have it washed away when the flood tide comes sweeping down after a heavy spring rain.

Sometimes the soft dirt is washed out from under the house, and in other cases the mud walls simply collapse under the impact of the rushing waters. In either case the folly is the same. The wise builder selects his foundations with care.

It was concerning this very matter that Jesus was talking when he said that a man could not build a successful life out of an "abundance of . . . possessions" (Luke 12:15). Life calls for a broader foundation than that. No man has ever yet succeeded in making a great God out of little gadgets.

Of one thing we can be very sure. The floods will come. No man has ever yet invented any satisfactory way of insulating life against trouble. And though the mansion on the boulevard is spared some of the tragedies that befall the tenement, the tenement is emancipated from some of the woes that stalk the mansion.

It is a great fallacy to believe that "your purse is your best friend." It is very comforting to a parent to know that he has provided economic security for his family; but if he is wise, he knows that the dike is still full of leaks. Even a great fortune is often insufficient to buy even one more hour of life or one shield from the shame of disgrace.

Frugality, thrift, prudence, industry—these are virtues of the finest quality, but he who has nothing more than these, fine as they are, may still be poverty-stricken and helpless in his hour of dire need. It can happen that a man, having given all his energy to the task of amassing a fortune, may discover in a crisis that his money has cost him too much.

⁹ *As Jesus passed on from there, he saw a man called Matthew sitting at the tax office.*

IT IS RATHER startling to discover in the midst of a scripture dealing with the subject of Jesus' ministry to the needy the story of Matthew sitting at the seat of the customs—as though he were one of them!

It is not so very strange after all, however, for it often happens that the rich man is the poorest man of the community. So often a rich man's fortune has cost him everything—health, happiness, family, reputation, peace of mind, friends, even his soul.

"If I had your money, I would have a time," said a man of modest means to a man of wealth. "Yes," said the rich man wearily, "I suspect you would have a time—a very little time."

The probabilities are that some of the well-placed Roman officials who knew Matthew very intimately were quite shocked when they heard that he had gone off after the wandering young prophet from Galilee. They shook their heads and said to one another, "It's too bad. He was a nice fellow too. Had a good future ahead of him—just getting well started. He could have been one of the big boys someday." But of all those in authority in Galilee that day, the Capernaum tax collector is the only one whose name we know today. He made himself immortal by shaking loose from the customs house when Jesus called him.

The biggest bargain Matthew ever made was that one he completed the day he pulled the lid down on his desk and, turning his back on an attractive business career, set off after a great ideal.

Albert Schweitzer was famous as a musician and as a scholar, and might have gone down in history as an authority in several fields as a result of fine character and research. But the day he turned his back on an honored professorship, fame, and social standing in order to become a missionary in an obscure community in darkest Africa, he achieved immortality. By turning his back on much, he achieved more.

Life consists of the ability to distinguish between the interesting and the important, between the good and the alluring, between the eternal and the temporary.

We hear much about the underprivileged of the earth, but the overstuffed are entitled to a share of our sympathy also. There can be no "full salvation" that does not include salvation for the poor rich man. And that is stewardship.

ONE MAN WHO LEFT ALL

⁹ He said to him, "Follow me." And he rose and followed him.

THERE HAS been a tendency among modern teachers and preachers to deprecate the sacrifices those early disciples made when they became followers of Jesus. We have spoken lightly of "a few fishermen, with fish scales in their hair and the smell of stale fish upon them, who left a few little boats and some rotten nets."

At least one of the little band was a man of considerable economic importance. Matthew, the head of the tax office in Capernaum, was a highly placed officer of the Roman government who must have employed a rather large corps of secretaries, accountants, appraisers, and clerks. Someone who ought to know has estimated that he had to deposit a cash bond of perhaps as much as $400,000 with the Roman treasury, and then had to provide almost as much more as working capital.

The Roman government was exceedingly careful in its choice of revenue officers, particularly of those who collected the customs at the intersections of great trade routes. The Capernaum office was one of the most important in all of Palestine, and an enormous amount of traffic went down over the routes that followed a line just at the edge of the city. Caesar was ruthless in dealing with defaulters, and Matthew undoubtedly had been chosen because of his ability as an administrator.

Enjoying a post of great responsibility in the taxgathering organization of the empire, Matthew had a right to expect some advancements. Undoubtedly his office was highly profitable. To relinquish such a post and go tramping over the country in the company of a wandering preacher called for a personal commitment that went very deep. Whatever the opportunity may have been for Matthew in Capernaum, the chief of the taxgatherers seems to have seen something even greater in discipleship. At any rate, he left one of the "plums" when he walked out.

The record of Matthew's decision as it appears in the New Testament is extremely abbreviated. But one can easily imagine all the struggle of soul that went on within the man as he turned his back on his "all" and accepted Jesus' invitation. Let no man think it was an easy decision. Great discipleship is not achieved by casual choices and offhand decisions. It was because of the very fact that he "left all" that Matthew became an apostle. That is what happens when our consecration goes to the very roots of our lives.

³⁶ *When he saw the crowds, he had compassion for them, because they were harassed and helpless, like sheep without a shepherd.*

THERE IS something about the Christian gospel that has made the Christian lands of the world vast reservoirs of mercy and concern, out of which relief has flowed in a veritable tide during recent years.

At the moment Jesus sent his friends out teaching the gospel of the Kingdom, the doctrine that a man was his brother's keeper was unheard of outside Jewry. According to the ancient records more assistance was given to the poor and more mercy was shown to the suffering among the Jews than anywhere else in the world, and yet even among the Chosen People there was a callousness that would be utterly reprobate in our modern world.

Today's world, even partially under the influence of Jesus, cannot suffer anywhere without efforts being made around the world by Christians to relieve that suffering. It is an eloquent comment on the basic character of Communism that, in the midst of the world's suffering since the war, not one shipload of assistance has gone from Communist countries to stricken peoples except as a bribe for political action or intrigue. But the democratic nations, in particular the Christian states, have poured out their treasure. Britain, out of her own desperate need, has rendered aid in amazing amounts; and the generosity of the American people is proverbial. The relief that streamed out of Sweden at the close of the war represented heroic sacrifices by a hard-pressed people.

In the average study of comparative religions offered to college and university classes, little or no mention is made of the fact that it has been the Christian nations which have supplied relief and the pagan states which have received it. In all the records there is no instance, so far as I can find, of any shipload of wheat, food, clothing or other form of assistance that has ever gone out of any pagan port in the direction of the famine-stricken. But the report of starving millions anywhere on the face of the globe starts the shipments out of Christian harbors.

There is something about Jesus' "compassion" that has seeped down into the souls of his people. They may have failed to measure up to his ideals, and their acceptance of their stewardship has been fractional, but the gospel bears fruit. And that fruitage is the world's hope.

CONSECRATION IS A CONTINUING PROCESS
Matt. 10:37-39

³⁸ He who does not take his cross and follow me is not worthy of me.

A SIXTEEN-YEAR-OLD girl had come to her pastor somewhat troubled about the matter of her consecration. "Why do I have to make so many new consecrations?" she inquired, just a bit impatiently. "I did it at the youth camp a year ago, and again this summer, and then tonight in the young people's meeting we were called upon to 'put everything on the altar' again. Why isn't once enough?"

"Well, Dottie, it is just a little like Christopher Columbus' voyages to the New World," the preacher replied. "You remember that when he finally arrived at the tiny little island of San Salvador in 1492, he raised the flag of his monarchs, Ferdinand and Isabella, and claimed the land in the name of Spain. Then when he went on to Cuba, he did the same thing again. On each voyage, when he arrived at a new spot, he made a new dedication. Life is a little like that, if we are Christians.

"A year ago last summer when you made your consecration it was complete, up to that moment. But after that you met a new boy friend, you faced some new problems, you had some new responsibilities thrust upon you. The consecration of a few weeks ago, like the earlier one, was up to the minute. But this fall you have faced some new problems and duties of which you never dreamed a year ago, or even three months ago. In the young people's meeting tonight you were asked to raise the cross over these newly discovered areas of life."

This is precisely what the doctrine of stewardship contemplates—keeping one's dedication abreast of his life. It means an acceptance of every responsibility as a challenge to consecration. It is a blanket agreement with God aimed to cover every new circumstance, decision, and possession.

Two young women, by an odd circumstance, passed through a series of similar occurrences. One was a consecrated steward and the other a Christian girl who lived more or less haphazardly. Both came into possession of some unexpected funds about the same time. One was prepared for her good fortune, for she had dedicated "everything" in advance and had a program into which the little bequest fell quite naturally. In the case of the other, the surprise precipitated a spiritual crisis. Her struggle to decide "the right thing" was something rather painful. She had no cross raised in preparation.

²⁶ *When the plants came up and bore again, then the weeds appeared also.*

IT IS COMMONLY agreed among the best scholars that the parables of Matthew were, for the most part, directed at the Church as warnings, challenges, or inspirations. We know that the synoptic gospels were written during the years that the infant congregations were being formed; and since the gospel writers were primarily concerned with the problems of contemporary Christians, it is altogether natural that they should use those stories and teachings of Jesus which were most applicable to beginners.

The parable of the wheat and the tares is admittedly one of the most difficult to interpret. Without a doubt it carried significant implications for first-century Christians that would not be impressive for the twentieth century, even if they were understood. But there is one teaching that, though it certainly is not the central lesson of the table, we can consider very seriously and profitably.

All of us live in tare-infested surroundings, and what we do about the tares determines in a very large part the issues of life.

Earl C——— had been an active and valuable member of the church in the community from which he came. When he deposited his letter with the congregation in the new community, his new pastor hailed his arrival with great delight, for it was a small church and the addition of even one strong leader was a great gain. For a time matters went well with Earl. As a branch manager he proved successful and was given a substantial increase in salary. An influential club of executives invited him into membership. Several big business leaders called him by his first name; a local hospital asked for the use of his name on the list of its advisors. Meanwhile the family was regular in its church attendance.

The first break came when he had to make an out-of-town trip and miss two Sundays at church. Then an emergency at the plant kept him at his office all one Sunday. The fresh young habits he was forming suffered severely. The pressure from the head office grew greater, and he had to spend increasing amounts of time at the office getting his dictation done. His larger salary called for wider social activities, and at the end of the year he had dropped out of church entirely. He had sowed his own tares. He tried to blame it on other people but never quite succeeded.

No man is ever more surely his own enemy than when he is sowing tares in his own life.

[31] Another parable he put before them, saying, "The kingdom of heaven is like a grain of mustard seed which a man took and sowed in his field."

A PALESTINIAN mustard seed was not, actually, the smallest of all the common seeds, though it was very tiny. It was, however, so small that it was used in popular speech as the symbol of all small things, Jesus himself used it in that sense when he said, "If you have faith as a grain of mustard" (Matt. 17:20).

When fully grown, the mustard plant became a bush of perhaps as much as ten feet in height, and one of them in the midst of a vegetable garden had the appearance of being very large—big enough to afford hospitality to the birds.

Jesus' purpose in using the parable was not to teach any lesson in agriculture but to emphasize a profound spiritual truth concerning the kingdom of Heaven. It is as though he had said, "Do not let the small and inconspicuous beginning of the Kingdom deceive you. Though there are but a few of us, the day will come when we shall take the world."

The great developments in history, in so many instances, have had very small beginnings. No one could have guessed, for example, that he was watching the development of a religious movement that would ultimately number tens of millions of people if he had by chance looked in on a little meeting of a dozen or more youths of Oxford University who had earned for themselves the nickname "Methodists." And no one could have dreamed that he was watching a world movement coming to birth—one which would eventually cover the globe—if he had stood at a street corner in London's east side and watched William Booth conduct a street meeting of the Salvation Army. Six women met in a small room in a Boston church and organized the first society of what has become "the largest woman's club in the world"—the Woman's Society of Christian Service of the Methodist Church with upwards of two million members.

It wasn't much—just a few dollars—but it was one schoolgirl's tithe that was forwarded to a rural missionary in Cuba who, in turn, used it to help defray some expenses in a youth camp where a boy dedicated his life to the Christian ministry. And who can say what a plant that tiny little mustard seed became?

Let no man despise himself, his efforts, or his gifts because they are small. Jesus entertained great hopes for mustard seeds, for consecrated plain people, and for small gifts that became great because they were dedicated.

He told them another parable. "The kingdom of heaven is like leaven which a woman took and hid in three measures of meal, till it was all leavened."

IT IS NOT a little strange that a striking phrase like "the kingdom of heaven," which was so frequently on the lips of Jesus, should have had so little attention from the Church Fathers down through the centuries. As a matter of historical record it did not come in for any serious and consecutive study at the hands of the scholars and commentators until during the last three quarters of a century. Yet Jesus described it by the use of a long list of figures, of which that of "yeast" is one of the most dramatic.

If one were to judge contemporary life by noise and size, he would be forced to the conclusion that prize fights, horse races, athletic contests, and sensationalism are the governing factors, because they attract crowds and get newspaper mention. But half a dozen far-sighted individuals meeting in a private office at the public library, or as many politicians in a "smoke-filled room," may exercise ten thousand times the influence.

The kingdom of Heaven is a quiet power that does not advertise itself but continues to exert pressure on life from a thousand angles every day. Teachers, preachers, editors, radio commentators, housewives, labor leaders, students, and all those who influence their fellows can find their places in its ranks and their work in its program. Literally millions of Christians make tens of millions of decisions every day on the basis of their honest and sincere answers to the question "What would Jesus do?" Tens of thousands of groups come together every day and ask for the guidance of the Holy Spirit before they tackle the problem that is of concern to them. It is impossible to imagine what this world would be like if suddenly the "leaven of Christ" were to be withdrawn from the life about us.

It is of the utmost importance, however, that we note that the action of the yeast begins *after* it is injected into the dough. It is helpless and fruitless until the mixing process has begun. A Christian missionary, returning from the field of his labors during the war, was asked, "What is going to become of the Church over there?" "It will go on," he replied. "The Holy Spirit has not been evacuated— only a few missionaries. As long as there is one man left in whom there lives the Spirit of Christ, the Christian Church is still alive." Like the yeast, it is still active as long as there is one cell left.

GOOD THINGS HAVE DIFFERENT VALUES

Matt. 13:44-51

" The Kingdom of heaven is like treasure hidden in a field, which a man found and covered up; then in his joy he goes and sells all that he has and buys that field.

The little land of Palestine lay athwart the great trade routes of the ancient East over which the commerce of three continents— Europe, Asia, and Africa—flowed in a tide. It was the only country that furnished a highway for merchants and traders whereon food and shelter might be had.

Because of the same topographical circumstances the little land of Palestine has been a battleground since the dawn of Mediterranean history, and the name of Armageddon, the great plain on which some of the historic conflicts have been waged, has been given to the bloodiest struggles. The plains and valleys of the sacred land have throbbed to the tramping hosts of every great world power of the East for the last five thousand years.

In the absence of vaults, banks, and other devices used for protecting fortunes, it was a common practice of rich men of that ancient day to bury their treasures in some secret crevice along the walls on the limestone hills during periods of danger. If perchance misfortune overtook the owner and he were killed or carried off without revealing the identity of his hiding place, the treasure could easily be lost. Jesus' story of the hidden treasure is that of some poor plowman who came upon such a treasure-trove, quite by accident, and sold everything he had in order to buy the field and claim the gems. The ethics by which he came into possession of the field are no part of Jesus' teaching. Instead, he makes it plain that some things in life are so superb, so splendid, and of such great worth that all a man has is a small price to pay for them.

Great living consists of distinguishing between values. As the ancient writer of Proverbs once said,

One man gives freely, yet grows all the richer;
    another withholds what he should give, and only suffers want.

(Prov. 11:24)

There is a kind of spending that enriches a man, and a kind of thrift that impoverishes him.

True giving—that kind of which God approves—has the effect of enlarging the soul of the giver, of broadening his horizons, of making tender his sympathies. Then there is that false kind of giving that results in vanity, pride, and actual emptiness of soul. Just as there is bad religion as well as good religion, so also there is bad giving as well as good giving. The wise steward discovers the difference.

⁴⁵ *The kingdom of heaven is like a merchant in search of fine pearls.*

A RATHER amazing system of international banking was in vogue around the shores of the Mediterranean in Jesus' day. Under this system fishing firms, like that of Zebedee and the one of which Peter and Andrew were the proprietors, were able to carry on commerce with merchants in great cities of Europe, Asia, and Africa. Letters of credit were carried by special couriers from city to city, and drafts were drawn in at least a dozen directions.

The vast majority of the commerce of the time, however, was conducted on the basis of cash payments, in which gold, silver, and other precious things were offered in exchange. Because pearls could be carried about easily, they were used extensively as a medium of exchange when transactions involved large sums of money.

The merchant in Jesus' story may have traveled as far as the Persian Gulf, or even to India, in search of gems; for quite evidently gems were his business (Rev. 18:12), and his keen eyes were quick to note an exceptional stone. The plowman of another parable (Matt. 13:44) evidently stumbled upon his treasure quite by accident; but the clever old lapidary had made a deliberate search for the finest jewel known to the craft, and was prepared to stake everything on possessing it.

It never occurred to the merchant of gems that he was making any sacrifice when he sold all that he had in order to own the treasure. That was because he knew the supreme value of the prize he was acquiring. The incomparable beauty of the pearl made it a profitable possession, regardless of its cost.

Such is the kingdom of Heaven—the supreme spiritual value known to man—the possession of which represents the highest achievement possible to a human personality. Anything, therefore, that helps establish the Kingdom within one (Luke 17:21) is worth more than any sacrifice that may be required if one is to possess it.

At this point tithing as a method of giving exhibits its greatest value. It becomes a spiritual exercise that produces such abundant benefits that the tither becomes oblivious of the cost of his gifts. The spiritual graces engendered in the giver are worth more than all the tithes.

It is one of the weaknesses of modern Christians that they do not put a sufficiently high value on Christian graces in contrast to economic advantages.

⁴⁷ The kingdom of heaven is like a net which was thrown into the sea and gathered fish of every kind.

THE GREAT French liner had anchored a mile or more offshore, and a little party of tourists was taking advantage of the delay of a few hours by visiting the small Mediterranean coastal town. Loitering along the broad sandy beach, they saw the parable of this scripture re-enacted before their eyes.

Two picturesque little sailing vessels had been circling in the sea for two hours or more, with a long net strung out between them. Finally they turned toward shore and, as soon as they were in the shallow waters, the crews of fishermen leaped overboard and began dragging the heavy net in after them.

Great excitement prevailed along the shore, with little boys shouting and older men offering their advice and comment. When at last the final lengths of the net were brought in, a strange assortment of fish floundered and struggled on the sand. Then began the wild scramble of the fishermen.

According to the ancient Levitical law of the Hebrews (Lev. 11:9-12) a Jew was not permitted to eat any fish except those having scales and fins, and this same rule prevailed among the fishermen on that sandy shore that morning. With amazingly dexterous hands the fishermen sorted their catch, throwing the edible fish into great baskets and tossing the prohibited ones back into the sea. It was a calculated catch in which the worthless were separated from the worthy, and the verdict was final.

The fishermen among Jesus' disciples had participated in exactly this kind of operation on the Sea of Galilee on countless occasions, doubtless, and were quick to sense the significance of its various implications.

The Pharisees among the Jews promised the nation that if the day ever came when all the people kept all the Law for even one day, then the Day of the Lord would come. They were struggling desperately to produce a "pure" Israel that would be in every respect ceremonially clean. But Jesus said that the net would be spread out widely and that the good and the bad would be taken. Then would come the judgment, and the bad would be thrown away.

There is something very sobering in the parable for the man who has been accepting his stewardship lightly and discharging his duties carelessly. What seems like a calm, can become a storm so quickly; what has seemed like the indifference of God, can become the judgment.

¹⁸ *But what comes out of the mouth proceeds from the heart, and this defiles a man.*

JESUS PUT HIS finger on the very center of the problem when he said that it is the thing that comes up out of the heart of man (the psychologists would probably say it comes up out of the subconscious) that defiles him, not the thing that he puts on the outside. Our ability to draw a clear line of distinction between the spiritually profitable and that which is spiritually dangerous marks us as mature personalities.

Nothing is more sorely needed in modern society than a clean-cut Christian philosophy of money. Every gambler, exploiter, tax-evader, gouger, grafter, and extortionist is the product of a wrong attitude toward money. Some of the worst abuses of our times go back to our unchristian attitudes toward possessions.

The economists make a very significant contribution here. They tell us that money, which is no more than a symbol for stored-up labor, is only a medium of exchange. The individual produces more than he consumes and stores up the surplus in the form of cash, credit, or other tangible assets. To come into possession of money without giving services in exchange is to be a parasite or perhaps even a thief.

The grocer who stocks his shelves with goods and has them ready when the housewife needs them has rendered a service for which he is entitled to compensation, but the speculator who jacks up the price by some clever manipulation of the market and collects off society is an altogether different type of businessman.

The thrifty man who accumulates savings that he loans to an enterprising manufacturer for the purpose of assisting him in expanding a useful business is entitled to the wages his stored-up labor earns, this compensation being called either a "dividend" or "interest." But anyone who takes money from the community without rendering service in return becomes a public charge.

The basic contribution Jesus made to the question was the doctrine of stewardship, by which a man is held responsible for his management of money. There can be no general rise in moral values until our attitude toward money is spiritualized. The Christian Church is under no more sober obligation than it is in this connection. It must teach a Christian philosophy of money.

¹⁵ He said to them, "But who do you say that I am?"

JESUS CHRIST presents the most insistant problem any man ever faces. It is not necessary that we make up our minds about Hannibal, Disraeli, Darwin, or Marie Antoinette. Our attitudes or opinions concerning any other character of history have little bearing upon our private lives. But any man who proposes to master life and live it at its highest level must face up frankly and courageously to the question of what attitude he is going to take toward Jesus Christ.

What we do about him depends, of course, upon what we think about him. Jesus himself put the central question to Peter when he asked, "Who do you say that I am?" Peter had to make up his mind. It would have been useless to quote another man's opinion. In precisely this way every man works out his own salvation.

There are so many ways of declaring our beliefs. We can, of course, learn the answers in the catechism and repeat them glibly with little or no concept of their vast implications. Or we can borrow our opinions from other people, say that we believe the "fundamentals," and go on living an unaltered life.

It is easy to agree that Jesus is the greatest figure in human history, the race's supreme teacher, and a perfect example for all men. But having admitted all this, we can go on refusing to do his will or live according to his principles.

If any man proposes to make him Lord, however, he must make him Lord of all. Jesus Christ has never been content with a fractional discipleship.

A genuine Christian discipleship consists of the establishment of Jesus as the master of all of life. This includes our possessions. To declare that we believe that Jesus is the Son of God implies that he is also the Lord of life. If this be true, his interpretation of the role of money gives the only true, accurate, scientific, and enduring attitude available to man. To reject this is like rejecting the law of gravity or the law of chemical cohesion. It is to live in open rebellion against one of the basic laws of the spiritual world. There can be but one outcome in such a case as there can be but one outcome in rejecting or violating the laws of chemistry.

No one would ever think of becoming a successful chemist on the basis of a defiance of the laws of chemistry: but we defy the principles of Christ deliberately, thinking we will be successful.

¹⁷ *Jesus answered, "O faithless and perverse generation, how long am I to be with you? How long am I to bear with you?"*

CARE IS needed in interpreting this scripture, for no little injustice has been done Peter, James, and John by those who have charged them with spiritual failure because they could not heal the stricken boy after having witnessed the Transfiguration. As a matter of fact, they had nothing to do with the matter. The nine who had not been to the mountaintop, and who had not seen Moses and Elijah talking with Jesus, were the ones who failed. No one knows what they might have been able to do if they had gone through the great experience which the three had shared.

It is a fact, of course, that genuine spirituality must be translated into action or it ceases to be spiritual. It is a dubious type of spiritual culture that can go into ecstasies over a "great" sermon and then ignore all appeals for service and help. Jesus was at war with the complacency of his times as certainly as he was opposed to the outright wickedness of the generation which crucified him.

There is something very wrong with the spiritual life of a congregation that can go to church every Sunday morning and remain oblivious to the impoverishment of life that is going on under the very shadow of the sanctuary. One can even raise some questions about the propriety of elaborate expenditures for stained glass when millions of our fellow Christians and their little children are starving in refugee camps.

Jesus charged the nine disciples with a lack of faith, and that is a serious matter; but he would probably charge the modern Church with a lack of concern, and that is a matter of the utmost seriousness.

It would be embarrassing to some Christian families if the Lord Christ compared the amount spent for dog food with the amount contributed to world evangelism. The price of a theater ticket would work such miracles on the mission field where little children are to be fed. It is so very easy to assume that we have done all that is expected of us when we have divided our small change with the Church or given our annual contribution to the Community Chest.

If our Christian faith is a matter of our eternal destiny, then our Christian giving cannot be a matter of unconcern, either to us or to our Lord. There are still stricken lads at the foot of the mountain, and there are mountains all about us.

¹² If a man has a hundred sheep, and one of them has gone astray, does he not leave the ninety-nine on the hills and go in search of the one that went astray?

ONE OF THE most direct routes to ineffectiveness is by way of in-definiteness.

A young preacher with an exact and scientific mind was experiencing some difficulty in persuading his officials to agree to a survey of the community in which their church operated. "We know enough about this neighborhood now," one of them said.

"But if the shepherd whom Jesus commended had not taken a survey, he would never have known that one of his sheep had wandered off down the mountain, and he would never have gone searching for it all night until he found it," the youthful clergyman replied.

It is even possible for us to become so general in our statements concerning stewardship that the doctrine loses its definite meaning. This is what tithing does: it pins the doctrine down to facts and figures.

"I do not keep any exact record, but I am very sure I give more than my tenth," an otherwise methodical and careful businessman said. "I like to feel that my giving is spontaneous and that it springs from a feeling of gratitude. If I kept books on God, I would feel as though I were losing something spiritual out of my life." But the same man assigned a fixed amount of money to his wife each month, and kept an accurate record of it without feeling that it marred their personal love for each other in any way.

In the case of personal devotions it is hard to be exact. One does not pray a specific number of minutes each morning, nor does one read a precise number of scripture verses. At the end of any one year it is impossible to take a precise spiritual inventory to determine whether or not we have made any spiritual growth. But we can keep an accurate record of our giving, and we can balance that against our income and discover the exact ratio. Definiteness in such a case can be very creative.

Planning one's benefactions on an exact scheduled basis precisely as one would plan any other business operation, is both good Christian statesmanship and good stewardship. Balancing one's giving so that the really important causes get the larger gifts and the lesser causes get the lesser contributions is the only responsible way of giving that a consecrated man can really commend. Tithing always contributes to that result.

³³ *Should not you have had mercy on your fellow servant, as I had mercy on you?*

IT WAS A common practice of the preachers and teachers of Jesus' day to drape their teachings with a story, and rich men, kings, landlords, and slaves were in common use as characters. This parable, which appears only in Matthew's Gospel, is the story of a forgiven man who was unforgiving.

When a certain king began invoicing his kingdom, he discovered that one of his satraps owed him an enormous sum of money upon which no payments had been made. Apparently it was a loan and did not represent any defalcation. When it proved that the underling could not discharge his obligation, the king dismissed it with a wave of his hand and wiped the slate clean.

The freed debtor, however, was an altogether different type of person, for when he discovered that some petty officer serving under him owed him a trivial sum, he forgot all about the generous treatment he had experienced at the hand of his king and threw the poor wretch into prison.

Jesus uses the story to illustrate the contrast between the treatment we receive at the hands of God and the treatment we accord one another. The lesson he endeavors to teach is that the generosity we receive should be matched by the generosity we extend.

The amount owed by the satrap amounted to nearly a million dollars, and the debt of the petty officer amounted to no more than twenty dollars, but the contrast between the souls of the king and the satrap is proportionately wide.

Let that one who complains that "the church is always asking for money" consider the deep obligation he owes to the forgiving heart of God. Who of us can say he is not in debt to the world of which he is a part? How many injuries have we worked on friends by our thoughtlessness? How many pains have we inflicted by our self-centeredness? How many weak ones have we brushed roughly aside as we have contended for our own designs or our own advantages? How many tears have we brought to the eyes of innocent people by our ruthlessness?

Yet the loving heart of our Christ is gentle and generous enough to forgive it all. Who are we, then, to resent the claims that the poor, the ignorant, the defrauded, and the debauched make on us? What justification can we offer to a generous God for our own miserliness?

⁶ *What therefore God has joined together, let no man put asunder.*

THE PASTOR of a famous downtown church in a great American city who has had vast experience in dealing with estranged couples said, in discussing the problem of marital discord, "I have discovered that at least 85 per cent of the people who come to me for advice do so as a result of difficulties arising out of either money or sex, and I have made it a rule to probe into their financial affairs at the outset. Sex maladjustments very often settle themselves once we can bring the couple to an amicable settlement of their financial disagreements."

It is a highly significant fact that the amount of money a couple has to spend is seldom the cause of the difficulty. Instead, it is a disagreement as to the management of their funds that results in friction.

"We always had trouble inside our home until we began tithing," a young husband said. "Perhaps it was because I assumed the right and responsibility for making all the decisions on the subject of our expenditures. I thought that was the husband's function. I overlooked the fact that my wife was a typical American girl who had been accustomed to handling her own funds and deciding on her own expenditures. To have her ask me for money seemed to me to be a perfectly natural procedure, but to her it was humiliating in the extreme. The result was argument, ill will, controversy, and constant misunderstanding.

"Then one Sunday morning our pastor preached on the subject of tithing and distributed some tracts dealing with the matter. We brought the tracts home and, when we sat down to dinner that day, began talking about the question. It was the first time in two or three years that we had really discussed our financial problems together in an objective way.

"I think it was that first conversation on tithing that opened the way and started us on the road toward an understanding of our problem. I am sure that it resulted in my wife's getting her first clear picture of our financial situation. She had always assumed we were making more than we were in the business. To tithe with any accuracy, we had to keep an account, and this systematic handling of our funds resulted in the most satisfactory decisions on the subject of money we had ever had. I have much to be thankful for besides the joy of giving."

²² When the young man heard this he went away sorrowful; for he
had great possessions.

THE YOUNG MAN of this scripture started out in life under two very
serious handicaps. He had inherited a powerful position from his
father, and he had been charged with the management of money
he had not earned. Two such demanding and exacting factors in any
young man's life can become a very serious matter.

In the report of the incident as it appears in one of the other
Gospels (Luke 18:18-27), the young man is described as a "ruler,"
and according to Jewish practice the only way in which he could
have come into such a line was by inheritance. The fact that he was
very rich also indicates that he had succeeded his father in the
management of an ample estate. Young men of that day were in no
position to amass large wealth by their own efforts at any early age,
for there were no patent rights, copyrights, oil wells, stock markets,
or movie salaries.

The young man seems to have been a very attractive individual
and probably made friends easily, for he captured Jesus' interest
from the start. But he was possessed by his possessions and was quite
unable to shake himself loose from his inheritance. That which his
father had probably thought would free him from all anxiety became
the thing that entangled him and tied him down to a grubby life.
His great wealth made great living impossible for him.

When Jesus suggested that he divest himself of his wealth and
give himself in service to the poor, he probably said within himself,
"What would father say?" A hand reached out perhaps from some
grave to hold him back from high spiritual adventure and achievement. His decision was a heartbreaking one, for the scripture says
that he went away "sorrowful," and we know that Jesus was greatly
depressed by the experience.

The most tragic role in the drama is taken by the old father whose
name never appears on the program. He thought he was doing well
by his son, when in reality he was imposing a crushing burden upon
the lad. He had bequeathed a fortune to his son, but he had given
him no philosophy by which he could maintain his independence of
his wealth. He left him money, but he left him no tradition of
benevolence. The boy found it hard to give money away, for he had
never seen it done.

GOD DOES NOT BARGAIN   Matt. 20:1-16

Take what belongs to you, and go; I choose to give to this last as I give to you.

THIS PARABLE has proved to be one of the most difficult to interpret of all those Jesus left to us. On the face of it there seems to have been an injustice in paying the men who had worked all day the same wages that were paid to those who worked but one hour. But the parable is not a lesson in labor relations. Instead, it is an assurance to men that God does not drive hard bargains with those who trust him.

The goodness of God is offered to everyone who will accept it. The relationship between God and man is not at all that which exists between a man and his servant, a boss and a hired hand. Rather, it is the relationship that exists between a father and his children. No man needs to bargain with God in the hope of wheedling some favor from him.

The true tither does not give his tenth for the purpose of bribing God to provide him with prosperity. The tither who has really caught the vision of stewardship gives his tithe in recognition of the fact that God is the owner of everything and that man is his steward, responsible for the management and administration of that which God has committed to his care. It is an evidence of our recognition of a moral and spiritual relationship that is the most sacred fact in a Christian's life.

It is a mistaken interpretation of tithing that to pay the tenth constitutes some kind of economic insurance. One good man who had tithed through more than a third of a century said, "I would be afraid not to tithe. God might withdraw his favor from me." And in that he expressed a common mistake in the application of the doctrine of stewardship.

No man can bribe God with the tithe any more than a child can bribe his parents to love him. The love of God is available to every man. It pursues him and woos him even in spite of his rebellion and indifference. Whenever we establish the right relationship within ourselves, the love and blessing of God flow in upon our lives correspondingly.

No man can buy the favor of God with benevolence. A small fortune spent on a stained-glass window or some other good thing does not change God's opinion of the giver. But he can be greatly pleased with the stewardship which represents a determination to manage our possessions as though we were God's personal representatives—as indeed we are.

118

³⁰ He answered, "I go, sir," but did not go.

THE SCHOLARS tell us that there are numerous hidden meanings in
this parable, and that the Pharisees with their elaborate ritual and
the Sadducees with their manipulations of the Temple system are
both deeply involved. All this may be true, but these facts do not
constitute the value of the parable for a Christian of today.

The basic meaning of the story is inescapable. The Church includes in its membership all too many who give intellectual assent
to the great Christian doctrines and then live in absolute defiance
of the fundamental Christian attitudes.

A vast emphasis is being laid today on questions of doctrine, and
of course straight thinking in the field of religion is as important
as clear thinking in the field of economics. But there is a grave
danger that we shall assume that a man is a citizen of the kingdom
of Heaven for no better reason than that he wears the label of
orthodoxy, even though he manifests the spirit of the moral outlaw.

There is a vast amount of practical atheism in our world and among
Christians, or at least among those who solemnly call themselves
Christians. We say we believe in God, and in Jesus Christ his Son,
and then we live as though there were no God and as though Jesus
did not know what he was talking about. We say that he preached
beautiful ideals, but that they are not practical, and that they cannot
be made to work in such a world as the one in which we have to
live. This is a good deal like saying that the law of gravity is a
beautiful ideal but that it will have to be brushed aside because we
want to erect a building of fantastic design that defies the law
of gravity.

We talk about defending Christian civilization and then we with-
hold the contributions upon which the Church must depend if it
is to press the campaign to a successful conclusion.

We stoutly declare we believe in the Church, and then we pay
more for our membership in the country club than we do for the
religious education of our children.

We complain about the spread of Communism and then soberly
assert our unbelief in foreign missions.

We spend less for all the Protestant missionary programs in one
year than we spend for tobacco or cosmetics, and then bemoan the
ineffectiveness of the Church of Jesus Christ. In the light of such
facts the parable is strangely modern.

[35] *The tenants took his servants and beat one, killed another, and stoned another.*

THE SCHOLARS say that this story is an allegory rather than a parable, and that each element in it has some symbolic meaning.

The owner of the vineyard is God, they say, and the tenants are the religious leaders and authorities of Jewry. The servants who were sent to collect the rent represent the Old Testament prophets, the beloved son is Jesus Christ, and the killing of the son is his crucifixion. This doubtless was the meaning of the story as it was told among the little, scattered Christian congregations of the first-century Church.

But our interest in the parable (or allegory, if you prefer) is in its message to us, and that seems to be perfectly clear so that no one need misunderstand.

The vineyard that the "householder" planted is the lovely land we have inherited from God and our fathers, and what a marvelous world it is! Its forests have been trimmed, its fields have been brought to productivity, its mineral resources have been surveyed and uncovered, its highways have been paved, its swamps have been drained, and its harbors have been dredged.

The humblest of us enjoys advantages and benefits which were beyond the reach of kings and queens only a few score years ago. Radio and television have brought the greatest music of the centuries and some of the most profound wisdom of the ages into the sacred precincts of the most unpretentious home. The martyrs have paid the price for our faith; they have made it safe and comfortable to be numbered among the Christians.

And now our Christ comes asking that we, the beneficiaries of the sacrifices and martyrdoms of the ages gone, spread out into this modern world the good news that has transformed our world, that it may similarly transform the whole world.

There is something very dismaying about the indifference of the modern Church to the missionary program. There was a time when we talked about rescuing brands from the burning, but today the whole world is on fire. Already Communism has swept over and is consuming half the world. The Christian missionary program is no longer a device for saving the souls of the heathen (though that is still an important part of the task, of course) but the one hope of saving the world for faith, freedom, decency, human rights, and common humanity. We are on trial exactly as the ancient servants were.

⁴⁰ When therefore the owner of the vineyard comes, what will he do to those tenants?

A GROUP of high-school youngsters, somewhat pressed to provide a devotional program for their Sunday evening meeting, hit upon a sensitive subject and determined to do it in a fresh fashion. They proposed a scene from the Judgment Day. The whole affair was rather crudely done and left much to be desired in the way of graceful English and professional stage settings. But the essential message of the presentation was very effective.

A rich man had come up for judgment, according to their story, and Saint Peter was hearing the case. Numerous witnesses testified to the fact that he was a community leader, a good churchman, a leading citizen, and a successful man in his profession. Then a witness for the prosecution was put on the stand. He testified that he was the man's checkbook and described how he had been ready to relieve the poor, assist with colleges and hospitals, send help to the mission fields, and do many other good things; but he had never been permitted to do so.

Among the most telling points the witness made was that the accused had been appealed to many times, but, like the priest in the story of the good Samaritan, he had passed by on the other side. Of course there was another side to the argument. Those of us who are older know that rich men are no more stingy than poor men; they only handle more money. Generally speaking, our communities are deeply indebted to a few men of wealth who think of their abundance as public trusts to be employed for the benefit of their fellows. Rare indeed is that town that does not owe a park, hospital, school, or social agency to some rich man who was keenly aware of his social responsibilities. But the basic point the youngster made in the drama is one we cannot afford to ignore. Our money will testify *against* us at the Judgment if it has not been administered as a stewardship.

What evidence our checkbook will offer in that final day depends upon the instructions we give it today. This is the message of Jesus' parable, and it is the meaning of good stewardship. It may be a bit fantastic to think of God's putting us on trial, but at least we ought to make sure the evidence will be in our favor. This is the plain teaching of the scripture in the matter of money.

¹⁴ Many are called, but few are chosen.

THERE IS the oft-told story of the old Negro who complained about the collection because his pastor had assured him that "salvation was free"; to which the preacher offered the rejoinder that "a drink of water may be free, but someone has to pay for the pump."

Something of this principle appears in the story of the wedding feasts to which the loiterers and the neglected from the highways and hedges were invited. One of them, arriving in filthy clothes and an unkempt condition, was ushered out because he had not gone to the trouble to show what little respect he was able to exhibit for the occasion. Even a destitute wedding guest could have shown a decent bit of self-respect for the happy occasion and the generous invitation he had received, if he had made some effort to make himself presentable.

We have long preached an assuring gospel in which we have told men very confidently that God loved them—even sinful men— and not one word of that message needs to be retracted. But to it must be added a word of strict warning that the God who loves sinful men also expects something of them.

It is not that sinners can buy the love of God, or that they can strike up a bargain with the Almighty. Our heavenly Father could make more gold and hide it in the mountains if that were what he needed. He could produce more jewels if jewelry were capable of making him happy. Just as the photographers advertise that "your friends can buy anything you can give them except your photograph," so it must be said that God can create anything for himself, but he cannot have your love and reverence unless you give them to him.

Love without gifts is a poor pretense. He who truly loves seeks the opportunity to give. Sinners who have been invited to accept the forgiveness of God never discover the full magnitude of the gift bestowed upon them until they undertake to offer God something in return. In our giving we discover the wonder of God's gift.

God can get along without our gifts, but we cannot get along without giving. The wedding feasts would have meant so much more to the thoughtless guest if he had made a bit of decent preparation. It cost him so heavily to go to the wedding without the wedding garment, but the pity of it is that he never knew how much he missed.

³ Practice and observe whatever they tell you, but not what they do; for they preach, but do not practice.

THE PERSON who finds himself catapulted into a position of leadership soon discovers he is no longer a free individual. He belongs to the public. Those whom he proposes to lead have rights he cannot ignore in making personal decisions.

The moment any man becomes pastor of a congregation, he loses his freedom to live as he pleases. From that time on his life is expected to exhibit the ideals of the people to whom he ministers. He is expected to be the embodiment of all the best they profess to believe. If he fails to measure up to the standards of the congregation (and that often applies to his economic standards), his effectiveness as a leader is undermined.

The scribes and Pharisees who sat on Moses' seat were the accredited moral and spiritual leaders of Israel, to say nothing of the fact that they bore the responsibility of being "leading citizens." The censure Jesus laid upon them derived from the fact that they assumed their positions insured them rights without responsibilities. To him such an interpretation was utterly immoral. He put the emphasis where it has rested from that day to this for Christians.

There are professions to which men give their lives to which a greater stewardship adheres than is the case in other lines of work. A schoolteacher, for example, is expected to be more than one who is capable of imparting information. He is expected to be a superior sort of person. For anyone to enter the ranks of the teaching profession with no expectation of assuming the stewardship that is a part of the work, is to accept money under false pretenses. This is one of the penalties of teaching, but it is also one of its richest rewards.

A layman who has been made a member of the official board of his church is no longer an "average layman." He becomes a member of the congregation from whom the people have a right to expect a superior exhibition of the idealism for which the church stands. Any person unwilling to assume this responsibility in behalf of the good name of the people, and of Christ, has no moral right to accept the office.

Not the least of the various aspects of this stewardship is the obligation of the church official to set a standard in the matter of giving to the support of the Lord's work.

JESUS ENDORSED THE TITHE   Matt. 23:13-24

²³ *You tithe mint and dill and cummin, and have neglected the*
weightier matters of the law, justice and mercy and faith; these you
ought to have done, without neglecting the others.

IN THE MIDST of their Babylonian captivity the Jews were compelled to find answers to some very troublesome questions: "Why
was the nation, dedicated to the worship of Jehovah, destroyed?"
"Was Jehovah too weak to protect his people?" "Had God deserted
his chosen people?" "How did this terrible thing happen?" "Was
there any way in which the nation could be restored to God's favor
and to their homeland?"

The best brains and the most devout hearts among the exiles
struggled with these problems for years and finally agreed upon
an answer. "The people have sinned and forfeited the friendship
of God," they said. "But they can reinstate themselves if they will
return unto him and obey his ordinances."

It became then the duty of the leaders to define the law, to
make plain the way in which the nation had sinned, and even
plainer the way in which they might repent and be restored.

In setting forth the conditions of redemption and restoration an
elaborate system of ceremonies and sacrifices was prescribed by the
priests, prophets, scribes, and doctors of the law. Conspicuous among
these conditions was a program of tithing which was, in part, a
revival of the ancient practices and, in another part, a series of
refinements suggested by the exilic leaders of the nation.

So meticulously did the Jew of Jesus' time tithe that he actually
counted out the grains of pepper he put on his food, setting aside
every tenth grain as his offering to the Lord. In a hundred other details he was as scrupulous and exact. The total result was something
very burdensome.

In commenting on the whole situation Jesus approved the principle of the traditional tithes in unequivocal terms, saying, "These
you ought to have done." But at the same time he insisted that good
religion went much further and probed much deeper than any
such surface concerns. It is quite evident that he recognized the
basic spiritual value of the tithe, as an acknowledgment of God's
sovereign rights, even though he might have amended some of the
practices if he had been asked for a precise opinion.

The Christian who assumes that the "free" grace offered by
Jesus excuses him from the payment of the tithe in harmony with
the ancient tradition has misread his Scriptures completely. In no
word on any occasion does Jesus even hint that this acknowledgment of God's sovereign ownership should not be made.

²⁴ *You blind guides, straining out a gnat and swallowing a camel!*

IT IS NOT unusual to hear some Christian say, in excusing himself for not tithing, "I do not believe in the system. It smacks too much of legalism."

Now it must be admitted that the hazard of legalism is involved in tithing. There have been those, for example, who have given their tenth for no better reason than that it seemed like good business to trade 10 per cent for larger profits, greater prosperity, and an increased income. There have been others who have tithed because, as they expressed the matter, they were "afraid not to." They have had the strange notion that God is a shrewd bargainer who must be treated as one would treat a shifty horse trader. All such concepts of giving and of God, of course, are utterly mistaken and unchristian.

G. Ernest Thomas tells of someone who was experiencing some difficulty in figuring out precisely what his tithe was. "I am not exactly sure what my income is," he said. "Then suppose," his friend suggested, "that God should offer to give you an increase of 10 per cent on this year's income? How would you figure it? If you know a way to get an additional 10 per cent, you should be able to figure out what you ought to give as 10 per cent."

The person who undertakes to strike a close bargain with God is almost certain to end up in legalism of a distressing and unrewarding sort. The steward who gives because of his enthusiastic loyalty to the causes in which God is especially interested is not apt to experience such an unhappy ending.

To give in order to satisfy the demands of a law—even a law of God—is to miss the great joy of giving; but to give as an expression of devotion, as an act of worship, as a sharing with the One who gave his life for us, is to enter into the joys of our Lord. Legalism leads to arid living; loving loyalty leads to exhilarating joy.

The ancient Jew, trained in the strict legalism of temple ceremonialism, would strain out the body of a dead gnat that had fallen into his food in order to avoid the charge of having eaten *unclean meat.* Then he might turn about and practice gross injustices on his fellows and feel no twinge of conscience, a spiritual process Jesus likened to swallowing a camel. Legalism has a way of distorting all moral values.

SOME JUDGMENTS ARE AUTOMATIC   Matt. 24:40-42

⁴² Watch therefore, for you do not know on what day your Lord is coming.

THE JUDGMENT DAY has been a favorite theme with a multitude of Christian writers and theologians down through the centuries, and, it must be confessed, some of the theories that have developed have been little less than fantastic. But quite irrespective of one's theology, there are some indisputable things that can be declared concerning the subject.

Judgment is automatic in the case of that one who feeds his soul on the hateful, the cynical, and the bitter. It is as impossible for one to grow in Christian graces while his mind is thus occupied, as it is impossible for the wheat to choke out the tares or for abundant crops to grow in shallow soil.

Judgment is automatic in the case of that one who shuts his heart against the appeal for help that comes from the needy, the weak, and the oppressed. An atrophy of soul results from callousness and indifference which is as inevitable as the action of the law of gravity and as constant.

Judgment is automatic in the case of that individual who does not hunger and thirst after righteousness. Jesus told the story of unresponsive soil (Matt. 13:4) upon which good seed fell without producing a harvest, and all of us are familiar with that church attendant who has listened to great preaching and continued small and petty. Elbert Hubbard once said, "You can send your son to college but you cannot make him think." One can be exposed to great books, great music, great preaching, and great dreams; but if he does not maintain an open mind and a hospitable heart, it profits him nothing.

There is something very necessary about the practical pursuits of life, such as making a living, providing for one's old age, perfecting one's skills, and meeting one's economic responsibilities. But to become occupied with such matters to the exclusion of the great things of the soul, is to smother the finest and best things of life.

Blessed is the man who, recognizing the inescapable responsibilities of life, refuses to allow them to crowd out the things that are necessary to the soul.

The man in this parable who was taken was as surely responsible for his fate as the one who was left, and the woman who was taken from her grinding at the mill was as much the architect of her destiny as that one who was left. So much of life is automatic.

³ When the foolish took their lamps, they took no oil with them.

THE CONFIDENT expectation that Jesus might return at any time to resume his messianic mission (the scholars call it the *parousia*) was perhaps the most distinguishing characteristic of the first-century Christian Church. This parable of the girls who missed the wedding party because of their lack of proper preparation is one of the stories which gained great popularity among the early disciples because it presented the sorry situation of the unprepared in such graphic terms.

A Palestinian wedding was a great occasion, in which an entire community might join. The festivities were elaborate, and a bridegroom's standing in his town or village was measured in terms of the entertainment he furnished (John 2:1-11). The entire celebration was considered so significant that the chief participants were excused from numerous religious duties and observances for a fixed period of time, and scholars were expected to forsake their study of the Torah because attendance upon the festivities was considered more important as a duty and as a privilege.

The ten neighbor girls who set out for the feast were not invited guests, unless it is understood that the whole community were to be guests. They were just like girls anywhere under similar circumstances. They wanted to attend the wedding. Nothing, perhaps, stirs feminine hearts more deeply than such an event. And all would have been welcomed if all had made the proper preparation. That is the point of the story. Five of them had not.

Their failure was in no sense due to their ignorance nor to any whimsy on the part of the bridegroom. Rather, it was due to carelessness and stupidity for which they alone were to blame. They brought their disappointment down on their own heads.

The anticipation of a speedy return of the Lord Jesus, at least in the terms on which the infant Church expected it, was unjustified. In fact it has not happened even yet, after nearly two thousand years. But there is a truth in the parable which is of as much value to the modern Church as it was to the early Church. There is a preparation for which each Christian is responsible and which includes a complete dedication of his entire life, including his total possessions. Without such preparation, there can be no return of the Lord Christ to the heart of the believer.

ALL DO NOT START EVENLY   Matt. 25:14-15

¹⁵ *To one he gave five talents, to another two, to another one, to each according to his ability.*

AMONG THE Jews of Jesus' day a talent was an amount of money equivalent in value to about $1,000, but the word has come down to us meaning some special gift, ability, skill, or capacity. This is another instance in which a scripture story has contributed a highly polished word to our common speech.

In most of Jesus' parables he makes but a single point, yet in this one, which is closely paralleled by Luke's story of the pounds (19:12-27), several truths are pointed up. At the outset it is conceded that life does not start evenly for all men. Some are unusually favored, while others must find their way on the basis of a single talent.

We work a serious injury on that young person to whom we say, "You can have anything you want—if you want it badly enough." Some skills, proficiencies, triumphs, and honors are quite outside the range of possibility for some people. No amount of effort, determination, persistence, or training will enable them to achieve in the fields for which they are not naturally endowed.

The reverse side of that fact, however, is of the utmost importance. *Every individual is capable of contributing something of value and importance to the life of all.* The humble artisan who frames the picture with a fine sense of appreciation may actually contribute almost as much to the pleasure of the viewers as does the artist who did the painting.

A banquet was being held in the swankiest hotel of the city, and to it every man who had been employed twenty-five years or more by a certain transcontinental railroad had been invited as an honored guest. There were traffic managers, division superintendents, general passenger agents, and engineers present, all beaming with satisfaction. Also present was at least one section foreman whose job for more than thirty years had been to inspect and maintain a stretch of track less than ten miles long.

In the course of the evening this "common laborer" was introduced and asked to make some remarks. His "speech" was one that no one, having heard it, would ever forget. "I was not cut out to be a big shot," he said very simply; "but in all the years I have worked my section, there has never been an accident on it, and there will not be any as long as I am on it." That was stewardship at its best!

¹⁸ *He who had received the one talent, went and dug in the ground and hid his master's money.*

THE SCHOLARS are not agreed as to the precise identity of the audience to which Jesus told the story of the talents originally. But that it was told for the benefit of one-talent people is quite evident, for they are the ones who furnish the audiences, public opinion, markets, sales resistance, hysteria, votes, subscription lists, mob scenes, and mass circulation.

Like the servant in this parable the one-talent man is subject to peculiar temptations that are all his own. The five-talent man may be seduced by a superiority complex, a passion to rule, or insatiable greed. But the one-talent man must stand constant guard against an inferiority complex, a lack of respect for his one talent, and the temptation to surrender even his one talent to some five-talent tyrant who offers to trade him "security" for support at the polls or in the ranks.

It has been the one-talent people who, rather than risk a solid defense of their one talents, have turned governments over to dictators and their souls over to false prophets.

The servant in the story knew what everyone else knew—what the five-talent and the two-talent men knew—that the lord of the manor was a hard man. But he allowed that fact to terrify him, whereas with the other two servants the same harsh fact had served as a stimulant. It is quite possible that the poor chap resented the discrepancy that had been shown in the different trusts assigned.

The pitiful collapse of the life of the one-talent man was due to the fact that he undertook to escape the responsibility for administering even his one talent under the cover of the hardness of his lord, whereas the real reason was his candid confession: "I was afraid" (25:25).

Being a man of only one talent was something for which he was in no wise responsible. But being afraid was something for which he was entirely responsible.

"I am not a money maker as my brother is," a man once said to his minister; and he spoke the truth. "But I do not propose to allow any man to outdo me in faithfulness in the administration of what I have. My tithe will not amount to a large sum of money, but no contribution will carry with it more sincerity of purpose or more honesty. The dollars I give to the missionary may be few, but I am going to enjoy thinking they pay his passage the last miles he has to travel in order to get to his field."

[32] *Before him will be gathered all the nations, and he will separate them one from another as a shepherd separates the sheep from the goats.*

MODERN LIFE is desperately in need of a revival of the sense of personal responsibility. We have grown so accustomed to turning to the state for the solution of all our problems that it comes as something of a shock to many people to be told that they must accept the stewardship for their own lives.

In this scripture Jesus plainly teaches the doctrine of responsibility—a principle without which there could be no moral universe. He says, in effect, that a day is coming when nations, individuals, and even civilization itself must be prepared to give an accounting of the way they have administered life. In keeping with this principle he tells the story of men who were called to explain the fidelity with which they handled the possessions entrusted to them.

The story has a broader implication than merely the matter of money, of course. But there is great danger that, in "broadening" our interpretation of the scripture, we shall lose sight of its essential economic considerations. Unless we can be trusted to administer our money according to the Christian ethic, we can hardly be trusted to be loyal to the larger implications of the gospel.

George Dayton, a devout layman of Minneapolis, operated the city's leading department store for many years. Being a strict Sabbatarian he issued orders that the blinds of his show windows should be drawn on the Sabbath day. "I cannot in conscience allow my windows to be selling my merchandise while I am worshiping in the house of the Lord," he explained to his pastor. That was personal responsibility operating at a high level.

A young businesswoman, urged to invest her savings with a cooperative investment organization that managed a wide variety of stocks, asked, "Will any part of my dividend be derived from the liquor or tobacco business?" When informed that the company did own some shares in a distillery and a block of stock in a big tobacco company, she replied, "Then I cannot invest. My money belonged to God before it came into my hands, and I am sure that my Lord would be very unhappy if I put it to work for such a business." That also was stewardship operating at a high level. The solution of most social problems is one of the responsibility of individuals.

[33] *He will place the sheep at his right hand, but the goats at the left.*

A LONG LIST of lessons can be drawn from this remarkable story of the talents, and all of them would be valuable. But Jesus makes at least one of them inescapably plain. To the man with five talents and the one with two, quite irrespective of the amount of money they handled, the master of the estate says, "You have been faithful." This was the standard by which all three were judged.

The man with the one talent was never expected to match the achievements of the other two, but he was expected to be equally faithful. His failure was not a matter of bookkeeping but of dependability. It is conceivable that he might have won a word of praise if he had earned even one half a talent, or if the special circumstances had imposed upon him an unusual hardship in handling the funds entrusted to him.

The poor fellow was not rebuked because he had tried and failed, but because he had not tried. He did not do the thing he was capable of doing; and when he faced the fact of his failure, he tried to cover it up with excuses. It is always so much easier to blame someone or something else, rather than to accept the responsibility ourselves.

A part of the justice of God is that he never expects the impossible. And faithfulness is always one of the foremost of the possibles. One may try and fail and still win the approval of God, but one cannot succeed even in generous measure and fall short of the possible and hope for the approval of God. According to the logic of the story, the five-talent man would have suffered a rebuke at the hands of the master of the estate if he had won three talents, for that would have been 40 per cent failure even though it was mathematically superior to the achievement of the two-talent man.

Christians subject themselves to a serious hazard when they begin comparing their giving, their services, or their contributions with those of other people. God has given each individual his own quota, and no man can estimate his duty by measuring his neighbor's duty.

The poor man can earn the censure of God and the rich man may earn the praise of God, but whether it be censure or praise does not depend upon the size of the subscription but upon the degree of the faithfulness each exhibits. Strict faithfulness lies within the power of every man.

JESUS' ADDITION TO THE TITHE   Matt. 25:34-40

⁴⁰ *The King will answer them, "Truly, I say to you, as you did it to one of the least of these my brethren, you did it to me."*

Bishop Costen J. Harrell, in an extremely helpful little book entitled *Stewardship and the Tithe,* has emphasized a very important point in connection with the whole matter of tithing. "The Christian's offering differs from the tithe of the Old Testament," he says. "It is given to further a cause. A Christian tither, like the ancient Hebrew, brings a tenth in grateful acknowledgment that

> All things come of Thee, O Lord,
> And of Thine own have we given Thee.

But something is added. His offering is not used to make a feast nor, as the Jewish sacrifice, to be burned upon an altar. *It is dedicated to serve a human need.* This is the distinctive contribution which the New Testament makes to an ancient and creative idea, and is another instance where the gospel of grace fulfills and completes the law of Moses." [1]

When the ancient Hebrew presented his fat ram at the altar to be burned as a sacrifice, it was with the thought that God was like a man in this respect—he enjoyed good food. Therefore the finest and fattest of the herd was offered. As it lay upon the altar over the fire, the fat began to stream out on the hot coals and blaze furiously. This indicated to the mind of primitive man that his god was delighted. When the fat had all been rendered out of the carcass and only the lean meat was left, he concluded that his god was satisfied and that he might now eat to his heart's content. It was something like a sanctified Jack Spratt arrangement.

To this idea of pleasing God, Jesus added the idea that one might please him by serving the poor, the needy, and the imprisoned. It was as if he had said, "If you really want to make your Father in Heaven happy, do not pile your sacrifices high upon the altar, but take the fat lambs and tender oxen and give them to the poor. Serve the needy and the unfortunate, and God will accept it as a gift presented to him personally."

This identification of sufferers, the stricken, and the unfortunates with the first interests of our Father in Heaven is something very revolutionary in the field of religion. It not only makes worship something very tangible and exact, but also makes our stewardship concrete and inescapable. It is one of the distinctive contributions of Christianity.

[1] (New York and Nashville: Abingdon Press, 1953). Used by permission of the publishers.

[32] *As they were marching out, they came upon a man of Cyrene, Simon by name; this man they compelled to carry his cross.*

THERE IS something very dramatic about the way Simon of Cyrene, a black man, was drawn into the crucifixion of Jesus. He seems to have been an innocent bystander who was pressed into service for no better reason than that he was available and that he was strong. From the very fact that he was picked to carry a staggering burden, one gets the impression that he must have been a huge man; and, his home being in Cyrene in North Africa, we can judge that he was a black man. A little later in the New Testament story (Rom. 16:13) there is a reference that many scholars have accepted as suggesting that Simon's family became prominent members of the Christian community (Mark 15:21).

The story is told of a San Francisco prayer meeting many years ago in the course of which the pastor asked of his people, "If you had the chance to be any person in history other than Jesus Christ, who would your choice be?" Various answers were made; one man wished he might have been Peter at Pentecost, and a woman said she would like to have anointed her Lord's feet. But a stranger arose and said, "If I had my choice of all those whose eyes beheld my Lord, I think I would rather have been Simon of Cyrene, and have borne his cross for him down that last awful mile. But maybe I have a chance to do that today, perhaps even yet tonight, in San Francisco." And with that he left the church.

The next day the pastor discovered that the stranger was one of the wealthiest and most prominent industrialists of the city whose name was associated with a long list of public benefactions. He had slipped into the service in the hope of not being recognized, and in this he was not disappointed; but his testimony made a profound impression on the people.

Giving to the Lord's work is one of the ways we have of helping to lift his cross. It is this fact which makes the period of the collection of such profound spiritual significance in the worship service.

Suppose that next Sunday morning the pastor should announce that the moment had come when some Simons were needed to bear the cross for Jesus, and that the offering would be taken as an opportunity for the people to share in the burden of the cross. Would that make any difference in the spirit of giving?

STEWARDSHIP OF REMOTE REGIONS   Matt. 28:18-20

[19] *Go therefore and make disciples of all nations, baptizing them in the name of the Father and of the Son and of the Holy Spirit.*

THERE ARE those Christians who find it difficult to feel any sense of stewardship for those who live in the remote regions of the earth. They are so far away, and their lives never seem to touch ours. It seems incredible to believe that what they think, or the way they worship, has any bearing on how we live. But the war made it inescapably plain that no man lives outside the orbit of the Christian's life, no matter what his native land may be.

Previous to Pearl Harbor and the shock of December 7, 1941, it was common to hear even Protestant churchmen say, "I do not believe in missions. Those people have a religion that suits them, and we have no right going over there and trying to force ours down their throats." If any mention was made of the cult of emperor worship in Japan, for example, such Christians were apt to reply, "Well, it is silly, of course, but if they want to believe in it, what business is it of ours?"

Then back from the atolls of the South Pacific and from the Aleutians, as well as from beyond the Arctic Circle, the word began to come back that "no Japanese ever surrenders." The reason, we were told, was that the Japanese soldier had been taught that, if he died in defense of his emperor, he was destined to some kind of sainthood in the life that is to come. The result was that young men embraced death exulting in their hope, and becoming in the meantime the most dangerous enemy the American man had ever faced on the field of battle.

Meanwhile, back in Japan, the 300,000 Christians who had been converted as the result of the investment of a tiny trickle of missionary money, constituted the core of the peace party. Their pastors, bishops, and leaders kept the flame alive even during the darkest days, and were prepared to take conspicuous posts of leadership as soon as hostilities ceased.

No one can guess what the effect on the world's history might have been if that peace party at the outbreak of the war could have numbered one million Christians. It is a fact, incidentally, that the Christian missionary program for all of Protestantism throughout fifty years had cost less than one battleship. Suppose the Christian Church had invested the cost of two battleships in the missionary enterprise. It would not have impoverished Protestantism, and it might have saved the tragic losses in the Pacific.

[11] *A voice came from heaven, "Thou art my beloved Son; with thee I am well pleased."*

WE HAVE BEEN so long accustomed to thinking of Jesus as "the Word . . . made flesh" (K.J.V.)—the Saviour of the world—that we are in danger of forgetting a very simple fact concerning him which is of prime importance.

Up to the moment that he presented himself for baptism at the hands of John the Baptist, he had never been anything but a carpenter—a highly respected citizen of Nazareth (Luke 2:52) and one widely known (Matt. 13:56), but not a teacher of the law (John 7:15) nor one of the rulers of the local synagogue. When the voice from heaven said, "Thou art my beloved Son; with thee I am well pleased," the tribute was paid to a *carpenter,* and not to a preacher.

The son of the Nazareth household had won the approval of God by the faithful performance of his daily duties as a craftsman, by the way he had handled the business of the carpenter shop, by the way he had treated those who worked under him, by the fair treatment he had given to those who came to him for his professional skill as an artisan. Had there been any sharp practices employed in the management of the business, it is inconceivable that any such tribute would have been paid. Had there been any just cause for complaint on the part of those whom he hired to assist him, the compliment would never have been given him. Had anything but the strictest honor characterized any aspect of the business, the voice at the baptism would have been silent.

We may make a serious mistake when we say there is no difference between the call God extends to the man he wants in the ministry and the call he extends to that one who is to do the necessary secular duties of life. There is a sense of destiny that adheres to the pastoral, the priestly, and the prophetic functions, that does not appear in other lifeworks; but faithfulness in the secular vocations is as necessary—and as commendable in the sight of God—as the same faithfulness on the part of the minister of the gospel.

When the voice from heaven uttered those words of appreciation and commendation, the praise was spoken for One who had worked inconspicuously and conscientiously at an everyday task and had kept faith with a stewardship that is still required of even the anonymous workers of the world. No man is ever out from under it.

¹⁷ Jesus said to them, "Follow me and I will make you become fishers of men."

MARK USES AT least one significant word in this scripture. He quotes Jesus as saying, "I will make you *become* fishers of men." Our Lord did not promise a miracle but a transformation, though it often happens that a transformation *is* a miracle. No man who believes in the Lord Jesus Christ and accepts a stewardship for all of life will ever be the same man thereafter.

In the lives of many Christians the payment of the tithe is a rock wall against which they wreck their spiritual lives. They become convinced of the legitimacy and wisdom of tithing, as a method of giving, but they are not quite able to bring their consecration up to the point of accepting the stewardship. They are frightened at the thought of "giving away so much money." The result is almost invariably tragic.

A young farmer who was prospering conspicuously became very angry one morning because his pastor preached effectively on the subject of tithing and called upon his people to adopt the tithe as their standard of giving. He vowed he would leave the church if "another sermon like that" were ever preached from the pulpit of their little church.

The preacher, hearing about his threats, went to see him. "Is your quarrel with me or with your Bible?" he asked the young man. "If it is with me, then perhaps *we* can settle it; but if it is a controversy with God, then *you* will have to settle it."

Said the farmer, "I do not know whether the Bible teaches it or not; but even if you could prove to me from the Bible that it was my duty to tithe, I would not do it. I am making too much money. I can't afford to give a tenth of my income."

From that very hour he began to lose the radiance of his Christian experience, for it should be said that he had been a man of genuine piety. But the light of joy went out of his eyes. He became uncomfortable at church and more uncomfortable away from church. Like many another, he blamed his spiritual depression on his preacher; but the tragic outcome was that within a year he had lost all the spiritual satisfaction out of his life and was soon outside the Church.

At the same time, another young farmer accepted the principle of the tithe as a part of his Christian consecration and the amazing way in which he "became" thrilled all the people. It was not only that he became a great giver, but also that he became an evangelistic layman.

[31] *He came and took her by the hand and lifted her up, and the fever left her; and she served them.*

THIS LESSON throws a spotlight on a fascinating characteristic of Jesus that has been all too often overlooked—his concern for the forgotten. We have talked about him as the healer of the sick, the friend of sinners, the lover of little children, and the divine son of God, but we have not given sufficient consideration to his interest in those whom the world has forgotten.

In the midst of a busy street scene, with the crowd pressing in upon him, he asked for the trembling woman who had touched the hem of his garment (Luke 8:44-47). The cry of a leper was sufficient to cause him to turn aside (Mark 1:40); a woman off the street received attention that was not given even to his host (Luke 7:36-39).

Simon Peter was a prosperous fisherman of Capernaum who seems to have lived on a rather ample scale, with a town house in Capernaum. One of the members of his household was his mother-in-law. When Jesus appeared in the home following his visit to the synagogue, someone dropped the word that the dear old lady was ill, and immediately Jesus asked to see her. There he extended his healing touch and, restored, she immediately joined the other women and began helping serve the dinner.

This world is full of the neglected, the overlooked, the anonymous needy, and those who have no one to help them down into the pool when the waters are troubled. To them the Church of Jesus Christ owes a special ministry that can be assigned to no other institution and no other people. Our Lord must have been highly pleased, for example, when the young people of a certain little church organized for the purpose of bringing a little sunshine into the lives of the neglected in their community. Night after night their "teams" appeared, sometimes in shabby little homes—there to spend an evening reading to the blind or visiting with elderly shut-ins. There was nothing spectacular about it, but it was so very Christian. For that matter, there was nothing very spectacular about Jesus' climbing the stairs to an upper room wherein there lay an elderly woman rolling and tossing with a fever. But it was just like him.

All of which is to say that we have not discharged the full measure of our stewardship when we have paid our tenth. Concern for the neglected must be a very personal matter.

ANY MAN CAN BE GOOD SOIL Mark 4:1-9

[8] Other seeds fell into good soil and brought forth grain, growing up and increasing and yielding thirtyfold and sixtyfold and a hundredfold.

I HAVE NEVER tried to play a musical instrument in my life, and I cannot sing a note. But I do help furnish an audience for the best music offered in this town."

The speaker was the manager of an important wholesale establishment who served on the board of managers of the symphony orchestra, assisted with the management of the affairs of the public library, and was treasurer for the board of trustees of his church. He had never preached a lay sermon from the pulpit of the church, but he was always at his post as an usher unless he was in bed because of illness.

Without an audience the musician would be a very helpless person; without a readership the best writers would live a life of futility; without someone to enjoy them, prize-winning flowers would come to their maturity without purpose.

One of the interesting facts about modern scientific agriculture and engineering is the way poor soil can be made into good soil. Atomic scientists declare that when the vast powers of the atom are released upon the face of the earth in peace-time enterprises, it will be possible to redeem hundreds of millions of acres of waste soil, making it as productive as the bottom lands of the Mississippi Valley.

One of the prime objectives of the salvation that Jesus came to bring to the earth is the restoration of souls so that they may become children of God and, as such, productive persons capable of being good soil.

There is a stewardship of the soul for which every Christian is responsible and to which all too little attention has been given— the cultivation of a spiritual soil that will provide a seedbed for redemptive and creative social interests and ideas.

"One of the things of which I am especially proud," said a Texas pastor, "is the way the people of my church assume their responsibilities in this community. We have some of our strongest people on some of the most important and useful boards and commissions in this city. They help organize the Community Chest; they head the Red Cross drives; they work for the success of school bonds; they serve on the boards of hospitals and orphanages. And everywhere one of our people appears, there Jesus Christ has a representative he can trust." His is a church with a strong sense of stewardship.

²⁶ *The kingdom of God is as if a man should scatter seed upon the ground.*

THERE IS something very reassuring about Jesus' assertion that "the earth produces of itself." It is as if he had said, "You can depend upon the earth to do its part."

The Gospel of Mark uses a phrase that might be translated "the automatic earth." The farmer plants the seed and then goes off to sleep, confident in the fact that nature will take up the process from that point and carry on to completion.

There is an inevitability about the earth—about all of life, for that matter—that is both a reassurance and a warning. Inject one drug into the bloodstream and you get one result; inject another drug into the same bloodstream and you get an entirely different result. There is no variability shown because of the patient's politics, economic status, or social prominence.

The psychologist speaks very positively in the matter. One mental or spiritual attitude will produce one result, and another mental or spiritual attitude will produce another result. The law in each case is inexorable; the results are entirely predictable. And the significant fact is that we are entirely free to choose our attitudes. Having chosen them, however, we have no power to choose their effects. Those are automatic. Our attitudes, like the earth, produce of themselves.

Just as it is impossible to gather figs if we have planted thistles (Matt. 7:16), so also it is impossible to experience peace of mind if we feed our minds on fear. A vigorous and reasoned religious faith becomes a mental and spiritual antiseptic that cleanses the mind and makes one's life safe from anxiety.

"I do not pretend to tell you how it works," he said. "I can tell you only that it works. Ten years ago, as a result of a very personal consecration, I dedicated all my possessions to God and agreed to give one tenth of my income as a token of the fact that everything belonged to him. I have since that time used my best judgment— the best decisions I could reach after prayer and careful thought. And because I have moved in the confidence that God responded to that kind of faith, I have lived without fear. Never in my life have I been so free from anxiety as since I made that vow. I have not bribed God with my tithe, but he has co-operated with me."

[28] *The earth produces of itself, first the blade, then the ear, then the full grain in the ear.*

MODERN LIFE with all its variety and richness is the result of a partnership in which man plays the role of the junior partner. The major responsibilities and decisions are all in the hands of God, who plays the role of the head of the firm. He carries the chief load; he is the proprietor.

The farmer drops the seed into the soil and then waits for God to bring the rains, start the chemical reactions, germinate the seed, and maintain the species. The little sprout must be guided to the light, and God does that. The tiny white rootlets must choose the right elements out of the soil that they may produce "after their kind," and God shows them how to do it. The first little green leaves must sort out the elements in the air, and God teaches them that lesson. Meanwhile man waits and sometimes fumes.

Many men of science are very humble today, though they were a bit cocksure just a few years ago. The moment they cracked the atom, they became aware of the fact that they were tampering with a universe that is quite beyond their power to manage. The atom is throbbing with powers that stagger the imagination. No scientist, however learned or clever, will ever be able to put one ounce of energy into an atom. He only releases what God has already put there, and the terrific impact of that atom upon man's conceit is something very sobering.

Every power with which man works is a power that has been given him, is one he has appropriated but not created, and was originally the property of the senior partner of the universe. Man writes no laws for the universe; he only discovers them and, when he is very wise, he obeys them. The scientists are never creators, only discoverers and exploiters.

The success of the junior partner in this world will depend upon his willingness and ability to accept the judgment of the senior partner. His happiness will depend upon his capacity for co-operation with the divine. His wealth consists of that which has been entrusted to him for purposes of administration. His capital consists of the trustworthy elements of the earth with which he works; his achievements are only possible in proportion to his obedience to the will of God.

³⁹ *When he had entered, he said to them, "Why do you make a tumult and weep? The child is not dead but sleeping."*

HUNDREDS OF years before the development of the modern science of psychology Jesus employed the strictest psychological principles in working his miracles of healing and in dealing with the disturbed. In this story of the stricken ruler's household he did a simple thing without which there could have been no healing. *He put the wailers outside.*

William E. Hocking once said that "panic is pagan," and no truer word of warning has ever been voiced for Christians.

If we really believe in such a God as Jesus taught us to call "Father," then there is no place for the wailer inside the congregation. There may be a large section of seats reserved for the waiters— those who wait upon the Lord to renew their strength—but for the hopeless, the cynical, the timid, and the terrified there is no room.

Deep down under modern life there is a terrible sense of fear and anxiety. The threat of atomic warfare hangs like a deadly pall over all the earth. The scientists, better than any others, know they have uncovered a power that is so fantastic and terrible that the race is now in a position to commit suicide. The threat of a godless manipulation of such power strikes terror into the souls of men around the earth.

It was into a similar terror that the Church of Jesus Christ was thrust on the day of Pentecost, and from that day to this its message has been one of "Begone!" to all wailers. Unlike any other world religion that looks backward to a golden age that is gone, Christianity looks forward to a golden age—the kingdom of Heaven —that is to come, and sets up *hope* alongside of faith and charity as one of the three major Christian virtues.

It is not the responsibility of the pulpit alone to preach the gospel of hope in the midst of a terrified world. That is a stewardship that every Christian must assume. Our trust is not in atomic weapons, but in the might, the power, the righteousness, and the eternalness of the Lord God. The Christian who lives in terror has taken his eyes off the open tomb whence came our Lord that first Easter morning.

Let us send out our missionaries, build our schools and hospitals, organize our churches and Sunday schools; but let us also raise our voices on every possible occasion declaring our hope.

³⁸ *He said to them, "How many loaves have you? Go and see." And when they had found out, they said, "Five, and two fish."*

THE MULTITUDES swarmed over the side of the mountain and spilled far down into the valley, for of the men alone there were at least five thousand. The day was fast spending itself; the evening shadows were lengthening; the people were hungry; and it was miles away to the only source of supplies. It was a critical situation.

Gathering his little band of friends together, a dozen of them, the Master inquired about the matter of food and was told that their total stock consisted of five loaves of bread and a couple of fish. There were twelve of them, grown men with vigorous appetites, so that such a stock could provide no more than a scanty lunch even for them.

It is not difficult to imagine one of them suggesting that they slip off by themselves, under the shadow of some great rock, and eat the little store. At least they would not be flaunting their food before the hungry multitude.

In the midst of the hopeless situation, Jesus taught one of his major principles. *The Christian is responsible for no more than faithfulness.*

Each of the five loaves and both the fish were requisitioned. When they had been put at the Master's disposal, he was completely satisfied. He did not upbraid them because there was so little, because there were no more than five loaves. Had one of the disciples, purely as a precautionary measure, held back one of the fish, the story might have been very different. He asked only for all *they* had, and they turned the total over to him. It seems reasonable to suppose that at least a few more loaves and fish might have been gathered up if they had taken a survey of the five thousand men present, but at any rate that was not done. The disciples were stewards only for those loaves and those fish which happened, at the moment, to be in their possession. And under the miracle of Jesus' touch, *that was enough!*

It should be said over and over that God has put enough provision into the hands of Christians to do everything in this world's work he expects the Church of Jesus Christ to do. Every mission could be financed, every hospital could be built, and every sanctuary could be provided, if God could count on a faithful stewardship among his people. Faithfulness is all he asks of any man.

[37] *They said to him, "Grant us to sit, one at your right hand and one at your left, in your glory."*

IT IS NOT surprising that the two disciples should have besought Jesus for special favors. In the first place, they were his cousins, and they probably felt this gave them an advantage of some sort. In addition, they had enjoyed his confidences on many occasions— he had shown them numerous preferences—and this may have given them the impression that they had an inside track. But they made the mistake of thinking that the enterprise Jesus was launching was designed for someone's personal advantage.

This same mistake has been made a great many times since those two untrained and inexperienced brothers made it. There are those among us even today who seem to think that spiritual authority is something that can be bargained for.

There was a certain rich man who fared sumptuously every day, tithed of all that he possessed, and prided himself on his superior business judgment. And for all this the Lord seemed to have rewarded him generously in terms of this world's goods, so much so that he was sure he spoke with unusual authority on any question concerning which he had an opinion.

And behold it came to pass at the church board meeting that an outspoken young man spake unto him, saying, "Brother, thou hast been a generous man, and thy benefactions have saved many a crisis in this congregation in the days that have gone by. But all of thy money, if given to this church, would not make a wrong thing right; nor would it make crooked thinking straight. Therefore when thou sayest 'I give the largest amount of money of all the men in this church and therefore my ideas should prevail,' thou art not doing the cause of Christ any great service. For thy generosity we honor thee, but for thy mistakes we hold ourselves commissioned of God to oppose thee."

It is one of the marks of the generous man that he is, almost without exception, a humble man who seeks neither power nor prestige because of his gifts. It is always dangerous when a church or any other religious society evaluates the importance of an idea because of the financial ability of the one who advances the idea.

There is so much that money will not buy, so many propositions that money cannot prove, so many enterprises that money cannot justify, so many devious designs that money cannot sanctify. Price tags have a way of stunting life.

⁴⁰ *To sit at my right hand or at my left is not mine to grant, but it is for those for whom it has been prepared.*

AMONG THE fishermen of Galilee—and their total number was very considerable—James and John would have passed as a pair of fortunate brothers destined to get somewhere in the world. They were the sons of a rather prosperous old fishing captain who operated an imposing enterprise catching, salting, and shipping the fresh water fish of the lake to various European cities, where they commanded a premium price as a rare delicacy. On the day Jesus called the brothers to join him in his preaching, they were heirs to an established business that they had every reason to believe would care for them well as long as they lived.

As the sons of a well-to-do fish merchant they were able to live above many of the struggles of life with which plain men contend, and this seems to have produced in them just a little disposition to make demands on life. It did not seem unreasonable to them to ask that they be given special consideration when the time came for the Master to make up the roster of officials in the new regime he was to set up. Besides, they were his cousins, a fact that seemed to give them the right to expect something extra.

They did not know that one's status in the kingdom of Heaven was something to be earned—that it was not something that could be conferred. Even Jesus could not give it to them, nor could their father's fishing business make them heirs to privilege. They would have to acquire their own status by their own efforts and on the basis of their own qualities of character.

According to every reasonable expectation their father would eventually bequeath to them some fortune in the form of fishing boats, a saltery, nets, and valuable trade and banking connections in a dozen foreign cities. They would come quite naturally into positions of leadership in the commercial life of Capernaum by virtue of the fact that they were sons of their father, and he a well-to-do man. But the kingdom of Heaven of which Jesus preached required them to earn their standing and their power on the basis of their own character and merit.

This is what Jesus meant when he told the ambitious brothers they were asking for something he could not give. Whatever of power or place they were to have would have to be earned by their own living and the way in which they exercised their stewardship over all of life, including their inheritance.

⁹ Those who went before and those who followed cried out,
.. "Hosanna! Blessed be he who comes in the name of the Lord!"

JESUS' VISIT to the Temple on the occasion of his last trip to Jerusalem, which ended in his crucifixion, was one of the most significant acts of his entire life. Once that he stood inside the sacred precincts, the entire system there in vogue was on trial.

Nowhere in all the world was there to be found a more shameful organization set up for purposes of greed than that which prevailed in the Temple. By a variety of devices the revenues had been built up to the point where they amounted to perhaps as much as $20,000,-000 a year, all of which was funneled through the hands of one rich man and his sons and son-in-law. They were responsible to no one, gave an accounting to no one, and could be questioned by no one. In one way or another they levied tribute against every Jew in the world, outside of ancient Babylon, there being nearly ten million of them scattered throughout the civilized world.

The obligation of the people to give to the support of God's causes is one of the most delicate and intimate aspects in the whole field of religion. Gifts offered to God are the most sacred things human hands ever handle. To prey upon such funds for the sake of private profit is one of the blackest sins of which the human heart is capable.

It is a fact, however, that enormous sums of cash go to church every Sabbath and come away again in the pockets of the worshipers. God not only knows and evaluates the honor with which the ecclesiastical stewards handle the sacred funds after they have come into the possession of the church, but he also knows the thoughts of the worshiper as he sorts out the money just before the collection plate is passed.

When God enters his holy temple next Sunday morning, we may be very sure he will make an estimate of the amount of money belonging to him that is carried in and carried out. It is a tragic thing when a man goes to the house of God, sings praises, offers prayers, meditates upon the Scriptures, and then carries an undue proportion of God's cash back home. Failure to recognize one's obligations—one's stewardship—is as serious a sin as to fail to offer a penitential prayer.

When God goes to church, he knows exactly how much each worshiper could give if he would.

¹¹ *He entered Jerusalem, and went into the temple; and when he had looked round at everything, as it was already late, he went out to Bethany with the twelve.*

IT MUST have been a very sobering experience for the disciples that day they went into the Temple with Jesus and watched as he "looked round at everything."

Having been reared and trained in the carpenter shop in Nazareth he would certainly have noted anything about the place that may have been in need of repair. And he would have been quick to reckon the lack of reverence it represented. Stained walls in the house of God must be almost as offensive to the Almighty as stained souls among the worshipers, because they represent a lack of reverence for holy things.

As one who wore a seamless robe (John 19:23)—a costume worn by an upper-level, middle-class man—Jesus would not necessarily have been clothes conscious, but he doubtless saw the plain and humble dress of the poor and made a mental note of their humility and worth. No rich man's robes, on the other hand, deceived him in the least, "because he knew all men and needed no one to bear witness of man; for he himself knew what was in man" (John 2:25).

The Gospel of Mark says that he "sat down opposite the treasury" (12:41) and watched the people drop in their offerings. Neither the poor widow nor the rich merchant was aware of being watched, of course, and that is part of the value of the story. They were quite off-guard, natural, and unpretentious. Jesus took them at their own worth, and surprised them all with his high estimate of the giving of the poverty-stricken widow. There is something just a little disquieting in remembering that Jesus watches us every time the collection plates are passed.

Our Lord was the only one in the Temple that morning who had the right to look around and watch other worshipers. He must have been quick to see those whose worship was perfunctory, delighted when he saw the sincerity of the truly penitent, and overjoyed as he saw the radiance in the eyes of those who had made their peace with God.

It must not be thought, of course, that his eyes were only for the worshipers. He saw also the priests who functioned at the altars, and was quick to note all the evidences of professionalism they betrayed. He knew whether or not their hearts were in their ministry that morning; he was first to sense any hypocrisy on their part. There was nothing that escaped his eye when he looked around.

¹⁷ *He taught, and said to them, "Is it not written, 'My house shall be called a house of prayer for all the nations'? But you have made it a den of robbers."*

JESUS' CONTROVERSY with the Temple authorities was not over the fact that a financial transaction was taking place in the house of God, but because a holy occasion was being exploited in the interest of private profits.

All too often the lowest point in a Christian worship service is that period during which the collection is being taken. The best that can be said of it is that funds are being gathered in an orderly and dignified fashion. But the element of worship is completely lacking.

At the close of one offering as the ushers stood with the collection plates in their hands before the altar, the pastor came forward and offered a prayer over the gifts that was quite unique. "Attend, we pray," he said, "the various portions of this offering as they go on their way. We are bringing them to thee in humility and sending them out with care. Bless those dollars that are going to China to assist in the work of those courageous servants of the Cross who have gone over to do our work for us in thy name. Bless that portion of the offering which is to provide care for little children, that which is aimed to bring other men into a saving knowledge of thee, and that which will be expended in behalf of world peace."

At least a dozen interests of the people were mentioned, each with simplicity and reverence, with the result that the people lifted their eyes at the close of the prayer with the feeling that they had actually shared their goods with God.

But that was not all of the pastor's prayer. "There are those who have laid their gifts upon these thy plates today, O God," he continued, "who prayed as they worked this week. Their gifts have been made possible by honest toil and careful stewardship. There is a girl here this morning who on last Tuesday between three and five o'clock clerked behind a counter as unto thee because she had dedicated her earnings for those two hours to this offering this morning. Make this hour of worship as sacred and as holy in her heart as those two hours last Tuesday when she clerked to the glory of God and earned her gift for this morning."

Such praying over the morning's offering cannot fail to make the act of giving a very sacred experience in the life of every giver, which is as it ought to be. We have not really given unto God until we have prayed for the gift.

NO MAN NEED BE CONFUSED Mark 11:27-33

²⁸ *They said to him, "By what authority are you doing these things, or who gave you this authority to do them?"*

JESUS TAUGHT men to believe in a God who is eminently fair and reasonable. "If any man's will is to do his will," he said on one occasion, "he shall know whether the teaching is from God." (John 7:17.)

We come upon one safe principle at this point that any man can understand. *God does not expect us to walk out into the dark until at least the first step is perfectly plain.* The end of the trail may be in the darkness, but if the first step is clear and the direction is right, then we are expected to move forward.

A very great many people pray for guidance somewhat as the characters in these two scripture stories came to Jesus. They want to present an appearance of piety, but they are not ready to accept the disciplines of devotion.

We pray for the Church and its missionary program and ask for guidance that we may see clearly to do our part. Then we hear a sermon on tithing, or we listen to a missionary describe the whitened fields that confront him every day, and we shrink from the duty that becomes immediately evident.

If any man really wants to know what his duty is in the matter of giving, he will find explicit directions in the Bible. Passage after passage sets forth the doctrine of the tithe. Many of Jesus' parables are a forthright discussion of some aspect of the problem of possessions. He who wants to know God's mind in the matter will find outcroppings on scores of the pages of Sacred Writ.

Every time we hear a sermon or read an article that sets forth some aspect of the world's need of Christ, we can be sure that God is offering us guidance. Whenever we get the news that one of God's enterprises is in danger of its life, that can be construed as an SOS call to us.

Few of us need any more guidance in giving than we now have. God has put his property into our hands for management. He reminds us every day of our stewardship. He thrusts the sorry pictures of need before our eyes. He calls to us from the hymns which we sing and the sermons to which we listen.

In all too many instances the prayer we say we are offering for guidance, is actually a plea that we may be relieved from the duty that is perfectly plain.

[34] *When Jesus saw that he answered wisely, he said to him, "You are not far from the kingdom of God."*

SHE WAS AN elderly woman who had known much more than an average share of trouble. Her husband had died after a long and lingering illness that had consumed the family savings. Her own health had failed in the years that followed to the point where she was compelled to live out her days in a wheel chair. Her only support came from an old age pension and the small amount she could earn doing a little art work.

She was a steward! By means that no one was ever quite able to understand, she contrived to save a tithe, from her pathetically small income; and from week to week she would send a small gift to some missionary working in Africa, Mexico, Cuba, Korea, or South America. In the course of twenty years she established contacts clear around the world.

"It has been the greatest experience of my life," she said to a friend. "In fact, it has been my life. When I pick up a paper and read of something happening in Havana, Manila, Buenos Aires, or Seoul, I say to myself, 'I have an interest in that city. I have holdings there.'"

And it did even more than provide her with a holy joy. It had the effect of broadening her horizons. Day after day, as she sat alone in her wheel chair, she looked out through the thick walls of her little house to the fields that are "white for harvest." She managed somehow to escape from the wheel chair and go roaming in far lands.

One day she sent a dollar to a section of the world of which she knew little or nothing. As soon as the money started on its way, she contrived to get a book from the library that gave her an insight into the lives of the people among whom her dollar was to work. The next time her pastor called, she told him with radiant voice about "those folk my money is working for."

Sometimes the neighbors pass and see her gazing out the window and find it difficult to understand how she can smile so much of the time. "She is such a great sufferer," they sometimes say; "yet she seems to have so much to live for, and she knows so many interesting things about so many interesting places." They do not know about the way she has gone adventuring for others with her tiny gifts that have become so transforming and creative. As the Old Testament says, her "line is gone out through all the earth." (Ps. 19:4 K.J.V.)

42 A poor widow came, and put in two copper coins, which make a penny.

A BEAUTIFUL car pulled up beside the curb, and a well-dressed woman wearing an attractive fur coat alighted and hurried up the steps to the church office.

"I just stopped in to leave my missionary offering," she said as the pastor greeted her. "I will not be able to be here Sunday, and I thought it ought to go into the thank offering."

With complete courtesy the pastor asked—even insisted—that she step inside his inner office. There he showed her to a seat while he dropped into his chair behind the desk, opening the envelope in the meantime and staring down at a single one-dollar bill.

"I know it isn't very much," the woman said, laughing a bit mirthlessly, "but it is a widow's mite, you know."

The pastor hesitated for a moment, then looked the woman squarely in the eye, and said, "I wonder if I dare tell you the truth. This is not the widow's mite. It is mighty little from a widow who has as much as you have.

"The widow in Jesus' story was a desperately poor woman. As she approached the treasury into which the rich and the strong were tossing their gifts, she probably felt very humble and insignificant. Some of those about her were dropping in great and rich gifts. But two mites, worth no more than a few pennies, were all she had in the world. And these she dropped into the box at the Temple door.

"Jesus did not pay high tribute to her gift because it was a small one, or because she was a widow. Rather, it found favor in his sight because it was *all she had!*

"If one of the rich traders or merchants of Jerusalem had dropped his entire fortune—all he had—into the treasury that day, Jesus would have commended him in the same terms. The thing that impressed the Master was not the size of the woman's gift, but how little she had left after she had given.

"Now, of course, this dollar bill will do a full dollar's worth, and you will get a full dollar's worth of blessing out of it. But if you have any desire to give the widow's mite, you will have to give that lovely car that is standing outside, and you may have to wear a cloth coat instead of this beautiful fur. I do not think God expects any such gift from you, but he does expect a worthy one at least."

[28] From the fig tree learn its lesson: as soon as its branch becomes tender and puts forth its leaves, you know that summer is near.

THEY ARE legion who can see the evil portents of the times; their radio comments, best sellers, editorials, and lectures command good fees. But the essentiality of Christianity—that which makes the faith of the Christian different from that of any other man on earth—is its confident expectation of better days to come.

The parable that is reported in this bit of scripture from the Gospel of Mark is unusually refreshing. Set in the midst of a depressing prediction of doom, it declares that the believer is to consider the case of the fig tree as it breaks into bud in the spring-time, as though life were to *begin all over again!*

The first-century Christian Church was bitterly aware of the wickedness of the world in which it was taking root. But it had a faith that Jesus was soon to return, take up his ministry again where he left off, and establish the reign of God in the affairs of men. It was that faith that nourished it and kept it alive during the persecutions through which it was compelled to pass.

With the passing of the centuries without the fulfillment of that hope in the fashion expected by those first-century Christians, the deeper meaning has appeared, and we declare with complete confidence today that God is active in the affairs of men and that the coming of the kingdom of Heaven on earth is inevitable because God has ordained it and Jesus announced it.

The poet Shelley in his "Ode to the West Wind" sings exultantly, "If Winter comes, can Spring be far behind?" And this theme is the essential Christian confidence that Jesus expressed in the parable of the fig tree, which puts forth leaves when "its branch becomes tender" as a sure sign that summer is near.

"I am an old man, and I have watched many dreams fade," he said as his pastor visited him while he lay on what proved to be his deathbed, "but I am grateful for the fact that I have made my major investments in those causes that cannot fail. I have put my money into missionaries, colleges, youth, and institutions of healing." What a glorious testimony!

"You are a young man, and I am old," an aged preacher once said to a man in his thirties. "You are beginning the climb, but I am at the crest of the mountain, and from where I stand all is clear in the west." That is the Christian's testimony, even in dark times.

[33] *Take heed, watch; for you do not know when the time will come.*

IN A CERTAIN city there lived a woman who arose very early every morning with the confident expectation that her Lord might return that day. Her house was a spacious one, and the best room in it had been made up as a guest room, with the finest of linens on the bed and the loveliest of lace at the windows. All the furnishings were of the purest white.

This devoted woman, for she was devoted, made it her first task in the morning, even before she had eaten her breakfast, to change the linen on the bed, dust every piece of furniture, and clean the white-enameled floor "in anticipation of his coming."

"I want my Lord to make my home his headquarters," she explained to her friends, "and I intend to have his room as perfect and as pure as it is possible for me to make it when he arrives."

One cannot fail to commend the reverence the good woman paid to her Lord, even when her judgment stands condemned. In another city not far removed there lived a humble woman who occupied a small house quite simply furnished. She too revered her Lord and endeavored, in her way, to prepare for his coming. But she held an entirely different concept in her mind.

One of the little rooms in her home presented much of the appearance of a relief agency. It was stacked with castoff garments in various stages of repair. Many hours of her spare time each week were spent in the room putting little garmentts into shape for tiny children; and two or three evenings each week were spent delivering packages, assisting tired mothers, and baby-sitting where there was no money for such service. And it was all done in the name of her Lord, a fact no one was ever allowed to forget.

An old preacher was questioned on one occasion as to what his program would be if he were to know that Jesus would return on a particular day. "I would do exactly what I have already planned to do," the little man said, "for my plans were made in the hope of pleasing God in the first place, and I see no reason for changing them."

The best waiting on the Lord is that which proceeds as though God were at one's side already. The best giving is that which is offered as though God sees. The best praying is that which assumes that God actually hears.

 ³⁴ *It is like a man going on a journey, when he leaves home and puts his servants in charge, each with his work, and commands the doorkeeper to be on the watch.*

THE STORY is told of an old Scottish preacher who prayed very fervently every day, "Lord, keep me alive as long as I live."

Jesus told the story of a householder who went off on a journey and, as he was leaving, charged his doorkeeper to be constantly on guard while he was gone. In the threats already gathering about his head the Master could see signs of the persecution that was to befall the Church; and about the time Peter's secretary was writing down the gist of the old fisherman's preaching in Rome these threats were becoming very real. The security and the survival of the movement depended upon every Christian (the scripture says "all") living on the alert.

Halford E. Luccock says: "There are so many forms of sleepwalking—the glazed eyes which never notice that one's ideals are being whittled away, one's purposes being pared down; never notice the evil forces in the world, gaining strength. *Watch and pray* against the sin that so easily trips us up, the compromise with wrong, so reasonable in the beginning, so deadly in the end. *Watch,* lest we neglect the renewal of life in communion with God, lest our sympathies harden! *Watch,* lest the great opportunities for service to God's kingdom come and pass by, unseen and unseized." [1]

There is something very tragic, if not actually sacrilegious, about the life of the Christian who is alive in this year of our Lord, and yet is not alive to the hazards with which the kingdom of God on earth is threatened; who can spend more for dog food than for missions; who can hand out tips hilariously and give to the cause of religion grudgingly; who can look upon club dues as necessities and gifts to God's causes as charity; who can support wasteful habits without regrets but cannot make a pledge to his church; who can buy a new car every year and be unable to afford a good solid book that deals with some great theme of the faith; who can pay three dollars for a ticket to a football game and drop a quarter into the collection plate on the Sabbath; who can laugh about money wagered and lost on the races and complain that the "preacher is always talking about money"; who can treat the crowd with a flourish of generosity and ignore the call of his fellow Christians afar.

Millions now living are already dead.

[1] *The Interpreter's Bible* (New York and Nashville: Abingdon Press, 1951), VII, 865.

THE CHRISTIAN OUGHT TO BE DESPERATE

Mark 14:32-42

41 He came the third time, and said to them, "Are you still sleeping and taking your rest? It is enough; the hour has come; the Son of man is betrayed into the hands of sinners."

A YOUNG CLERGYMAN was in conference with the managing editor of a great metropolitan newspaper—a man who had a reputation for being a skilled craftsman in his field, a courageous crusader, and a political leader of high principles. He could not, however, be called a churchman in any sense ef the word.

"If I were a Christian," he said, "and if I really believed the things the Christians say they believe, I think I would be desperate. I cannot understand how any man can believe such doctrines as the Church preaches and be complacent in a world like ours."

Stewardship, reduced to its simplest terms, is a matter of taking our faith seriously and experiencing something of the spirit of desperation.

The gospel of Jesus Christ can never be substituted for the present chaos until Christians are ready to accept it literally, take it seriously, and work at its tasks with something like desperation.

In no land in the world, so the experts say, are the Communists in a majority. In at least one land dominated by Communist philosophy it is reported that the hard core of the party consists of no more than three thousand persons; yet they are able to dictate to the government, which represents and governs three million. Each individual among those three thousand, however, is strictly disciplined and counts not his life dear unto himself.

The Christian who is really desperate allows nothing, however small, to continue long outside the area of his consecration. He views everything he possesses as a sacred trust committed into his hands to be employed in behalf of the cause of the kingdom of God. If he owns anything that can be used in the interest of the Kingdom, and if he has any skill that can be used in furthering the cause of the Kingdom, that possession and that skill are put completely at the disposal of Christ. No haggling, no bargaining, no halfheartedness!

Halford E. Luccock once said that it is impossible to read the Acts of the Apostles without getting the impression that those early Christians were fighting something, that they were engaged in a tremendous enterprise, that they were desperate men.

³ They were saying to one another, "Who will roll away the stone for us from the door of the tomb?"

A VERY GREAT deal of precious spiritual energy is wasted by those who worry over stones that have been rolled away by the time they get to them.

Long before they had reached the tomb, the good women who were on their way to complete the last sad rites for their crucified Lord began, like many another before and since, to worry about the stone they were sure they would find covering the entrance to the grave. The last thing they had seen on Friday night was the soldiers rolling the stone into place. It had been a heavy affair that had taken the best efforts of several strong men, and they knew they would be no match for it with their frail strength. Their concern was very natural and quite understandable.

They were right in one respect, however. They kept on walking in the direction of the tomb. Had they allowed the prospect to terrify them out of their purpose, they might never have seen with their own eyes the glory of the Resurrection. God always comes out to meet those who go forward, even when they cannot see the end of the road.

"I had no idea how I would come out," the widow said. "It seemed as if my income could not possibly meet all the demands I was laying upon it, and to take out a tenth for God's work seemed like taking out so much. But as my pastor explained the matter, and as I read my Bible, I became convinced that it was the way to give, and even though I could not see the end I made a beginning. In fact, I do not think I ever thought my way clear through. I only thought my way into the habit of tithing, and God has seen me through.

"It seemed to work in strange ways from the beginning. I cannot say I ever experienced a miracle. No one died and left me any inheritance. I did not suddenly come upon some new sources of income. I did not get a raise or a promotion. But the nine tenths seemed to go farther than the ten tenths had, I kept my bills paid up currently, and to my surprise I did not have nearly so much concern over my financial affairs. Once that I had put everything into the venture and had accepted the proposition on faith in God, I experienced a sense of relief and confidence I had never known before. Now, after several years, I would not even consider returning to the old haphazard way of giving."

The stone had been rolled away.

¹⁵ *He said to them, "Go into all the world and preach the gospel to the whole creation."*

IF ANY MAN trembles at the thought that the Christian Church has been charged with the responsibility for changing the life of all the world, let him remember, first of all, that God has provided ample funds for financing the enterprise and has already committed them to the keeping of Christian people.

It is not that the Church is poor, or that Christian people do not have the money. God never asks the impossible of any man or any congregation. Sufficient funds are now available inside the membership of any congregation to permit the people to do anything that God expects them to do, and do it well.

It is when we compare the expenditures of Christian people for missionary work with their expenditures for secular interests (sometimes actually harmful) that our embarrassment begins.

The tobacco bill for the average Protestant congregation, if it could be applied to the cause of Christian evangelism throughout the world, would triple the giving of the people. The money spent for dog food by tens of thousands of Christian families would multiply their gifts by ten if placed at the disposal of the missionary society. In one church the pastor discovered that the amount of money expended by eleven men for tickets to one football game was nearly double the entire contribution of the group to all the missionary and benevolent work of their church for a whole year. In the case of their wives two "permanents" a year would have represented a 25 per cent increase in their missionary contributions if an equal payment had been made to the church treasurer.

A certain amount of exercise is good insurance, and in the case of golf it is a social opportunity as well, but there are preachers standing in Christian pulpits and preaching missionary sermons who probably spend more for green fees and golf balls than they contribute to their denominational missionary program.

There is scarcely a Protestant denomination whose missionary contributions are equal to the cost of one daily newspaper a family throughout the year. And as for our expenditures for gasoline, tips, cosmetics, movie tickets, and fads, only God can keep the books!

If Jesus' parable of the talents means anything, it means that we have been entrusted with the funds with which to carry the gospel to the ends of the earth; failure to do so means that we shall have to sit down with God and have the books opened before us.

⁴⁸ *He has regarded the low estate of his handmaiden.*
For behold, henceforth all generations will call me blessed.

CONCERNING THE economic background of Mary and Joseph we know next to nothing. The head of the Nazareth household seems to have been a man of some economic importance in the town, for he is referred to as *the* carpenter (Matt. 13:55), as though he might have been something like a commissioner of public works in the town of about eight thousand population. The home was doubtless a simple one but also one freed from the threat of dire poverty. In later life Jesus is known to have worn a seamless robe (John 19:23), a garment that was commonly used by the upper middle class.

Nothing is known of Mary's girlhood aside from the fact that she was chosen by God to be the mother of our Lord. That is sufficient evidence concerning her character and personality. There is an old tradition to the effect that she was an orphan who had been responsible for the care and rearing of younger brothers and sisters. One of the latter, very probably Salome, the wife of Zebedee and the mother of James and John, was with her at the time of the crucifixion of Jesus (John 19:25).

From the Magnificat (Luke 1:51-53) we catch a glimpse of her mind and discover her to have been one who felt keenly the sufferings of the poor and nursed within her heart a strong spirit of social protest.

From Jesus' frequent references to the prophets in the course of his preaching, it is evident that he was steeped in their philosophy. Their protests against injustices and the rapacity of the rich had quite evidently been a part of his intellectual and spiritual fare from childhood. From his numerous references to household matters, as sermon illustrations, it is reasonable to assume that his mother had taught him much and had colored his mind with her interpretations of the teachings of the prophets. It can almost be said with certainty that he had received from Mary his concern for the poor, though we know that Joseph was a like-minded person, being described as a "just man" (Matt. 1:19). In modern terms this would mean that he was a devout and fair-minded individual.

Out of such an environment the Son of the household would certainly acquire a high sense of social responsibility in economic matters. This was a part of Mary's bequest to him.

[1] *In those days a decree went out from Caesar Augustus that all the world should be enrolled.*

IN CONNECTION with our Christmas festivities we often overlook the fact that the birth of Jesus occurred at the very moment when the East was in the throes of an economic crisis. The infant Saviour's first contact with this world was made at a time when the economic pressure upon the plain people was extremely severe.

The people were being "enrolled" as part of a world-wide economic survey and tax maneuver manipulated by the Roman Empire. Caesar Augustus in an attempt to determine just how much might be extorted from the world in the form of taxes had ordered that a census should be taken, a decree that stirred up no little resentment, particularly among the Jews.

It was a process involving something far more than a mere listing of the inhabitants of the empire. Every man who was the head of a household was expected to present himself at the town where the citizenship rolls were kept, and where he might be able to prove his descent. There he was to deposit with the properly accredited officers an itemized statement of all the property he owned. This list was then transmitted to the publican of his home community and formed the basis of the tax assessment levied against him. Joseph, the head of the Nazareth household and the manager of the carpenter shop, went to Bethlehem (for he was the lineage of David [Luke 2:4]) with an invoice covering every ax, adz, plane, saw, hammer, and chisel he owned. There he registered, filed the invoice, and prepared to pay the tax which might be levied against him. If any unlisted materials were found in his possession, for which he could not give a satisfactory explanation, he would be fined an amount equal to twice the value of the unlisted goods. This system put Joseph completely at the mercy of his local publican, for by various subterfuges the helpless citizen could be assessed sums that amounted to confiscation, and there were always soldiers near at hand to assist in the collections.

It was for the purpose of enrolling in this grim business that Joseph and Mary journeyed to Bethlehem, and it was in the midst of a period of seething unrest that Jesus was born. It must have been hard for Jesus to dissociate his mind from the subject of taxes after such an introduction.

*⁷ She gave birth to her first-born son and wrapped him in swaddling
cloths, and laid him in a manger, because there was no place for them
in the inn.*

TAKING CARE OF travelers—providing them with shelter and hospitality—was the innkeeper's business. His place was small, but
under any ordinary circumstance it was plenty large enough. Bethlehem was a rather small town and the traffic was light. Certainly the
keeper of the little hostel could not be expected to maintain a
great establishment for the accommodation of the crowd that came
only once in a decade.

The decree of Caesar Augustus had filled the highways of all
the East with travelers—many of them people who did little traveling. Every Jew had to go back to the land of his ancestors where
he could prove his citizenship and identity by the family records.
He was supposed also to submit to the officials a complete inventory of all his property so that the taxgatherers back home might
know how much they would be able to extort from him in taxes
for the empire.

The Bethlehem inn was crowded to suffocation when Joseph and
Mary arrived, but that was not the fault of the innkeeper. Nor was
it evidence of the callousness of the other travelers. It was only that
Bethlehem was under the necessity of taking care of more travelers
than it had room for.

Out of the several scores of houses that made up the little village,
it is highly probable that one might have found at least a few with
empty rooms that night. It is quite probable that the other householders lay down for the night with untroubled consciences, saying
within themselves, "We have an inn, don't we?" and feeling that
this relieved them of any responsibility.

It is impossible for the police force of any city to enforce all the
laws and keep all the peace. It is equally impossible for the relief
agencies to dispense all the charity and meet all the needs of the
suffering. Upon every man's doorstep there lies some responsibility
for the hungry who will never be discovered by the social agencies,
for the burdened and the sick who will never find their way to
the charity wards.

There are times and places into which the individual citizen must
thrust himself if suffering is not to result. The Christian has not
done his full duty when he has paid his pledge to the Community
Chest, nor has the Church accounted for its stewardship when it
fails to know the relief needs of those who live under the shadow of
its spire. All the responsibility cannot be laid on the innkeeper.

OUR FATHER'S BUSINESS Luke 2:46-49

⁴⁹ Did you not know that I must be in my Father's house?

A MODERN mother, sensitive to her responsibilities for the care and oversight of her children, finds it difficult to understand how Joseph and Mary could have traveled all day without knowing that the boy Jesus was not with them. To anyone who has watched an oriental caravan stretched out for two or three miles along the highway— the camels and donkeys plodding single file, attended by their drivers, with a swarm of children bringing up the rear—the answer is simple. The whole caravan moves as a unit, and families never get together as family groups until camp is made for the night.

When the frightened parents finally found the lad in the Temple, and Mary had upbraided him for the anxiety he had caused them, Jesus gave utterance to a remark that must be set into the philosophical foundation of his entire life. "Did you not know," he asked her, "that I must be in my Father's house?"

By his parents' training and by his own commitment, made by the time he was twelve years old, Jesus had come to the basic decision of his life. He assumed that his parents would know that any decision he made would be for the single purpose of doing God's will. If they could guess what that will was in any situation, they could know what he would be doing and where he might be found. It seemed like a simple proposition to the young lad, and he could not understand how his parents could possibly have been confused.

There are three implications in the boy's question that are of the utmost significance to anyone honestly desiring to make a success of his spiritual life. First, God is a divine Father whose love can be depended upon, and to whom the welfare of his children is of first concern. Second, he is sponsoring causes and approving attitudes that are designed to produce a superior quality of life. Third, man's chief delight in life will be experienced by those who most perfectly do the will of God and co-operate with the Father most intelligently and enthusiastically.

There are aspects of the life of Jesus that no man can ever hope to share—his peculiar divine nature, his access to the Father, and his superb understanding of the divine Mind. But any Christian can share in Jesus' determination to do the will of God with singleness of purpose.

Jesus answered him, "It is written, 'Man shall not live by bread alone.'"

OUR GENERATION is in grave danger of being led astray by the bread philosophy that is enjoying such vogue today, and the Church is confronted with no more delicate decisions than those it must make when it protests against social injustices and attempts to protect spiritual values.

It should be noted, of course, that Jesus did not say that man could live without bread. It is possible to assume an indifference toward social and economic problems that is nothing less than a betrayal of basic spiritual considerations. But it is also possible for the Church to protest against economic sins of society in such a way that the impression is left that bread is the final measure of life.

That society should order its affairs so that all men may find doors of opportunity open before them is both good sociology and good economics, and the responsibility of the Church in this area is clear. It should always take a position in favor of enlarged opportunity. For the Christian Church to ignore the significance of bread in the life of the race, or for it to shut its eyes to the struggles of the poor and underprivileged is to abdicate its function as the spokesman for God. Social protest must always occupy a large place in the mission and the message of the Church.

But when all men have been guaranteed economic security, and when the good things of life have been equitably distributed, the central function of the Church to serve as a redemptive agent in the life of sinful men still remains.

The Church itself is not altogether removed from the insidious temptation of bread. It is not uncommon for churchmen to measure the effectiveness of their church in terms of money, which is only another name for bread. To judge a church by the amount of money raised for the budget may be interesting, but it may also be inaccurate and misleading. Souls cannot be saved at so much a head; life cannot be redeemed by bank balances or a surplus in the current expense treasury. To boast that our musical program costs the most, or that our sanctuary is lighted by the most expensive stained glass is to come dangerously near to the paganism against which Jesus protested when he was face to face with the tempter. The virus of secularism makes its appearance in the sanctuary almost as often as in the office of the sales manager.

¹⁶ *He came to Nazareth, where he had been brought up; and he went to the synagogue, as his custom was, on the sabbath day.*

OF ALL THE experiences through which Jesus passed in the course of his ministry among men, perhaps none was more dramatic or revealing than that which occurred on the occasion of his return to his old home town of Nazareth and his occupancy of the pulpit in the local synagogue. He had gone out of the community as a highly respected businessman, quite without professional religious training, to become one of the preachers associated with the movement inaugurated by John the Baptist. He returned as a famous person who had suddenly come under the eye of all the nation. It was quite natural that his old friends and neighbors should have a great interest in hearing what he had to say.

No local synagogue had what could have been called a pastor who filled the pulpit regularly Sabbath after Sabbath. Instead, anyone qualified to speak to the people might be invited to do so by the local rulers or elders; and though a stipulated portion of the Law must be read, the speaker was at liberty to read any passage from the Prophets that might suit his purpose. Jesus' choice of the words from Isaiah (61:1-2; 58:6) was extremely significant. It was as though he were setting the key for all his ministry to follow. The scripture he quoted was an expression of his first concerns.

When all the theological implications of conversion have been fully admitted, it must still be said that the Christian is one who is characterized by certain concerns. When we commit our lives to the mastery of Jesus, we commit ourselves to certain purposes and objectives that he set up as being of first importance. It becomes, then, our responsibility to protect and promote certain ideals that Jesus declared were his own.

To declare one's faith in Jesus Christ as the Son of God, to claim him as one's personal Saviour, and yet to have no concern for those ideals that he announced as being his major concerns is to miss the whole objective of discipleship. To claim the grace of his salvation and to accept no stewardship for the propagation of his gospel is to hold a doubtful relationship to the Son of God. To sing his praises on the Sabbath in the house of God and to work quite indifferently toward the program for his Kingdom among men during the rest of the week is to be a fractional disciple.

[18] *The Spirit of the Lord is upon me,*
   because he has anointed me to preach good news to the poor.

THE KINGDOM of God, of which Jesus preached the hope, is a very inclusive doctrine that sets as its goal the redemption of all life. There is no interest or activity of man that does not come under its authority at one point or another. A man's time, his money, his talents, and his influence—all are vital to the fashioning and establishment of the Kingdom.

This means, then, that each individual is responsible for bringing into existence that portion of the Kingdom that lies just outside his own doorstep. The Spirit of the Lord presses upon each one of us at all times, because we have been called as pioneers of the Kingdom to bring it into being.

If the authority of the kingdom of God is ever established in industry, it will be because Christian men in positions of power inside the ranks of labor, and also inside the ranks of management, use all the strength of their influence to bring the attitudes and actions of their respective groups into harmony with the ideals of the kingdom of God.

If the authority of the Kingdom is ever established in international affairs, it will be because every man who has influence (and who of us does not?) exerts that influence upon all about him to produce, as far as it is possible for him to do so, a moral and spiritual climate that will make peace possible.

If the authority of the Kingdom is ever made effective in the field of community morals, it will be because each citizen of the Kingdom maintains an absolute loyalty to such morality as has the endorsement of God.

There is therefore no Christian who is not involved in stewardship. It is an essential part of our citizenship in the kingdom of God. It is as impossible for a Christian to be loyal to Christ and to "the world" at the same time as it is for a good citizen of a democracy to be at the same time a Communist.

The Christian teacher must think of himself as a Christian who happens to be working inside a schoolroom; the Christian employer must think of himself as one who happens, for the moment, to be serving the Kingdom inside the front office; the Christian youth is one who is the sole representative of the kingdom of Heaven in the precise spot on which he stands. The spirit of the Lord is upon each of us every day.

LIVING ON A BARTER BASIS
Luke 6:27-38

[35] Love your enemies, and do good, and lend, expecting nothing in return; and your reward will be great, and you will be sons of the Most High; for he is kind to the ungrateful and the selfish.

THERE IS NO more unhappy man among us than that one who is constantly involved in keeping books on life, always trying to strike a balance so that he may know whether or not he is appreciated, whether or not he is getting as much as his rights have earned for him.

There are those hostesses, for example, who keep careful books on the subject of hospitality. With meticulous care they list all their invitations—those invitations accepted (and their classification) and those rejected for any reason. Then once a year (or oftener) they give a dinner, invite all those who have invited them, and clear the slate ready for a new "season." It is all very sordid and very painful, having the result of polluting the entire philosophy of good will.

And there are those givers who keep books on God. "I cannot understand why this had to happen to me," a widow said. "My husband and I were always generous. We gave to every good cause. But I lost him, and I do not think it is fair." As though generous gifts to God's causes were a form of life insurance!

It is true, of course, that generous promises have been made to those who give to God's causes. But the good gifts promised are not immunity from pain, escape from sorrow, or a guarantee of prosperity. He who gives in the hope of bribing God in such matters is doomed to disappointment.

There is something very pagan in the type of giving that inspires gifts with the hope of them being exchanged for rewards.

The rewards of giving are generous. Within the spirit of the Christian who gives with Christian purpose, there develops an attitude of graciousness, mercy, sympathy, and purity that is abundant reward. The satisfaction that comes back to the benefactor usually exceeds the satisfaction that comes to the beneficiary.

To give and forget the gift is to find the bread returning upon the waters—sometimes in amazing forms.

To keep books on life is to become absorbed in benefits and to become insensitive to satisfactions.

Every Christian is responsible for an outpouring of his own spirit among his fellows. The Christian gifts that are calculated and apportioned on a quota basis are invariably robbed of something very precious.

[14] *He came and touched the bier, and the bearers stood still. And he said, "Young man, I say to you, arise."*

THOUSANDS OF sermons have been preached from Jesus' words to the young man, as though they were a challenge intended only for youth. As a matter of fact, the call to set one's heart and hope on something higher is the chief characteristic of Christianity.

The church is expected to take a more idealistic position on many matters than other institutions do. It is expected to conduct its business with a strict regard for principles of fair play, honor, and good will. A finer type of relationship should exist between two congregations of Christians than might be expected between two competitive business organizations.

"I don't know much about their theology," the banker said concerning a rather odd little company of Christians who were banded together under a strange name, "but I know they pay their bills promptly, they never resort to any begging schemes to raise their funds, and they seem to have a decent respect for a dollar. I like the kind of religion that does that for a congregation." And he was unwittingly paying a high tribute to the system of tithing upon which that congregation insisted.

"We are poor people," the pastor of the little congregation said, in talking about the fact of their unusually high giving for missionary purposes, "but God seems to have given us enough of this world's goods to enable us to do everything he expects us to do, when we return to him our tenth. We are able to pay cash for the things we need, and this saves us some money. We do not pay large salaries, but they are always paid promptly, and our workers enjoy the feeling of security when we offer them jobs at wages. By giving our tithes we have been able to raise the funds we have been required to raise, without being under the necessity of resorting to any scheme or method which might prove embarrassing to our Lord."

In the meantime some of the "orthodox" congregations of the city who looked down upon the little congregation because they were not "important people" were financing their programs with rummage sales, frenzied drives, and other devices even more questionable.

In no aspect of our church life are we under more searching investigation at the hands of the community than in the handling of our finances, and the challenge to us is "Arise!"

WHEN LOVE BECOMES EXTRAVAGANT   Luke 7:41-42

⁴² When they could not pay, he forgave them both. Now which of them will love him more?

THE STORY OF which this parable is a part is bristling with questions the scholars have never been quite able to answer; but we do not need to be concerned with them. Our chief interest is in the woman whose love for Jesus was expressed in an extravagant style, and in the Pharisee who was unable to comprehend the thing that was happening right under his eyes because he was spiritually blind.

There seems to be little question but that Jesus had numerous friends among the Pharisees (Luke 11:37; 14:1) in spite of the fact that he came into frequent conflict with members of their party. The Simon of this story seems to have been one such, even though he was either an ignorant or a careless host (7:44-46). The woman, however, seems to have been one with an evil reputation, but her intrusion is easily explained by the fact that an oriental dinner is a more or less public affair with many loiterers being permitted to look on.

Admittedly, the story is very sketchy and many details and sequences are lacking, but it appears that Jesus has in some way assured the shabby creature that her sins have been forgiven and in a transport of joy she tries to express her gratitude, much to the consternation of Simon, the starchy old host.

Simon's difficulty lay only in the fact that he knew what sort of woman she was; for he judged her by her class. Jesus saw her as an individual who was penitent; he therefore ignored the stigma under which she lived because she was a member of an outcast group. That was one of the Master's ways: he always dealt with individuals as such.

Overwhelmed with the realization that she was no longer an outcast in the eyes of the Galilean, she expressed her unbounded gratiture and with an utter abandon lavished upon him the expressions of her gratefulness. Two or three hundred dollars' worth of perfume poured out upon his feet was all too little with which to testify to her delirious joy.

Niggardliness and the joy that attends a sense of forgiveness simply do not go together. The forgiven man who calculates his contribution and who undertakes to bargain with God has failed, somehow, to experience the great deeps of divine pardon. It is almost as if one were to say, "By their benevolence ye shall know whether or not they know they are forgiven."

[15] *And as for that in the good soil, they are those who, hearing the word, hold it fast in an honest and good heart, and bring forth fruit with patience.*

THIS PARABLE, which appears in slightly variant forms in both Matthew (13:1-23) and Mark (4:1-20), was originally told for the purpose of inspiring hope in the minds of the disciples who watched and listened while Jesus taught but failed to win the multitudes. It is designed as something to inspire those who fear for the future of the truth, but there is an auxiliary meaning in it that deserves something more than passing notice.

It is not the seed or the sower that is being put to the test, but the soil and three kinds of souls—soils—are portrayed as failing to measure up: those who cannot hold up under the traffic of life; those whose lives are so crowded with little things that they have no power to sustain greatness; and those who are shallow and therefore unable to sustain any great purpose until it comes to fruitage.

Modern life is very hard on spiritual things. Secular life crowds in so ruthlessly upon the spirit. The mad rush, the excessive demands of economic interests, the crushing burdens, the competition which leaves so little time for creative interests of leisure—how quickly the soul becomes akin to the hard-packed path upon which nothing can take root.

Modern life is terribly crowded. So many problems to understand, so many new adventures to try, so many rival prophets to hear, so much conflicting advice to consider, so many gadgets to buy, so many fads to occupy one's time! And during all the meantime the great things of life wait for a hearing; the good seed falls so much of the time among the thorns, which choke it out. It is not that the seed is inferior, but that the soil does not discriminate.

Modern life is very shallow. Our interests are so short-lived; our thrills are so temporary; our concerns are so superficial; our consecrations are so transitory! Scarcely has a best-seller been read before it must be forgotten; scarcely has a reform administration been voted in before it is deserted; scarcely have we been warned before we sin again.

To man alone of all creatures has there been given the capacity to judge and administer life, and by our management we shall be judged. Only as we compel the lower to serve the higher, only as we master the economic in the name of the spirit, do we demonstrate our capacity as good soil to yield a harvest.

[18] Take heed then how you hear; for to him who has will more be given, and from him who has not, even what he thinks that he has will be taken away.

JESUS VOICED a sober and serious warning when he said, "Take heed then how you hear," as if to say there are many different ways of listening, as indeed there are.

There are those who listen only for those statements with which they can agree, for the evidence that supports the position they already hold. There are those others who listen only for those statements with which they can disagree, for the propositions they can contradict.

There are those who listen in the hope of getting light on life, and there are those others who, having caught a glimpse of the light, proceed as though they had never heard.

As much skill is required of the intelligent listener as of the intelligent speaker. Even a great teacher fails to impart transforming truth to the careless or the indifferent listener.

Every listener's mind is like a sieve: it retains those things in which it is interested and allows those other things about which it is not concerned to slip through. "I can give my audience great ideas," said a bishop who bore an impressive reputation as a preacher, "but I cannot give them the ability to distinguish between the useful and the useless." The listener must supply his own discriminating judgment.

It is impossible to excuse ourselves to God by saying "I did not know," if we had an opportunity to know and did not make the necessary effort. That one, for example, who had a chance to learn how to put the life belt on and did not listen to the ship's officer as he gave the instructions, cannot blame the captain if he finds himself helpless in the deeps in the midst of the storm.

The doctrine of stewardship and the tithing system have been presented from the pulpits of Protestantism for many years, and rare indeed is the Christian who has not heard them described and defined. If any man admits to himself that "it sounds reasonable" and does not thereafter accept his personal responsibility in the matter, he has exposed himself to the judgment of God.

A fundamental principle of law accepted in practically every civilized state declares that ignorance of the law is no defense in the courts. But in the providence of God we are judged by our *faithful obedience to the thing we know.*

Luke 9:57-62   THE GOOD STEWARD IS STEADFAST

[62] *Jesus said to him, "No one who puts his hand to the plow and looks back is fit for the kingdom of God."*

BENJAMIN OVERTON had been reared in a Christian home and had come up through the activities and under the influence of the Church. By all the usually accepted standards he was a good churchman.

Partly as a result of some vigorous preaching, and in part as a consequence of his mother's pronounced convictions, he had signed a tither's covenant and for a period of three years or more had given his tenth with systematic regularity. Then his business began to prosper in an unusual and unexpected fashion, and his business associates began to talk about him as "one of the community leaders."

At the close of a Sunday morning service he approached his pastor, his hesitant manner betokening the fact that he had something on his mind which was causing him no little uneasiness. Evading the preacher's eye and trying to assume the air of one who has definitely decided a matter that is still a troublesome problem, he said, "I have about decided that I will have to break that tithing pledge of mine, and I am asking you to return the card I signed."

The pastor, quite naturally, was concerned and said, "I am perfectly willing to do as you request, Ben, but would you mind telling me what your reason is?"

Overton shifted a bit uneasily, and then replied, "Well, to tell you the truth, I am making so much money that my tithe now amounts to a big item, and I doubt whether or not I am justified in giving so much away."

"Then I would be greatly alarmed about my own soul," the preacher answered, very soberly. "You are in an extremely dangerous position. You are about to barter away your spiritual life for the sake of extra profits that, according to your own statement, you do not need. Three years ago, when you signed that tithing covenant, you were a free man. At this moment you are not. Your property and your income own you. Your decisions are not being made in accordance with what you believe to be the will of God but by your bank balance and by your auditor's report. That means that something holy has moved out of the center of the picture and that something very secular has moved in and taken control. I know you are still 'orthodox' in your beliefs, but a new and pagan purpose has taken over and Jesus Christ has been dethroned. What a pity!"

FAITH AND SECURITY

> [1] *After this the Lord appointed seventy others, and sent them on ahead of him, two by two, into every town and place where he himself was about to come.*

LET THERE BE no misunderstanding in the matter. It took an implicit faith in Jesus for the seventy to go out on that first evangelistic campaign. The towns into which they were to go were unfriendly, the people were indifferent, and the days were very sure to be hard. Hunger, hate, ridicule, opposition, scorn, indifference—these were but a few of the attitudes with which they might expect to be greeted. And they did not have nineteen centuries of Christian experience to reassure them. But "the seventy returned with joy" (Luke 10:17). Their faith had been vindicated. That is what happens every time a Christian launches out on one of the Lord's sure promises. Security is an inevitable result.

A young preacher and his wife, with an assortment of college debts hanging over their heads, faced the question of tithing and agreed that the principle was reasonable. At first they kept an account of their income and their giving, but after a few weeks the wife said, "We have only accumulated another debt. We now owe the Lord $11.74. We will have to do it some other way."

A few days later she came up with a brave decision. The next $11.74 that came into the family's possession went into the "tithe box." Thereafter one tenth out of all money received was dedicated and deposited. Then came a day when a bill of $50 had to be paid. By borrowing what was in the Lord's box and adding it to the cash in their possession, the debt could be liquidated. By this time the accumulated tithe amounted to $29.35. "If we take it to pay on the $50, we will still owe it to God," the wife said. Whereupon she offered her solution. Instead of sending the money to pay the bill, they sent it to pay their missionary pledge, and their last $20 was forwarded as partial payment on the $50 obligation. "Now the Lord is as badly broke as we are," she said. "Let's see what happens."

In justification of her proposal the girl pointed to this very experience of the seventy. "They went out, not knowing exactly how it was coming out," she said, "and they came back rejoicing. I do not believe God will let us down when we do it as an act of faith."

And he did not. On the very day that the $50 note had to be paid, an unexpected turn of events made it possible for them to meet their obligation honorably. But the sense of security that attended their faith was worth even more.

[30] *Jesus replied, "A man was going down from Jerusalem to Jericho, and he fell among robbers, who stripped him and beat him, and departed, leaving him half-dead."*

IN JESUS' DAY the Jericho Road was a short little highway that wound in and around the barren hills stretching away from the Jordan up to the high land and mountains on which the city of Jerusalem stood. Today the Jericho Road runs completely around the world.

The thieves who infested those few miles between Jericho and Jerusalem were an unorganized lot, vicious and desperate, living by their wits with the hands of all honest men against them. The thieves who infest the modern Jericho Road are usually organized. Some of them occupy beautiful office suites at the hearts of great cities, and occasionally one of their leaders enjoys high social standing.

The chief of police of Los Angeles, William E. Parker, declared in a notable address before the peace officers of the nation's great cities that the thieves of the modern Jericho Road enjoy their immunity because they draw their patronage from so many good people. A devoted churchman himself, he said that if the church people of America would withdraw from all participation in horse-race betting, they would strike a body blow at syndicated crime throughout the nation. The vice lords have organized for the sake of the loot supplied to the bookies by otherwise respectable people.

On every mile of the modern Jericho Road there are those who are suffering from the terrible conflicts being waged between races, nations, and ideologies. Whatever our repugnance to Communism may be, there is one aspect of its program that ought to arouse the envy of every Christian. *It has succeeded in creating a fellowship among Communists,* and this sense of unity is its greatest single source of strength.

Every Communist looks upon the struggle of Communists anywhere as being something of immediate personal concern to him. The party member inside the United States is tremendously interested in the success of the movement everywhere else on earth, and the color of the skin of his brother Communist is of no significance to him if he is winning the fight for the cause.

The source of weakness inside Christianity is the lack of this same sense of unity. "What do I have to do with that man of color?" the white Christian is apt to say, and excuses himself on the grounds that he "does not believe in foreign missions." But the Communists do, and are making it pay.

[33] *But a Samaritan, as he journeyed, came to where he was; and when he saw him, he had compassion. . . .*

THE ROAD FROM Jerusalem to Jericho is seventeen miles long, and in that distance it descends thirteen hundred feet. Anyone journeying from Jerusalem to Jericho actually "goes down," and the route is still subject to some hazards. Josephus spoke of it as "desolate and rocky," and Jerome wrote of it in the fourth century as being infested with Bedouin robbers.

The Priests and Levites associated with the Jerusalem Temple had their specific terms of duty but at other times were at liberty to move about in the land much as they might please. It is of interest to know that a Jew would naturally expect them, as professional religious workers, to be more sympathetic toward one in trouble than other men might be. This was a marked contrast to the priests of other religions who were, for the most part, quite indifferent to suffering citizens.

The lawyer in asking his question "Who is my neighbor?" received a strange answer from Jesus. Our Lord did not tell the story of the good Samaritan for the sake of identifying the neighbor who was in need—the poor wretch who had fallen among thieves—but in order to describe the real neighbor, that one who went far beyond the line of duty in showing mercy on the unfortunate person. That the one he commended was a stranger in the land, a Samaritan trader traveling on a strange road, only emphasizes the point that the Samaritan did more than might reasonably have been expected of him. The amount of his charity was not large—about two days' wages for an ordinary workingman, and enough to compensate the innkeeper for no more than a few days—but it was indicative of the generosity of the man's mind and heart.

This is only another illustration of Jesus' way of interpreting discipleship in generous terms, of paying tribute to those who live to the limit. The woman of the street who broke a costly box of ointment was commended (John 12:3). Those who were under any obligation to forgive were to forgive "seventy times seven" (Matt. 18:22). If anyone forced another to go with him a mile down the road, he was to go two (Matt. 5:41). The true disciple of Jesus will not stop to count his costs to the penny. He will live and give and serve beyond the limits that might be expected of him.

⁹ And I tell you, Ask, and it will be given you; seek, and you will find; knock, and it will be opened to you.

EVERY FAMOUS person leaves behind him a large number of stories that are characteristic of his life, and with the passing of time some of these take on great authority. As they are told and retold by admirers and friends, they gradually conform to a type and are repeated for the purpose of emphasizing some aspect of the deceased hero's work or some phase of his thinking and idealism.

It was so in the case of Jesus. No stenographic records were made of his sermons, conversations, speeches, or public utterances. Instead, those who heard him speak repeated his remarks, retold his stories, and sometimes elaborated on his teachings. It was quite natural that the different Gospel writers, in sorting over the large amount of material that came to them from the various sources, should select those which seemed to them most convincing or most vivid.

Two stories emphasizing the importance of persistent prayer fell into Luke's hands, and both of them he used (11:5-13; 18:1-8) in slightly different settings. The importuning friend and the persistent widow both illustrate the same theme—that one can be sure of the open-mindedness and good will of God.

Because of the extreme heat encountered during the day it is the custom to travel much during the nighttime in the Near East, so that the arrival of a friend in the night was a common experience for a Palestinian householder. Probably every person who heard Jesus tell the story was familiar with the circumstances.

Jesus told the story for the purpose of illustrating a simple truth. God does not need to be labored with, cajoled, worn down, or high-pressured. He is utterly unlike a reluctant friend or an unjust judge, but can be relied upon to run out to meet the honest soul, just as the father of the prodigal ran out to meet the errant lad who was coming home (Luke 15:20).

That prayer should be persistent is, of course, true, not for the purpose of persuading God to help, but for the purpose of bringing about a change in the one who prays.

The prayer that does not drive a man back upon himself to examine his own motives, search his own soul, and weigh his own consecration, is poor praying. To pray for the Church, for example, without seeking light on the question of one's own responsibility for supporting the Church and its missions, is fruitless praying that does not deserve a divine answer.

¹³ *If you then, who are evil, know how to give good gifts to your children, how much more will the heavenly Father give the Holy Spirit to those who ask him?*

THE ANCIENTS believed that the gods, like men, enjoyed good food, and for that reason they burned their finest animals on their altars in the belief that the gods actually devoured the toothsome meat. To make a gift to a pagan god was, therefore, a relatively simple matter. We have outgrown that primitive concept, of course; but Jesus made it very plain that we can never outgrow the idea of making gifts to God. He described a service to "one of the least of these my brethren" (Matt. 25:40), as such a gift. The hunger, poverty, ignorance, disease, suffering, and need of the world are all his, and as we relieve them we relieve God.

In the light of this principle Jesus' words "how much more" become very impressive. The great love God bears for man implies an obligation on the part of man toward God that is at least comparable. If the love of God toward us is "more" than that which is bestowed upon us by our parents, then "how much more" ought our devotion to our heavenly Father be!

Inasmuch as everything we have comes from God—possessions, skills, facilities, aptitudes, intellectual gifts, health—is it asking too much to insist that each of us return to God some systematic gift as an expression of our continuing and filial love for our heavenly Father?

We are accustomed to refer to a mother's love as though it were the symbol of undeviating loyalty, but the ancients said, "As a father pities his children" (Ps. 103:13). Jesus pointed to the acknowledged fact of a father's love—the highest standard the world of that day knew—and then said of God, "How much more."

It is relatively easy to assure men that God loves them more, but to persuade us to return devotion to him in equal measure is an entirely different matter.

Perhaps one of the reasons for the low esteem in which men hold their responsibilities toward God can be traced back to the lowering sense of responsibility men entertain toward their parents. Modern society, with its emphasis upon the responsibility of the state, has gone far in relieving the child of his obligation toward his parents. Increased economic security has been purchased at the cost of decreased filial loyalty.

[19] *And if I cast out demons by Beelzebul, by whom do your sons cast them out? Therefore they shall be your judges.*

JESUS PUT HIS finger on the pulse of life when he said, "Seek, and you will find." We find in life precisely the thing we look for.

The suspicious person finds that which feeds his evil imagination; the irritable person finds that which irritates him; the jealous person finds food for his jealousy on every hand.

Our dominant desire largely fashions our personal world. If money is our first concern, then our world will be filled with dollar marks. If, on the other hand, we are moved by compassion, we shall find those in need of our ministry all about us. If honors are our chief concern, then our life will be made wretched by the jealousies and madness that honors inspire in the souls of the envious.

The demand we make on life has the effect of fashioning our world for us. If we demand that we be paid for all our efforts in hard cash, then our world soon becomes stern and brittle. If we weigh every proposal in terms of what we may expect to get out of it, we shall soon discover that the world has become niggardly and rough in its treatment of us. The scales of life seem out of balance, and we are the sufferers under such circumstances. As we make life hard for other people, we make it incredibly hard for ourselves, for life always has a strange way of coming back at us in the same packages in which we send it out to other people.

In training his disciples Jesus made every effort to help them open their lives to the Spirit of God, that it might inflow upon them with transforming effect. The mark of the Christian was this transformation. The apostle Paul put it very bluntly: "If any one is in Christ, he is a new creation; the old has passed away, behold, the new has come" (II Cor. 5:17). It was the chief purpose of Jesus to make new creatures out of men. He called it giving them the abundant life (John 10:10).

He has begun his own redemption who has set out to discover his dominant desire and bring it into harmony with the will of God. It means that everything thereafter—money, love, work, ambition— is fitted into its proper place in relation to that great major purpose. The psychologists speak of it as the "process of integration." Paul said, "One thing I do" (Phil. 3:13). Such a man is redeemed.

LIVING WITH A REASONABLE CONCERN   Luke 12:13-15

¹⁵ *And he said to them, "Take heed, and beware of all covetousness."*

THERE IS A very great difference between covetousness and a reasonable concern for a proper care of one's financial responsibilities. Many times we declare that we are concerned only over the welfare of our own families when actually we are driven by greed.

One does not need to have a huge income to be guilty of greed or take a wrong attitude toward possessions. One can be a miser on $50 a week or on an income of $500. It is not the amount of our income, but the attitude we take toward it, that becomes our undoing.

The voter who votes the straight party ticket because he hopes to share in a resulting economic advantage is at least distantly related to the traitor who sells his country's welfare to an enemy. The purveyor of entertainment that debauches the entertained is of the same moral status as the madam who operates a house of prostitution and as landlord who collects rental from the building in which evil operates.

The spirit of covetousness is so very sinister. It appears in so many places and assumes so many disguises that have the appearance of being respectable. The covetous are listed so many times as leading citizens, and are frequently paid high honors by the community, sometimes actually on behalf of their covetous enterprises.

Covetousness displays great skill in presenting itself as being reasonable. On so many occasions it says that it is primarily concerned with "the best interests of the town," "the good of the church," "the higher justice," or "the eventual welfare of all concerned."

The mother who absorbs the life of her child under the pretense of motherly concern may be as dangerous to the developing personality as the mother who actually neglects her little one. Both are seeking their own personal satisfaction at the expense of the child. The labor union leader who arranges to featherbed the job is of the same stripe as the industrialist who jacks up his prices and compels the public to pay an extra percentage in profits.

The real estate operator and the landlord who oppose slum clearance because it is "socialistic" may not be as patriotic as they are greedy.

Christian stewardship is the antidote for all covetousness and becomes the Christian's first line of defense.

ECONOMIC SECURITY WAS NOT ENOUGH
Luke 12:13-15

[15] *A man's life does not consist in the abundance of his possessions.*

ON THE FOURTEENTH day of August, 1817, a half-starved, destitute company of nearly three hundred German immigrants stumbled down the gangplank from a decrepit sailing vessel onto the dock in Philadelphia to begin life all over again as a religious colony in the New World. With the assistance of a committee of Quakers they were settled on a broad tract of fertile land in the Tuscarawas Valley in Ohio.

Finding themselves faced with an almost impossible economic need, they agreed to hold all property in common and share all goods alike. Then, lest there be more mouths to feed, the entire company agreed on a system of voluntary celibacy; and for a period of years no baby was born in the colony.

By almost superhuman efforts the economic problem was solved, and by 1854 the colony had cash and property assets valued considerably in excess of $5,000,000. Everyone was extremely well fed, well clothed, and comfortably housed. But no one owned anything, and all owned everything.

In the more than seventy years that the community existed as a "society," not one poet, painter, inventor, or educator was produced. For a period of many years the village church was closed with no religious service of any kind held. Toward the close of the experiment drunkenness became commonplace, and the moral fiber of the people disintegrated. Young men and women of promise and power left the colony to compete for a life and a living in the "capitalistic world" by which the society was surrounded.

There was something deadly about the economic security that had been achieved. The village schoolteacher—the only person in more than seventy years who ever went outside for any educational training—headed the revolt that eventually led to the disbanding of the corporation and the division of its assets.

Within the space of a few years the village church was reorganized and is thriving today among the descendants of the original settlers. The village school is crowded, and young people leave every year for advanced educational opportunities. Since the dissolution notable citizens—including authors, musicians, and business leaders—have been contributed to the life of the nation. But the original society demonstrated one fact: economic security is not enough to satisfy the human spirit.

[21] So is he who lays up treasure for himself, and is not rich toward God.

THE TRAGEDY IN the case of the man in the parable who built bigger barns lay in the fact that he had no great purpose in possessing. He was not growing grain with which to feed people; he was building bigger barns for the satisfaction of owning more.

Paul once said that it was the *love of money* for its own sake that produced all manner of evil. And bigger barns are another form of money. Both represent goods that are stored up awaiting consumption. To store for no better purpose than to possess is to miss much of the satisfaction which can be extracted from possessions.

Money is neither moral or immoral. But the desire to possess money can become such a terrible passion that it corrodes and corrupts all of life. That love of money which exaggerates ownership above usefulness is one of the most dangerous enemies of the soul of man, and the soul of any man is the best there is of him.

The rich man made the mistake of thinking that if he had bigger barns crammed full of goods he could then take his ease, but no man ever finds it easy to live because he has enlarged his barns. There is something about big barns that seems to rob life of all peace and serenity. Only when barns have been dedicated to a purpose bigger than they, is it possible to bring them under subjection and make them pay dividends in genuine satisfaction.

No man ever knows what it is to have peace of mind because he owns many things. Unless he has developed a passionate interest in something very much larger and more important than things, he is apt to find himself literally working for his possessions. Nothing is more tragic than this: a man made in the image of God becoming enslaved to things.

The story is told of a tombstone in an English churchyard on which were engraved these lines:

HERE LIES TIMOTHY PERKINS
BORN A MAN
DIED A GROCER

A thousand times a day each of us finds himself in need of the strength that only a triumphant spiritual life can provide.

[48] *But he who did not know, and did what deserved a beating, shall receive a light beating. Every one to whom much is given, of him will much be required; and of him to whom men commit much they will demand the more.*

REGARDLESS OF the fact that Jesus has not even yet returned to resume his messianic work as the first-century Christians expected him to do, it is necessary to read much of the New Testament scriptures with the expectation of the "second coming" in mind. Otherwise we shall overlook the meaning of many passages as they were intended to be understood by the generation for whom they were written.

In the allegory (vs. 35-38) and the two parables (39-40, 41-46) of this typically Lucan passage we read three distinct warnings. A day of reckoning is coming, the evangelist says, and all men will be judged according to the way they are prepared for the judgment. Luke as a slave (as he is generally assumed to have been) and as a Gentile dwelt much on the theme of the love of God that Jesus exhibited and taught. But there is no suggestion of any special mercy in any one of these three figures. Instead the Christian is enjoined to live constantly on guard.

The advice is good, whatever may be our opinion concerning the second coming of our Lord. We are under judgment every day; Judgment Day is only a spectacular version of the average daily test to which every man's life is subjected.

But suppose, for example, that Jesus should enter our office, home, workshop, or vacation resort today and ask for a look at our checkbook, our income-tax report, or our schedule of expenditures!

The story is told of a great dinner given to a thousand New York newsboys in a swank hotel one New Year's Day. The people who were to sit at the head table were shown in through a side door while the crowd of street urchins swarmed the hall outside the dining room. Each boy's dinner, including a huge piece of pie, was on the table awaiting him.

Suddenly the doors swung open and in they trooped. The first arrivals scooped up the pie and tucked it under their jackets until one little fellow, catching sight of Jacob Riis—the famous social worker who bore a striking resemblance to Theodore Roosevelt—cried out, "I know you. You're Teddy Roosevelt." Instantly every lad with stolen pie rushed to get it back on the table. He would not be caught in Mr. Roosevelt's presence with any such loot. It would be even more embarrassing to be caught by our Lord with disreputable dividends.

179

⁷ And he said to the vinedresser, "Lo, these three years I have come seeking fruit on this fig tree, and I find none. Cut it down; why should it use up the ground?"

WE HAVE BEEN so long accustomed to speaking of Jesus as being "meek and lowly," and we have laid so much stress on the fact that he is a "loving Saviour," that we have almost lost sight of a conspicuous fact concerning his ministry: he could be very stern when the circumstances required it.

No one ever saw the dangers that overhung the world more clearly than Jesus did, and no one voiced warnings more carefully. But he steadfastly refused to join with insurrectionists who would have bathed the world in blood. Instead, he laid down strict and stern conditions of life and called upon his followers to accept them and live as redeemed persons.

Because he was so intimately familiar with the laws of life, and because he knew that there is no broadmindedness or tolerance in them, he insisted that men who proposed to do the will of God should conform strictly to exact principles. He had never studied chemistry as it is taught in today's schools, but he was quite familiar with the strict disciplines of the material world. He knew that one could not gather figs from thistles or grapes from thorn bushes (Matt. 7:16), no matter how orthodox one might be. There is no magic by which the fixed laws of the earth can be outwitted; and if that principle holds true in the physical world, it is equally valid in the realm of the spirit. The parable of the fig tree constitutes a bit of very straight preaching.

A Palestinian "vineyard" contained fruit trees, vines, and occasionally vegetables. The story Jesus tells is of an owner who had waited in vain for a certain tree to demonstrate its capacity to produce fruit, but when he became convinced that it was unprofitable, he ordered it cut down. Like a modern soil conservationist he said to his head gardener, "Why should it use up the ground?" Jesus made our ability to produce fruits the acid test of life.

The production of fruit implies a strict disciplining of one's own life, of course, but it also implies one's usefulness in society. The person who attends only to his own business, never sharing in the costs of community life, is a poor steward and is living off public charity. As in the case of the fruitless fig tree, Jesus hints rather broadly that the fruitless individual will be dealt with very severely.

¹⁸ *But they all alike began to make excuses. The first said to him, "I have bought a field, and I must go out and see it; I pray you, have me excused."*

THIS PARABLE, which is paralleled closely by one in Matthew's Gospel (22:1-10), is intended to make but one point—the superiority of God's claim upon every man's life and interests.

Some important man (Matthew says he was a king) had arranged for a great banquet, had issued the invitations, and was prepared to serve his guests. But at the hour when they were supposed to arrive, their host discovered that all of them had allowed themselves to become involved in other matters.

The allegorical meanings of the parable may be left to the scholars who are learned in such matters. It is sufficient for the plain man to be reminded that nothing is more serious than the common way we have of giving priorities to the minor affairs of life.

"Sunday is the only day I have in which to rest," the tired salesman says, excusing himself for squandering his Sabbath and being quite indifferent to the fact that Sunday is also the only day he has for the cultivation of his own soul and the worship of God.

"If I do not provide for my old age, no one else will," is the excuse many a Christian gives for his failure to bear a proportional share of the financial burden of the Church, as though his generosity toward God were to deprive him of comforts twenty years later, or as though God would not honor faithful stewardship with his own prevenient care.

"But a man has to live," is the way one churchman explained the fact that he had taken employment with a firm engaged in a dubious business. To this his pastor very pointedly asked in reply, "Live, yes, but what for, and why?"

A young couple who had agreed between themselves to tithe set up their family books to include a column in which their tenth was to be accounted. Debts, family expenses, and the problem of new furnishings all conspired to drain off the dollars until one day they discovered that their unpaid tithe had become big enough to give them some concern. Thereupon they reversed the order and each Saturday evening when the pay check was cashed, the Lord's money was taken out first, like a firstling of the flock. This proved to be the beginning of a new order of affairs in their financial management.

⁴ *What man of you, having a hundred sheep, if he has lost one of them, does not leave the ninety-nine in the wilderness, and go after the one which is lost, until he finds it?*

ONE HUNDRED sheep was a considerable flock in the experience of the average Palestinian shepherd, for it was a very impoverished little country in which even one poor little lamb represented a piece of valuable property. The loss of one sheep out of the flock could represent something approaching a catastrophe in the life of the shepherd's family.

A young clergyman who was ministering to a downtown congregation that represented the city's polyglot population, reminded his brethren one day that "the shepherd would never have known that he was short one sheep if he had not taken a survey." While there is much truth in the witticism, the facts are that the Palestinian shepherd knew every one of his charges and called most of them by some familiar name, and they responded to his call.

There is something just a little touching about the statement that "the tax collectors and sinners were all drawing near to hear him." The late William L. Stidger was wont to say, "You can always be sure of the wistfulness of the audience, no matter how swanky the houses may be from which they come to Church."

The gist of the parable is that any man, no matter how unpromising he may seem to be, may be sure of God's concern in his behalf—may be sure that God is out looking for him. Every season sees some book coming from the presses that undertakes to discuss "man's search for God." And some of them are very profound and very helpful. But the essential message of the Christian gospel is that God is out in search of man, just as was the shepherd who sought his lost sheep *until he found it!*

If the Church of Jesus Christ is to represent our Lord accurately and sympathetically, it must be possessed of that same passionate quest for the "untouchables," for that is precisely what the publicans and sinners were in the society in the midst of which Jesus moved.

When a highly placed businessman of the West Coast arrived in the city that was to be his headquarters for the next ten years, he got in touch with a mission within the first hour and arranged to pay for a bed for "some poor fellow every night this year." In explaining he said, "I wanted to go to bed, thinking another man was sleeping in my bed every night."

⁸ Or what woman, having ten silver coins, if she loses one coin, does not light a lamp and sweep the house and seek diligently until she finds it?

THE INTERPRETERS of the Scriptures down through the ages have been guilty on many occasions of obscuring simple truths, beautifully and simply stated, as they have undertaken to unearth some dark and hidden meaning. By a process of allegorizing, meanings have been read into the parables of Jesus that never seem to have entered the Master's mind. In this scripture we have a parable that has been badly distorted again and again, whereas it is like a lovely little candle with but a single flame. It tells a simple story and tells it simply.

Since Jesus wanted to help men understand the enthusiastic love of God for men, even for sinful men, he told the story of a humble woman who ransacked her house and turned it completely upside down in her effort to find a coin she had mislaid. The love of God for a person who been "mislaid" is exactly like that, Jesus said. Our heavenly Father will go to any length to restore the mislaid person to his rightful place in life, in society, and in relation to God.

The parable is one of three that Jesus told, perhaps at different times and under different circumstances in his ministry. Luke probably collected them and told them all to illustrate God's concern for lost men, no matter how they may have become lost, whether they have just wandered off—nibbled themselves off the path, as an old shepherd once said of a sheep—been accidentally mislaid by some outside influences, or become lost through their own inexperience and waywardness as in the case of the silly youngster who hurried off into the far country.

This is the story of a poor woman with a tiny hoard that represented all her savings, a woman who became almost frantic when she discovered that one of the precious coins was gone. To a modern mind a drachma (a few cents) sounds like a trifle, and there are those who say some of us are not worth saving, but to the woman it was 10 per cent of all she had been able to accumulate above the costs of her bare existence. To lose a mere drachma, or even a child of the slums or of the forests of Africa, is a tragedy.

The love of God is like that. Our heavenly Father becomes desperately concerned when one of the humblest of us is mislaid, lost, out of circulation, or buried under the debris of life. Even a nobody is somebody in God's sight.

¹³ Not many days later, the younger son gathered all he had and took his journey into a far country, and there he squandered his property in loose living.

ALTHOUGH THE majority of those who have commented on this scripture have centered their interest on the silly youngster who skipped off to the far country and made a fool of himself, the story of the older son who slept every night under his father's roof and lived in an entirely different world from the old gentleman is of equal spiritual import. What we actually have in the parable is the story of two very stupid and very disappointing young men.

According to the Deuteronomic law (Deut. 21:17) the younger son was entitled to one third of the property upon the occasion of the father's death, two thirds of the estate going to the older brother. Such a division as the youngster suggested was not unusual in the case of families where the inheritance was a large one, and Jesus' audience was doubtless familiar with a number of such distributions.

There is nothing in the story to indicate that the boy was in any sense of the word vicious at the moment he made his suggestions. Instead, he was probably a self-confident youngster who found it difficult to live under the strict disciplines of his father's house and, in the supreme confidence that he was more than a match for the world, became eager to get out into life and try his wings.

Far countries, however, are very frequently rough and tough in their treatment of fledglings, especially those whose pockets are stuffed with money they have not yet learned to manage. By combining flattery, deception, sophistication, and hilarious applause (for which he paid generously when he picked up the checks), the far countrymen took the youngster to a rapid cleaning. It was all very neatly done—very thoroughly and very cynically.

The Greek word that has been translated "riotous living" in the King James Version and "loose living" in the Revised Standard Version, actually means "recklessness" or "dissolute pleasures." But Jesus seems to have used it in the milder sense of rashness and carelessness.

It may be that the old father ought to come in for some of the blame. There is an intimation in the story that he had considered his duty done when he had provided his sons with cash; it never seemed to enter his mind that he had any responsibility for teaching them the skills of money management.

²⁹ *He answered his father, "Lo, these many years I have served you, and I never disobeyed your command; yet you never gave me a kid, that I might make merry with my friends."*

No ONE CAN know what provocation the older brother may have experienced as he went about his day's work, quietly, methodically, patiently, week in and week out, endeavoring to the best of his ability to compensate his father for the loss of the younger son. It is quite possible that the constant watching of the road, the melancholy that no filial loyalty could dispel and for which the unobtrusive efficiency and faithfulness of the older brother could not atone, had the effect of embittering the young man who was the first-born. It is very easy for a self-centered parent to take dogged devotion for granted.

But whatever the cause, and whoever may have been to blame, the father and his older son gravitated in the course of the silent years into two different worlds. The younger son sitting at his father's table every day and dreaming of the adventures and the tinsel (which he mistook for pure gold) of the far country actually lived there long before he arrived in it. The older son, on the other hand, withdrew to a far corner of the family estate and there walled himself in with his jealous resentment. There was something almost equally pathetic in both cases.

It must be said for the younger brother that at last he "came to himself" and longed for his father's house. But the poor old gentleman seems never to have come to himself and longed for the intimate companionship of his older son. Had there been any intimate understanding between the two, then jealousy might never have eaten away at the soul of the stay-at-home. It apparently was a household in which everyone was at fault, at least to some degree.

The tragedy in the case of the stay-at-home son appears in the fact that he had set up a false and utterly impossible measurement for life. In every circumstance he asked, "What shall I get out of it? Am I getting what is coming to me?" He was always trying to strike a trial balance with life, and no man is ever more miserable than when so employed.

There is an old witticism that says, "The man who is wrapped up in himself always makes a very small package." And, one might add, "a very miserable one at that." The stay-at-home brother still held two thirds of the estate and whatever profit he had made, but he was very poor of soul.

⁴ I have decided what to do, so that people may receive me into their houses when I am put out of the stewardship.

THERE IS something very modern about this parable, in spite of its ancient setting. The inefficient manager of an estate feels he is under suspicion and, in an effort to protect his own position, indulges in dishonesty. Thinking that he may need friends, he settles with some of the tenants for fifty cents on the dollar, expecting to cash in on their gratitude when he falls on evil days.

It looked like a clever bit of stratagem at the moment. The manager of the estate was under severe pressure and counted on his wit to save him.

This is a strange parable on the lips of Jesus, for there is no word of rebuke for the crook and no intimation that he suffered because of his devious transactions. Instead, he seems to have been commended for his "prudence." But that is not the end of the story. Men cannot live by prudence alone.

A very great deal of the so-called cleverness of today is sheer stupidity. The half nude girl gets her picture in the paper, and loses something infinitely precious. The politician wins the votes of a majority and finds himself in office tied hand and foot. The president of the corporation covers up some of his assets, avoids paying his full income tax, and lives in constant fear of detection. The crook gets by with the thievery and has to give a cut to everyone who knew anything about it. The basketball player throws the game, collects his paltry payment, and the newspapers never find out about it.

But the books are not all balanced on Saturday night. The newspaper keeps a morgue, and some day an inquisitive reporter may begin digging into the files. The Justice Department becomes curious about the income-tax report, begins investigating, and issues a subpoena. The politician has to run on his record. The glamour girl discovers that newspaper clippings and a scrapbook are poor substitutes for a faithful husband and devoted children.

Money, applause, and majorities are so deceptive. Like the Arab they have a way of folding their tents and silently stealing away. The friends we make with the mammon of unrighteousness are so temporary and so expensive to maintain. There is a prudence that represents a judicious caution, and there is another prudence that is no better than self-deception; but it is not always smart to be clever.

[10] He who is faithful in a very little is faithful also in much; and he who is dishonest in a very little is dishonest also in much.

ONCE OUR attention has been called to the matter, it becomes rather amazing to discover how much Jesus made of little things. Instead of preaching on ponderous and abstract themes, as did the rabbis of his day, he dealt with problems that were both intimate and familiar. In picking his illustrations he used the woman who had lost a coin out of her betrothal band (Luke 15:8), the single sheep that had gone astray in the mountain (Luke 15:4), the boy who left home (Luke 15:11), the farmer who hired a hand (Matt. 20:6), the trader who found a valuable pearl (Matt. 13:45), the hen that gathers her chickens under her wings in the face of the storm (Matt. 23:37), and the mustard seed that becomes a great bush (Matt. 13:31).

Our Lord was very explicit in saying that not even a jot or tittle (small marks something like punctuation marks) of the law was to be repealed (Matt. 5:18 K.J.V.). He commended the man who gave a sufferer a cup of cold water (Matt. 10:42). In words almost incomparably stern he condemned the man who possessed only one talent and allowed even that to go unused (Matt. 25:28).

Faithfulness, he said, was not a quantitative but a qualitative virtue. The man who cannot be trusted with dimes makes a poor custodian of dollars; he who wastes minutes never finds his hours long enough. The individual who will defraud his neighbor out of a few cents is a dangerous risk where thousands of dollars are concerned. The citizen who cannot be trusted to respect property rights cannot be trusted to respect human rights.

The little land in which Jesus lived and preached was about the size of the state of Vermont, and the audiences to which Jesus spoke were far smaller than those that gather any Saturday afternoon to watch an intercollegiate football game; but the destiny of all the race was profoundly affected in that little land by what Jesus said.

"If I can teach my son to tithe his allowance of ten cents a week," the wise father said, "I may be able to implant in his mind a principle that will insure wise management of a great income some day." And that is exactly what happened, for the head of the great industry that does a business of more than $20,000,000 annually ascribes his lifelong rule of tithing to his father's example and instruction. "It was the best lesson in business management he ever taught me," the son says today. And his business associates agree with him.

[12] *And if you have not been faithful in that which is another's, who will give you that which is your own?*

A POPULAR luncheon club in a certain city had staged a giant community fiesta for the purpose of raising funds for the support of a fine piece of boys' work. The cause for which the money was to be expended was a worthy one; the members of the club invested a great deal of time and effort in the enterprise; and the city gave it generous support.

One of the features of the fiesta was the raffling off of an expensive automobile. The club had calculated that this one event would add at least $5,000 to their fund.

A raffle was in violation of the law in that state, but the club calculated on its influence with the law enforcement officials of the city to forestall any prosecution. The fact that these prominent businessmen were violating the law was known to every boy in town. Also it was known that the profits from the fiesta were to be devoted to the cause of combating juvenile delinquency. The spectacle of reputable businessmen breaking the law in order to make money which would pay for teaching boys to obey the law was one calculated to arouse some questions even in the minds of the boys.

A quick check of the membership of the club that sponsored the affair revealed the fact that considerably more than half its members were also members of some Christian church, Catholic or Protestant. Churchmen put on the show, broke the law, raffled off the automobile, and raised the moral issue of gambling for charity's sake.

Listed among the members of the club were some men who taught Bible classes in church schools of the city, but none of them ever objected to the violation of the state law. Also listed on the roster were two ministers of the gospel, but one of them said, "I do not like to inject my personal opinions into a thing of this kind." And the wrong was permitted to go on because no one raised a voice in protest.

Time and again during the last ten years the nation has been shocked by the revelations of the sinister influence of gambling on the life of the nation, but the bookies would have to go out of business in many cities if all the church people were to abstain from the dangerous traffic.

Every Christian either raises or lowers the moral average of the community in which he lives, and he also adds to or subtracts from the influence of the Church of Jesus Christ.

[13] No servant can serve two masters; for either he will hate the one and love the other, or he will be devoted to the one and despise the other.

IF LIFE IS governed by law, as all good science and good religion declare is the case, then it follows as the night the day that some things are impossible, being contrary to law. In this single bit of scripture Jesus describes one such situation. "You cannot serve God and mammon."

This is no arbitrary ruling on the part of Jesus, but a calm and dispassionate statement of a law of life. It is not the result of whimsy or caprice, but a basic principle upon which the whole moral universe rests. It simply cannot be done. No matter how clever we may be, no matter what age we may live in, no matter how we may try to gloss over our disobedience with pseudo-scientific language, and no matter how slow the retribution may be, a split loyalty is always fatal in the long run.

No man can run in two directions at the same time; no man can look in two directions at the same instant; no one can follow two impulses in opposite directions at the same time; no man can give complete loyalty to God and complete loyalty to mammon at the same time.

Life is constantly confronting us with choices. Much time and energy are expended every day in the process of deciding "either/or." The psychologists warn us very soberly against divided devotions, multiple purposes, and split loyalties; but long before science discovered the danger, Jesus undertook to warn the race against such. It is not a matter of opinion but a statement of fact that is involved. No man ever finds it possible to serve God and mammon.

He who owns property must defend himself every hour of the day against its demand that he serve it. All about us there are those who have surrendered to its demands. "I have to run the coal business," says the manager of a big concern, trying to excuse himself for having lost interest in culture, religion, art, and music. What he means is that he has committed himself to the coal business and that it is running him.

It is precisely at this point that tithing renders its most conspicuous service in the life of the Christian. The man who tithes as a matter of principle is one who has accepted his business and his property as a trust from God, his tithe being the token of that stewardship which is returned to God on a regular business basis. His tithing agreement is his declaration of spiritual independence.

LOVERS OF MONEY

14 The Pharisees, who were lovers of money, heard all this, and they scoffed at him.

IT IS A LITTLE difficult for a modern Christian to take an absolutely fair attitude toward the Pharisees of Jesus' day, for all we know about them is what we read in the New Testament and, it must be admitted, the Christian writers experienced many things that could have prejudiced them.

The Pharisees, as a religious party inside Judaism, were passionately devoted to the God of Israel, to the age-old principles of the Law, and to the highly involved ceremonialism that promised them the favor of God. That they had their faults goes without saying, of course; but that they had been a bulwark within the nation, holding it true to its national ideals in spite of terrific pressure from Roman secularism, must also be declared.

Nowhere else in the New Testament is it said that the Pharisees were an avaricious lot. As a matter of fact it was the Sadducees, their political rivals, who were the economic royalists, money lenders, landlords, and propertied class among the Jews. This sentence does not represent Jesus' opinion of them. Rather, it is what the scholars would call an "editorial comment" slipped into the record by Luke, the author of the Gospel. And Luke, it must be remembered, was not a Jew but a Gentile. His contacts with the Jews had been, for the most part, with those of the dispersion who lived in the great cities of the empire. So far as we have any way of knowing, he never made more than a single visit to Jerusalem.

We do know some of the unlovely characteristics of the Pharisees, however, and they suggest that there may have been those individuals among the group who were avaricious, money lovers, ostentatious, and greedy.

We know, for example, that it was common for them to contrive to occupy some prominent street corner at the precise moment that the Shema was to be recited, and that they tarried long at their prayers in the hope of attracting attention (Matt. 6:5). It was not uncommon to see them tossing their money into the offering box at the door of the Temple in such a way as to attract the most attention possible.

Nothing is cheaper or more tawdry than the ostentation that money makes possible. It is difficult to conceive of anything that would earn more of Jesus' scorn than the giving that is done for the sake of show. He who gives in that fashion must buy all the appreciation he gets.

[15] *He said to them, "You are those who justify yourselves before men, but God knows your hearts; for what is exalted among men is an abomination in the sight of God."*

As A WRITER Luke was disposed to gather up a number of Jesus' sayings that were related to a single theme and present them as a body of teachings, usually with little or no editorial comment between them. In 14:25-34 the sayings all relate to the question of discipleship, but in 16:10-18 the subject under discussion is money.

Because of the fact that we know nothing about the circumstances that elicited the comment from Jesus, it is difficult to know precisely all the meaning the words were intended originally to convey, but at least one point is perfectly plain. God's judgments are frequently very much different from man's.

The wealthy Pharisees, like many others since that day, assumed the right to speak with great authority on many subjects for no better reason than that they were rich. They seemed to labor under the impression that their possessions had conferred upon them a superior type of wisdom, an ability to think more clearly, or the right of final judgment.

It is a common mistake—common in that ancient day, as it is also common today—to ascribe great weight to the opinion of the man who owns much property. It has happened in many instances that the church has listened obsequiously while some rich man has spoken, allowing him to dictate the terms upon which he would contribute to the church's program. Plainly, this scripture is in condemnation of any such attitude.

In planning the work of the kingdom of God, any man's opinion is worth exactly what the facts and the logic warrant—no more and no less. It sometimes happens that the humble man who lives in a cottage under a mortgage is a better judge of the spiritual worth of an idea than the big industrialist who lives in a mansion on the boulevard. There are fields in which the rich man's judgment is invaluable, because of his economic knowledge and experience, but neither money, college degrees, nor political powers give any man a right to speak with authority in a field outside his special fitness.

To tyrannize over other men's minds and consciences on the basis of possessions is to invite the condemnation of God. To undertake to exert economic pressure on a pulpit, an editorial chair, or inside a broadcasting studio, to defeat or delay the truth is to set one's self up in opposition to God. Money has never bestowed any such right on any man.

THE BLIND RICH MAN   Luke 16:19-21

[20] At his gate lay a poor man named Lazarus, full of sores.

A BASIC PRINCIPLE in interpreting Jesus' parables is this: *each parable is the presentation of but a single idea.* Nothing does more violence to the original meaning than some effort to read hidden meanings, allegorical significance, or intricate theological meanings into them.

The case of the certain rich man who fared sumptuously every day while a poor wretch lay begging at his door is very simple. It could have been duplicated in actual life in Jerusalem or Antioch or Ephesus perhaps a hundred times every day. For that matter, Chicago, Birmingham, Seattle, or El Paso might furnish the scene and the actors if they were lacking elsewhere.

There is nothing in the story as Jesus told it to indicate that the rich man was also a wicked man. As a matter of fact, he may have been one of his city's leading citizens. Although Jesus says he "feasted sumptuously," he does not say that he was either a sot or a glutton.

It was only that he had no eyes or ears for the wretchedness that was spread out all about him—that crept up to his very door, in fact. The famous artists of a few years ago (Bassana, Doré, *et al.*) who pictured the rich man's servants as whipping the beggar away from the rich man's door, and the modern cartoonist who portrays a corpulent ruffian as grinding a poor man under his heel, are both wrong. Dives (the name that is derived from the Latin adjective meaning "rich") was probably something of a gentleman, perhaps a patron of the arts, a highly respected individual.

But he was blind. He never saw the beggar. He returned from the meeting of the hospital board so engrossed in the problem of the new laboratory they were building that he never even looked in the direction of the filthy fellow who was trying to beat off the street dogs that crowded about him as he lay on his vermin-infested pallet.

It is entirely possible that Dives consoled himself with the thought that he helped support the Community Chest, and that it was the responsibility of the case workers to take care of such persons. At least that was what one leading layman said when the problem of ministering to the poor came up in the board meeting: "Isn't that what we support social agencies for?" And he fared sumptuously every day also.

192

⁵ *Because this widow bothers me, I will vindicate her, or she will wear me out by her continual coming.*

THERE IS SOMETHING very like modern slang in the parable of the importunate widow and the unjust judge. It seems that a poor woman with a just cause had appealed to some minor local official who served as a judge. He was a callous individual who looked upon the woman as being something of a nuisance, and therefore ignored her pleas. But day after day she thrust herself in upon him, renewed her pleas, mixed tears and wrath in a vain effort to get justice, and made life so miserable for the scoundrel that he finally said, "Because this widow bothers me, I will vindicate her, or she will wear me out by her continual coming." The literal translation of the text is "lest she come at last and beat me."

The woman had no attorney, no vote, no influence, and no friend. But she could badger the judge with her persistence until he said to his friends, "I am taking an awful beating from her."

This is one of those parables that teaches by contrast. It is as though Jesus were saying, "If such a judge could be moved by a friendless woman who persisted in her demands, then how much more ought you to be assured that God will come to your assistance when you pray and when you earn his favor with your faithfulness!"

It happens very frequently as we pray that our minds are illuminated by our own petitions, so that we find ways of answering our own prayers. A man and his wife who had come to a crisis in their domestic affairs became engaged in a controversy that left both of them angry and bitter. Being Christians both began praying privately, and at first each asked God to "help the other see his mistake." Then, as they prayed, they began discovering their own errors. "I prayed God to show my wife where she was wrong, for I could not do it, and he ended up showing me where I was wrong." At least this is the way the husband described the healing of the breach.

"My pastor called on me to lead in prayer at the missionary meeting," one of the leading women of the congregation said, "and my prayer got on my own conscience. I had tried to pray honestly for the missionaries; but when I got to thinking about how little I had done to help them myself, I had to restudy my whole program of giving or else quit praying. God used my prayer as a window through which to pour light on my own need."

THE SELF-SATISFIED TITHER   Luke 18:9-14

¹⁴ *Every one who exalts himself will be humbled, but he who humbles himself will be exalted.*

THE AVERAGE modern Christian is in danger of judging the ancient Pharisee unjustly because an occasional member of the party was singled out in one or another of Jesus' parables to illustrate some subtle weakness of the supposedly religious man. The self-righteous individual of this story has done his kind great injury in the course of the centuries.

The Pharisees were, actually, the most seriously religious people of their day, and there were among them some very admirable and genuinely devout people. But there were also those who became very conscious of their spiritual superiority and took great satisfaction in the fact that they were "not like other men." Jesus was intent on showing that such individuals were greatly in need of something that he was prepared to give.

The Pharisee of the story was a man of exemplary life. He kept the law meticulously. In fact, he went far beyond the strict requirements of the commonly accepted code. Whereas private fasting was not required by the Law, he did fast. On Mondays and Thursday he abstained from food or ate sparingly, as a spiritual discipline. He also tithed. And again he exceeded the requirements of the Law. More than merely tithing his income, he tithed his possessions: 10 per cent of all he owned he gave away every year.

But his excessive devotion to the Law had not produced in him those spiritual qualities of life without which no man can claim to be possessed by the Spirit of God. When he prayed, he prayed "with himself." One of the very ancient New Testament manuscripts (Codex Bezae) says, "the Pharisee stood by himself and prayed," as though he felt too superior to be associated with ordinary men.

There are those rare instances of tithers who have assumed that, because of their tithing, they are somehow superior to other people. Their willingness to give largely has had the effect of making them self-righteous, and in a few extremely rare cases they have used their benevolence as a reason for demanding that their opinions be given exceptional consideration in determining the decisions of a congregation.

Christian living consists of an assemblage of virtues in which humility, mercy, love, charity, benevolence, honor, patience, long-suffering, and joy are blended. Blessed is the man who is able to maintain a decent sense of balance.

194

²² *When Jesus heard it, he said to him, "One thing you still lack. Sell all that you have and distribute to the poor, and you will have treasure in heaven; and come, follow me."*

THE CHRISTIAN doctrine of stewardship includes much more than the simple matter of giving. It includes all of a man's attitude toward property.

We make a serious mistake in our evangelistic efforts if we do not raise the issue of money at the outset of a young Christian's life. One of the very first questions any follower of the Lord Christ must settle is this: "What kind of mastery over my money am I to give Jesus?" Upon the answer to that query will depend a large part of his subsequent spiritual development.

A Pennsylvania insurance man, who has shown rare ability and zeal as a personal worker, says that he always puts the question of tithing into the middle of every conversation he has with a prospect. "If my man can get straight and clear on the problem of property," he says, "I find that it is not difficult to lead him on into a vivid Christian experience." His pastor reports that those whom he accompanies to the altar of the church, seeking church membership, become good stewards almost from the first day of their Christian life. And this is as it should be.

The failure of the rich young ruler originated in the fact that he had no great concept of the meaning of money. Because it was impossible in those times for a young man to accumulate a large fortune by his own efforts, it seems altogether likely that he had inherited his fortune. There was no other way by which it could have come into his possession at such an early age. His father had left him "very rich" in goods and lean of soul.

It is quite probable that the young man had never learned to give because he had never seen much giving. When Jesus invited him to become a generous man, it sounded very strange and very difficult to him, for he had never had any education along those lines.

The weakness of modern Christianity lies at least in part in this area. We are trained to deal with every problem except that of property. We are taught how to make money but not how to give it away. Christian parents who train their children in honesty and sobriety do well, of course, but the training is not complete until the child is given an understanding of this doctrine of stewardship.

[15] *When he returned, having received the kingly power, he commanded these servants, to whom he had given the money, to be called to him, that he might know what they had gained by trading.*

THE PREACHERS and evangelists of our fathers' day had much to say about a great Judgment Day—some far-off and terrible occasion—when every man would be required to stand before the bar of God and receive a verdict on all his life. In the hands of eloquent men such sermons could become both very terrifying and very reassuring.

In the modern pulpit, unfortunately, the theme of the Judgment Day is very seldom discussed. The reason may be that our fathers surrounded the doctrine with many a fantasy. But one cannot read the New Testament honestly and critically without becoming aware that the preaching of Jesus was highly colored with the conviction that a day of reckoning is coming, from which no man can hope to escape.

Perhaps our fathers laid an overdue emphasis on theology and logical conformity, so that the blessings of the final day of reckoning seemed to be reserved for those who reasoned correctly about the great doctrines of the faith. Or, in describing the fate of those who were found lacking, they may have drawn too liberally on overactive imaginations, with the result that they described the fate of the damned in terms too literalistic. But none of these "mistakes," if mistakes they be, can justify us for our silence on the fact of the final reckoning.

If the New Testament teaching has any meaning whatever, it means that, among other things, all men must give an accounting for the manner in which they have administered the property they have held in their possession.

As a matter of spiritual invoicing it will pay any man to imagine himself standing in the presence of God when the books are opened and the full record of his financial transactions is being studied. With all the facts before him and with all rationalizations and pretexts swept aside, the judgment will be reckoned up. All the various amounts spent for necessities, extravagances, pretenses, ostentation, minor vices, wasteful habits, and the advancement of the kingdom of Heaven—those causes in which God has a special interest—will be calculated with complete fairness and justice.

As a matter of fact, every day is a judgment day. Every dollar we hold in our possession stands up to offer its testimony concerning our stewardship. And each of us writes the verdict on himself by his own decisions.

³⁵ *The people stood by, watching; but the rulers scoffed at him, say-*
ing, "He saved others; let him save himself, if he is the Christ of God,
his Chosen One!"

THERE IS something so very sinister in the description of the curiosity seekers who thronged Calvary the day Jesus died there upon his
cross. Luke says, "The people stood by, watching."

No one in the crowd drove the nails through his hands; the
Roman soldiers did that. No one of the bystanders railed at him; the
rulers from the Temple did that. No one in the crowd shared in any
loot; the soldiers divided his garments among themselves (Matt.
27:35).

There was sufficient influence in the crowd to have saved Jesus
from the cross, if the people had risen and demanded that he be dealt
with justly. The Temple authorities and the Roman command knew
they could count on the apathy of the people.

The ineffectiveness of the Church in the midst of an age of crisis
is due to the large number of Christians who are content to stand
and watch. Oh, they may say that it is "too bad" or that "we ought
to have a law" or even that "somebody ought to do something." But
slums continue, exploitation goes on unrebuked, the Sabbath is
desecrated wholesale, the liquor traffic preys on American parents,
the radio and television industries invade the American home with
their insistence that men shall drink alcohol, and millions stand by
watching, saying nothing, and doing nothing.

God has put enough money into the pockets of American Protestants to enable them to finance every campaign he expects them to
put on, erect every hospital and school he has assigned to them, build
every church and mission the program requires, and promote every
reform this world needs.

In one great American city there stands a magnificent church. Its
architecture is superb, its services are dignified and ponderous, its
congregation is cultured and capable. But within a stone's throw of
the stately edifice, are squalor and wretchedness. Hundreds of little
children roam the streets, and some of them actually beg at the door
of the Lord's house if they can do so without attracting the attention
of the police. The worshipers drive through slums to get to God's
house on the Sabbath day, but no one suggests that anything be done
about the neighborhood. They only stand by and watch, and sometimes complain about "those terrible children that swarm about."

²³ He said, "I am the voice of one crying in the wilderness, 'Make straight the way of the Lord,' as the prophet Isaiah said."

IT IS RATHER remarkable that we know so few details concerning the life of John the Baptist, the prophet of whom Jesus said, "Among those born of women there has risen no one greater" (Matt. 11:11). His one appearance in the New Testament consists of the dramatic announcement of the arrival of Jesus, the Messiah.

The magnificence of his ministry consisted of an absolute fidelity and devotion to a single purpose. His life was never cluttered up with a series of conflicting emotions, objectives, or demands. He refused to allow himself to be called another Elijah, though his eloquence might have attracted a following that would have permitted him to lead an uprising of all Jewry. He did not even demur when asked if he were the expected Messiah. Instead, he denied the office emphatically and went on, under his own colors, content to call himself a voice in the wilderness.

Profoundly moved by the decadence of the life about him, John the Baptist was convinced that God was about to take a hand in the affairs of men and he therefore proposed to make that fact known to the nation. Whatever his name or fame, it is due entirely to this purpose. His friends appealed to his jealousy in vain; he could be imprisoned by a playboy tetrarch, and his life might be in dire jeopardy, but he could not be tempted down from his great objective.

His greatness consisted in his ability to do one thing superbly. His magnificence consisted in his willingness to play a secondary role with enthusiasm. He earned his place because he performed the stewardship of a single purpose with complete faithfulness. His life was never out of focus.

It is probably true that more Christians allow economic considerations to blur their spiritual vision than are deflected from high purpose by any other cause. Jesus never found fault with rich men because they were rich, but because they had not brought their riches under the authority of any great major purpose. The apostle Paul said it was *the love of money,* not money itself, that was the root of all evil.

Christian stewardship is that focusing of life which brings all of one's possessions, economic concerns, and financial management under subjection to the dominant desire to do the will of God. The Baptist was that kind of person.

⁴⁶ *Nathanael said to him, "Can anything good come out of Naza-*
reth?" Philip said to him, "Come and see."

AT ONE TIME he had seriously considered entering the ministry, but
circumstances deflected him from that purpose; to satisfy his inner
sense of mission, he therefore determined to become a faithful
layman. He taught a Sunday-school class, served on the official body
of his local church, and went as a delegate to two or three national
conferences of his denomination.

"I have made it a rule to tithe my income, for I learned that from
my father," he confided to a friend. "But I have the feeling that there
is something more I should undertake. A visit with a preacher friend
of mine has almost convinced me that I should tithe my time."

This had the effect of starting a serious conversation between two
Christian laymen that resulted in the tither's extending his covenant
to include his time as well as his possessions. Later in the day he
instructed his secretary to make no appointments for him to see
business callers on Tuesday afternoon and evening after three o'clock.
Still later in the same day he handed his secretary three names of
business acquaintances saying, "Make appointments with these men
if you can, and tell them I do not want to sell them any life insurance."

The following Tuesday afternoon he set out precisely as though he
were going to meet an insurance prospect. Instead, however, he
called on men with whom he had had business dealings for years and
with whom he had never discussed religion. With the same direct-
ness and winsome manner that had made him a top flight salesman,
he presented the case for Jesus Christ. When he returned home late
that night, he announced to his wife: "Well, I landed one of them."
The next Sunday he stood sponsoring an entire family as they came
into the church on confession of faith.

As a part of his victory he had persuaded the new convert to tithe
his income and help with the personal work. The next week the two
of them went together, and soon there were two teams of personal
workers.

No pastor or committee ever gave them any names or directions.
They used their own judgment, made their own contacts, and
followed their own leadings. Within the space of one year they had
brought more than one hundred new members and in excess of
$12,000 into the work of the church.

Suppose Protestantism—all the denominations combined—had
ten thousand such tithers of possessions, time, and talent.

JESUS' SHARING of the wedding festivities in Cana is but a foreshadowing of the very intimate relationship that the Christian Church bears to the Christian home, and the sober responsibility the Christian pastor owes to those for whom he officiates in this most intimate human ceremonial.

"In my forty years' experience in dealing with marital difficulties," said an old veteran clergyman, "I have discovered that at least 90 per cent of the trouble is traceable to either sex or money. One of the most common causes of dissension is the question of how the family funds are to be handled.

"One of the mistakes the average couple make in this connection is their failure to come to a clear understanding of what their bills are to be, whose duty it is to be to attend to them, what budgeted items each is responsible for, and how the personal bills of each are to be paid.

"The average girl who stands before me the night of the wedding has been a wage earner, in some cases for several years. She has become accustomed to a certain independence in handling her own earnings, and is usually as expert in handling funds as the young man is.

"If I can persuade these young people to set up their family finance on the basis of a sincere stewardship, with a definite amount set aside for contributions to religious and charitable giving, I feel that I have done much to insure the success of their matrimonial venture.

"When I have persuaded the young couple to view all of their income and possessions as a stewardship, under which they are responsible to God for administering their funds for the advancement of the kingdom of God on earth, including their own care and comfort, I have removed the first great cause of dissension, which is selfish fear.

"On numerous occasions I have had the satisfaction of seeing the spirit of discord driven entirely out of the home when I have been able to persuade the husband and wife to view all their possessions as a sacred trust received from their heavenly Father. Such a philosophy has the effect of preventing either of the two talking about 'my money' and 'my rights.' There is something very sanctifying about two people sitting down together to figure out the accounts and reckoning up 'God's share.' It means that neither says, 'This week I am going to get mine.'"

¹⁶ *He told those who sold the pigeons, "Take these things away; you shall not make my Father's house a house of trade."*

IT IS UNFORTUNATE that the facts underlying the episode of Jesus' cleansing of the Temple are almost completely unknown to the average reader of the New Testament. As a consequence the incident has been given many bizarre interpretations by some very good people.

As a result of the machinations of Herod the Great (a half-Jew) the management of the Temple and its services had fallen in large part under the control of the Sadducees, a political party consisting of some three thousand aristocrats, money-lenders, and landlords who made their home in Jerusalem. They were a compact group, utterly ruthless, allied for their mutual economic advantage.

One of their number, a wealthy schemer named Annas, had contrived to have himself named high priest; and by means of an annual bribe to Caesar, he had been able to perpetuate himself, his sons, or his son-in-law in office through a period of many years.

By an adroit use of the Sanhedrin, which was packed with Sadducees, Annas had been able to monopolize the sale of pigeons, sheep, rams, oxen, and all other animals used in the Temple services. He had even engineered the passage of a rule requiring that the wood burned on the altars should be of a certain sort, and he was the only man among the Jews who was able to supply it. This he did at a handsome profit to himself.

To one son he assigned the sheep concession, to another the ox concession, and to still another the privilege of managing the money changing. This in itself was a highly lucrative business, for no Roman coinage was permitted inside the Temple area, it being adjudged loathsome because it bore the image of Caesar; and nothing resembling a graven image could be tolerated inside the sacred precincts. The entire system produced an enormous annual revenue for which Annas was under no accounting obligation.

There is something very evil about the man or the party that uses sacred things for private profit. To be entrusted with the management of holy affairs is to be assigned a stewardship of the utmost importance. The church treasurer, the chairman of the finance committee, and the spender of trust funds are called of God as stewards of sanctities.

³ Jesus answered him, "Truly, truly, I say to you, unless one is born anew, he cannot see the kingdom of God."

NICODEMUS WAS one of the leading laymen among the Jews. As a member of the Sanhedrin his name commanded respect among all classes. His vote inside the body was vested with great authority. That he must have been a man of some wealth seems almost certain, for otherwise he could hardly have been found in such company. That he was educated and cultured goes without saying. Only such a one could have aspired to the post he filled.

It seems evident that Nicodemus was a spiritually-minded man from the fact that he sensed something in Jesus' words and acts that suggested divine power. He probably would have been a superb host, a charming conversationalist, and a skillful debator. Because of his official position his favor was courted by everyone.

All this, however, constituted an actual handicap when he came to deal with Jesus; for to have become a disciple he would have been under the necessity of breaking so many ties. He risked a good deal as it was. Annas and Caiaphas, plotting Jesus' execution, would have stopped at nothing if the old Sanhedrinist had gone over to the Galilean.

Matthew, the taxgatherer, could turn his back on a fortune and a future; but Nicodemus, the Sanhedrinist, must break with his social ties and honors. It sometimes calls for more consecration to give ourselves than it does to give our money. Matthew occupied a social status at the foot of the ladder for tax collectors were everywhere despised. Nicodemus, on the other hand, was a man who had arrived and who enjoyed honors and prestige. To turn his back on the Sanhedrin and all it implied called for heroic devotion of the first order.

A prominent businessman of a great American city became genuinely interested in religion and went to call on a clergyman to inquire concerning the way of salvation. When he discovered that it was going to be necessary for him to cut loose from certain "connections" in order to be a genuine disciple, he found it impossible to bring himself to the decision. In a terrible soul struggle he discovered that he belonged to his advantages. That was his trouble; he belonged to so many other things that he could not make the break.

Nicodemus was in one of the most difficult positions of any man who ever inquired of Jesus concerning the way of life.

¹⁰ *Jesus answered him, "Are you a teacher of Israel, and yet you do not understand this?"*

TIME, TRADITION, and Christian preaching in general have not dealt altogether fairly with Nicodemus, the highly respected Sanhedrinist who, according to the story told by the Beloved Disciple, came to Jesus by night. The cautious old scholar has been called a coward who was unable or unwilling to stand up in public and defend his real convictions.

At a later date Nicodemus is reported to have been associated with Joseph of Arimathea in providing for Jesus' burial. It is said that Joseph believed in the Galilean "secretly, for fear of the Jews" (John 19:39), and on the theory of guilt by association the old Sanhedrinist has been adjudged a coward. But nothing in the record supports this charge except that he "came to Jesus by night" (John 3:2), a fact that can be explained fully on other grounds.

It must not be forgotten that Nicodemus occupied a position of great authority and influence. He was learned in the law, a man of wealth, a venerated citizen, and a leader of the people. To him had been assigned great spiritual and civil responsibilities. His position required that he proceed with caution, for he was not a private citizen and his acts were therefore not private actions.

Jesus was creating a furor, and the Jews were at all times a yeasty people. It would have been a serious matter indeed if Nicodemus had lent his name to an impostor, but to condemn him on any other basis than that of facts would have been to betray himself as well as Jesus and the people. It can be nothing less than evidence of his independence of mind and conscience that he undertook to get the facts directly from Jesus himself.

Any Christian, whether he be a leader or a humble follower, is under a solemn obligation to exercise his influence with godly care. This means, of course, that one must inspect his contributions with the same careful scrutiny that he would inspect his theology. To be guilty of turning funds over to unworthy organizations or unchristian purposes is as certainly a sacrilege as to indulge in actual profanity.

To lend one's money to a questionable cause is a little like lending one's name. The honorable man does not do it carelessly.

Every man is the steward of his influence. Money being one expression of personality, one must therefore give "as unto the Lord." A cause we cannot pray for is one no Christian should help pay for.

[16] God so loved the world that he gave his only Son, that whoever believes in him should not perish but have eternal life.

THIS VERSE has been called "the entire gospel" on a good many occasions. It more perfectly expresses the whole Christian message than any other verse in all the Scripture. The universality of the gospel is in it; the amazing love of God is in it; and the hope of the world is in it. But the most revolutionary word in the text is that simple monosyllable "gave." It is the watchword of Christianity.

It is rather remarkable that Jesus, in all the conversations he had with men concerning God, never gave any description of the conference that must have gone on preliminary to his coming into the world. But this verse states very plainly that God took the initiative. His was an entirely free decision in which he was influenced by but a single purpose or motive. He *loved* the world and, as a consequence, gave it the incomparable gift of his Son, Jesus Christ.

It would have been impossible for man to have persuaded the Father to send the Son if that had not been his loving purpose. And there was little in the record of the race up to that time which might have induced him to show it such a favor. Only a God who loved humanity with a divine love could ever have been prevailed upon to make such an effort to redeem the human race.

He who lives as a reluctant Christian—giving his time, his talent, his life, or his possessions grudgingly—is one who has never actually realized the significance of God's love for mankind or the sacredness of the act of giving.

That service which is given thoughtlessly or carelessly is something of a sacrilege; that gift which does not represent genuine devotion provides the giver with small satisfaction. Unless giving can be spiritualized, it becomes a terrible burden.

There is a very real sense in which it can be said that the way we give is an index of our understanding and appreciation of God's gift to us. He who senses the divine quality of God's love as that love was expressed in the Incarnation does not need to be urged to give. The awareness of the grace of God is sufficient compulsion.

It is significant that God's love for man resulted in a gift to man. Genuine love is like this. It never asks "Am I getting all I deserve?" but "Am I giving all I can?" That love which expresses itself only in fine phrases is a low grade of love, even though it may be very artistic or literary.

CAPITALIZING ON CATASTROPHES
' *He had to pass through Samaria.*

Two ROUTES led from the fords of the Jordan back to Galilee. One of them, following along the east side of the course of the river, was safe but rough. The other, better traveled, led through Samaria; but, while it was much more comfortable, it was also much more hazardous. Jesus found it necessary to take the dangerous way back home.

Even strict piety does not protect us against all the hazards of life. Righteousness does not immunize us against pain or rise as a barrier against all catastrophes. Good people have to pass through their Samarias; the test of their faith comes in the way they make the journey. Such experiences can become highly profitable or extremely disastrous. It depends upon the individual and the way he makes use of his religious faith, what his Samarias do to him.

"I am going to cut my pledge to the Church, in spite of my every desire not to do so," a highly responsible businessman said to his pastor in the midst of the depression. "I am a tither, as you know, and the reverses I have suffered in my business have been so severe that I find myself quite unable to continue my ten dollars a week. In fact, as I study the situation I face just now, I think I am stretching a point when I repledge at the rate of one dollar a week. But we will try it out on that basis for a few weeks and see what happens.

"But I want you to remember that my lonely dollar represents my tenth and my stewardship just as certainly as my ten dollars did. It appears to me that God either does not trust me with as much as he once did, or that he is relieving me of some of the responsibility he once laid upon me."

Two years later that same businessman came back to his pastor, saying, "I think I can now restore my pledge to the ten-dollar level. Matters are going better for me financially. But they will never go better for me spiritually than they did during those days when I had to scrimp to give one dollar a week. I think my determination to go on tithing when my income was down was the greatest spiritual victory I have ever won. I do not believe I shall ever be afraid of anything after this."

In considering this text let us remember that Jesus was under the necessity of going *through* Samaria, not merely to Samaria. There is always a way *out* for the man of faith.

³ *In these lay a multitude of invalids, blind, lame, paralyzed.*

THE POPULAR philosophy expressed in the proverb, "Every man for himself," has come in for no little criticism at the hands of Christian commentators, as well it should. It is a fact, of course, that the apostle Paul once said, "Each man will have to bear his own load" (Gal. 6:5); but only three verses earlier in the same chapter he said, "Bear one another's burdens." Jesus made a great point of the fact that he would always accept the service rendered to the needy as a service rendered to him (Matt. 25:40).

It would be unfair to say that the people of Jerusalem were callous or brutal. As a matter of fact a very great deal of charity was shown to the unfortunates of the city by those who were fortunate. But the streets of the town were infested with beggars, the blind, the lame, and the afflicted—all of whom clamored for alms. And no one had ever made it his business to see that relief was extended in any systematic or organized fashion.

It was commonly believed that anyone stricken with certain diseases might be cured if he could be thrust into the pool near the sheep gate at the precise moment that the water was "troubled." There seems to have been some kind of mineral quality in the water that did have an actually beneficial effect. The poor wretch of this story had lain at the gate, almost within reach of the pool, for years without anyone offering to help him at the critical moment. It was all very pathetic.

The amount of emotional giving in this world is very great. It is relatively easy to appeal to the public for help in an emergency, and some of the outpourings are thrilling indeed. But the best giving is that which proceeds according to a plan carefully devised and consistently maintained.

The bitterest charge that can be made against us is not that we are niggardly, but that we are preoccupied. The good steward is one who makes a business of his helpfulness, who offers assistance on a systematic basis, who plans sufficiently in advance to be most effective.

The sin of the crowds that frequented the Temple was not that they were ungodly, but that they were thoughtless; they were not vicious but self-centered. Few of us go to the house of God without passing someone in need.

IT IS HIGHLY improbable that Philip ever realized the significance of that chance meeting with a little company of Greeks who came, saying, "Sir, we wish to see Jesus." Quiet-mannered man that he was, it is not likely that it ever occurred to him that he was in that moment the prototype of the millions of Christians who were to come after him and to whom the same query would be put.

This is the most searching question that can be put to a Christian. To the railroad engineer, for example, it means that the non-Christian says, "Sir, let me see how a Christian would run a locomotive." To a merchant the world says, "Let us see how Jesus would run a store."

But even more to the point is this question that the non-Christian world might put to the individual Christian: "Let me see how you spend your money."

The answer that the Church of Jesus Christ is giving to this intimate inquiry is not too encouraging. Of course Christian givers represent the hard core of generosity that supports every Red Cross, Community Chest, social agency, and relief program. It is the money that has been touched by the spirit of Jesus Christ that provides social settlements, private hospitals, many colleges, and other institutions. The record of the Church is not all bad. Much of the best can be said. But we still fall far short of our goal as Christian stewards.

The fact that the Communists have practiced a cruel deception on a hungry and needy world does not in the least excuse us, as Christians, from our utmost in generosity. The Soviet economy taxes the workers in Russia, and everywhere else that Communism is in power, to support the most aggressive "missionary program" now in operation anywhere in the world. Everywhere the word comes back that the Communists have plenty of money for their propaganda and their infiltration schemes. Unless the Christian democracies can find some way of matching this expenditure with free gifts in behalf of the Christian missionary enterprise, we can expect to suffer defeats all along the line.

There is a very intimate connection between the Greeks who came, saying, "We wish to see Jesus" and the modern world that asks, "How serious are you about your religion?" The sacrifices we make for the faith are an index of our seriousness.

²⁵ *He who loves his life loses it, and he who hates his life in this world will keep it for eternal life.*

ONE OF THE things that makes a vital Christian faith seem difficult to many people is its frequent insistence upon a paradox.

In the book of Proverbs, for example, we read:

One man gives freely, yet grows all the richer;
another withholds what he should give, and only suffers want
(11:24)

Or, again, Jesus says, "He who loves his life loses it" (John 12:25). Many, unaware of the strange ways in which the laws of the spirit operate, turn their backs on all Christian faith saying, "It does not make sense." But history and experience unite in saying, "It *does* make sense." The proof does not lie in logic but in the acid test of experience.

The generous man finds unexpected dividends returning to him because of his generosity—satisfactions he cannot buy with any other coinage. Albert Schweitzer spends his life away in an African jungle and becomes world famous. Toyohiko Kagawa goes to live in Kobe's slums and suddenly finds himself a world citizen. John Wanamaker and J. C. Penny, devout men, engage in the most highly competitive business in the world, give one tenth of their income to religious and philanthropic institutions (to say nothing of large amounts of their time), and become merchant princes in spite of their prodigal giving.

In the midst of hard times, when they seemed quite unable to pay their current expenses, a small congregation in Cincinnati became profoundly convinced that "the law of the tithe represents the highest New Testament standard of Christian giving." As a consequence a very large proportion of the people began bringing the whole tithe of their income into the storehouse.

But they also came to another conviction. "We must give as much for others as we give for ourselves," they said, and in accordance with that resolve they assumed a responsibility for missionary work that put many of the larger congregations of the city to shame. To the astonishment of everyone (and perhaps to their own surprise) they met those enlarged obligations with comparative ease and did "something extra."

In the meantime their own congregational affairs were straightened out, all questionable money-raising schemes were abandoned, and their credit at the banks soared to an all-time high. They had discovered a basic law of the spiritual life.

[35] *By this all men will know that you are my disciples, if you have love for one another.*

STATED IN ITS simplest terms Christianity is a philosophy of love, and the Christian is measured by his loves. Jesus put it very simply: "By this all men will know that you are my disciples, if you have love for one another." The non-Christian world may have some difficulty in understanding our theology, but it can recognize our dominant desires without the slightest difficulty.

If the chief purpose of any man is to pile up treasure, then he will not keep that fact a secret very long. If his major concern is with his possessions, it will not long remain a mystery to those who live alongside him. Those of us who are ready to trade principles for profits never conceal our preferences, and by all these things we are measured both among men and by our Father in heaven.

If the chief purpose of any man is to indulge his passions, cater to his appetites, and trifle with his convictions, that is very certain to come to light the first night out, or the first week he goes off on his vacation in a strange city.

If the chief purpose of the strong man is to seize power, he will make that fact evident to all the world at the very moment he thinks he is concealing it; and if another man's dominant desire is for applause, he will always be found among the noisy and the blatant, cultivating the friendship of the superficial and allying himself with the transient and the temporary.

If, on the other hand, any man's dominant desire is to do the will of God, he will soon be discovered among the heroic, the sacrificial, and the unselfish who live with a glorious abandon. In the meantime his neighborhood will be quick to respond to his sincerity and his transparent kindliness.

There comes at least one hour in every Christian's day when any Christian love that is to be shed abroad in his neighborhood will have to be shed by him. The good name of Jesus Christ has been entrusted to the keeping of every Christian. This is a part of the genius of Christianity. By its fruits it is known. As long as the Christian Church thrusts men and women out into the life of a community, charged with the spirit of love, it need have no fear for its future. Therein is our holy responsibility. The unlovely and the selfish person is as surely a heretic as the teacher of false doctrine.

FRUITLESS VINES AND STINGY MEN   John 15:1-11

⁵ *I am vine, you are the branches. He who abides in me, and I in him, he it is that bears much fruit, for apart from me you can do nothing.*

QUITE UNLIKE the Synoptic Gospels that report forty-two parables ascribed to Jesus, the Fourth Gospel reports none. The figure of the vine employed in this scripture is, properly speaking, an allegory and not a parable.

The central theme of the allegory, quite aside from a variety of interesting implications concerning the divine nature of Christ, is that the same life-giving spirit that was in Jesus is to be found in his true disciples.

According to this allegory it should be relatively easy to identify the Christian. He is the one who displays in his daily associations with his fellows and in his attitude toward God those same spiritual characteristics that made Jesus himself unique.

If we are to accept the plain teaching of the figure of the vine, it means that the Christian is not to be identified as the one who believes certain doctrines and is able to defend them with stout and reasoned arguments. Instead, he is the one who exhibits all the familiar characteristics of the vine; and the characteristics of Jesus—love, patience, forgiveness, generosity, compassion, grace, good will, reverence, and obedience unto God—are so well known and so conspicuous that they admit of no argument.

Only a little earlier in his book (14:15) the Beloved Disciple reports Jesus as having said, "If you love me, you will keep my commandments," which is to say that the one in whose life the life-creating spirit reigns will automatically keep the Lord's commandments because he will be actuated by the same motives, purposes, interests, and desires.

There is something incongruous about a stingy Christian, just as there is about salty sugar, dry rain, level mountains, or noiseless thunder.

That person who has his generous instincts under perfect control may have a theology that is as correct as a compass; but if he does not have the spirit of generosity that characterized the spirit of Jesus, then something is wrong with his attachment to the vine. If the need of a stricken world cannot move him to compassion, as it did in the case of Jesus, then something has interfered with the spirit rushing out through the vine into him, as one of the branches. This is a simple test any man can apply even to himself.

⁷ *It is to your advantage that I go away, for if I do not go away, the Counselor will not come to you; but if I go, I will send him to you.*

ON NO SUBJECT, perhaps, has there been more confusion inside the Christian Church than in connection with the question of divine guidance. The doctrine of the Holy Spirit has been appropriated by the cults, and such bizarre and extravagant claims have been made that sensible people grow apprehensive when the subject is mentioned.

We often become confused because we are not actually endeavoring to do the will of God. More than likely we are seeking some plausible reason for not doing the divine will that is perfectly plain to us. We say we are seeking for guidance, but as a matter of truth we are seeking some escape from guidance, our duty being perfectly clear.

Dave H——— had sold more than a hundred fat hogs and nearly half as many steers at a top market price and was feeling very comfortable as he took his pew in the little country church that Sabbath morning. The world looked good to him. A missionary was to preach; Dave was interested in world affairs; and there was every promise that it would be an interesting service.

As the sermon went on, the Holy Spirit laid it upon the heart of the farmer to give; but the size of the gift suggested terrified Dave. Certainly he had never given any such amount to anything before. But he could not escape the guidance.

"I really prayed hard," he told his pastor afterward. "But I guess that what I really asked God for was some way out. I wanted a decent reason for not giving, and I could not find one. I kept saying 'Lord, show me what I ought to do,' but what I meant was 'Lord, can't we settle for a little bit less?'"

As the service went on, Dave surrendered one position after another and finally arrived at the place where he was ready to give the amount that had frightened him so badly at first. "Then the devil got after me," said he, "and told me I was making a fool of myself, and I had to do something to get rid of him. So I decided to double my gift in order to have some peace of mind. When the devil remonstrated with me, I doubled it again. I just kept on raising my bid until I was sure the Lord was satisfied and the devil was completely routed. Since that morning I have never been troubled about how much to give."

> [8] When he comes, he will convince the world of sin and of righteousness and of judgment.

THE CULTISTS and fanatics are responsible for much misunderstanding concerning the work of the Holy Spirit. They have surrounded this fundamental Christian doctrine with so much mystery, and have made so may fantastic claims, that the plain promise of Jesus' words has been lost to sight.

The help that comes to us from the Holy Spirit does not consist of some cataclysmic experience, a dream, or a mysterious vision that comes out of nowhere. Instead, it is the constant pressure from within our own souls that impels us to holy action.

There is no Christian who is not tempted to generosity every day, nor is there any Christian who is not impelled by the Holy Spirit—by some wistfulness arising within his own soul—in the direction of holy living. It is easy to dismiss such impulses as though they were merely psychological experiences without spiritual significance. The voice of conscience is often ignored because we decide it is some "silly notion." But it is very dangerous to brush aside these splendid impulses. We may be offering an affront to the Spirit of God.

"I get tired of our preacher always talking about money," said one man who suffered greatly from tightened purse strings. "I never go to church that he does not ask for money for some missionary, hospital, school, or 'crusade.' I get tired of collections. I go to church to worship God and to get away from material things."

What he was confessing, without being aware of it, was that the Holy Spirit was speaking to him through his pastor, undertaking to guide him into a finer life, a bigger world, and a greater satisfaction in living. Because he was unable to summon himself to great generosity, he was suffering spiritually. His parsimony was having the effect of making him unhappy. He never refused to give to one of God's causes that he did not leave the church a restless, irritated, dispirited Christian.

There can be exceptions, of course, but it is a pretty safe rule to assume that the Holy Spirit has something to do with the case when a need rests upon our conscience. The man who has settled the question, and is giving on some proportional basis, experiences an altogether different spiritual sensation. With him it is not "How much *must* I give?" but "How much *can* I give?"

¹⁶ *He handed him over to them to be crucified.*

A VERY considerable debate has raged about the case of Pilate, the procurator who ordered the crucifixion of Jesus. There have been those who portrayed him as an outright coward, bullied and badgered by the Jewish hierarchy into doing something against which his soul revolted. There have been others who cited the fact that he was responsible for keeping the peace and being altogether unaware of the character of the accused, that he undertook to do the sensible thing—save a riot and probably life, and maintain the orderly process of government. The Jews were always a restless people, and the task of governing them was never easy.

Of one thing, however, there is an absolute certainty. Pilate was cloaked with sufficient authority, and he had enough soldiers at his back, to have saved the life of the young prophet of Nazareth, maintained justice, and saved himself from the condemnation of the centuries.

Rome boasted that any man in the empire might expect justice, and according to the moral standards of that day Caesar achieved no little success in the matter. The law and the legions went together, and Pilate had both. The good name of the empire rested with him and his administration of justice. So far as Palestine was concerned, *he was the empire.*

Any man who exercises authority over other men must accept responsibility for the measure of welfare they enjoy. The employer is responsible for so much more than the wages he pays to his employees; the landlord is responsible for so much more than the shelter he rents to his tenants; the worker is responsible for so much more than the eight hours a day he stands in his place in the shop.

The economists all agree that money is power. This means that the individual with even as much as one dollar in his pocket is in a position to exercise power. He can command services, possess property, build barriers, and exert some authority.

The money we control represents at least one measure of the responsibility we owe to God and to society. Our stewardship includes so very much more than responsibility for making contributions to good causes; it involves also the uses to which we put the money we employ as our agent. In that spot on which we stand, we are the sole representative of the kingdom of God.

[17] Peter was grieved because he said to him the third time, "Do you love me?" And he said to him, "Lord, you know everything; you know that I love you."

THERE IS NO more interesting spiritual case study in all the New Testament than that of Peter, who was transformed by the resurrection of Jesus. Between Simon, son of John, and Peter, the rock man of Pentecost, there is an almost immeasurable distance.

Reading between the lines of the book of Acts, we discover something of the secret of the old fisherman. In the course of his spiritual climb he threw all discretion to the winds and lived with abandon as a Christian. After the humiliating scene at the door of the judgment hall when he denied his Lord, his life moved over to an entirely new center from which he was never dislodged.

It is this new center that develops as a result of the transformed life to which every true Christian is expected to aspire. Jesus was speaking about it when he declared that "no one can serve two masters" (Matt. 6:24).

A young man just out of college and barely launched on a professional career went to a church service one morning and chanced to hear a sermon on tithing. Like many another youth he had maintained a more or less contemptuous attitude toward religion and a definitely critical attitude toward the Church. But the logic with which the preacher discussed the question of the tenth, and the earnest assurance he offered of spiritual values to be achieved by tithing, had the effect of arousing in him a profound interest. "If religion is good, then it ought to be good all the way," he said to himself. It is not ordinarily expected that a sermon on the subject of money would be the means of the conversion of a non-Christian, but that is exactly what happened in the case of this youth.

The first thing he did was to sit down and figure out what his income really was. Since he drew from four or five different sources, this meant that he made the first really systematic survey of his finances. In the process of figuring out what his income was, he suddenly found himself confronted with a serious question as to the legitimacy of his claim on certain funds. Having vowed his tithe, he found himself looking at money through entirely new eyes. For the first time in his life he began keeping accurate records. This led to more careful spending. After three years of such tithing he reported to his pastor, "That vow to pay my tenth has been my economic salvation. It has actually made a businessman out of me." Good stewardship has that effect.

[8] *You shall be my witnesses in Jerusalem and in all Judea and Samaria and to the end of the earth.*

AN AMERICAN clergyman was picking his way down the main street of a Polish village only a few weeks following the cessation of hostilities in Europe. The little town had been terribly battered by gunfire, and the road was littered with débris and fallen walls.

At one point, as the preacher and his interpreter were clambering over a pile of rubble that blocked the doorway of what had been the town hall, they came upon a little group of men who were trying to clear away the entrance and restore some semblance of order. The villagers were very evidently interested in the American and watched his every movement with great gravity. When the two of them were fifty feet or more along their way, the interpreter said, "I wish you could have understood what one of those men said about you as you passed."

"What did he say?" the preacher asked, greatly interested.

"You must remember," the interpreter said, "that you are the first American these men have seen for perhaps as much as ten years. You may have been the first American one or two of them have ever seen. That is why I was sure you would be interested in knowing that one of them said, 'There goes the United States.' You see, you are all they know about the Americans."

There is the doctrine of stewardship in a nutshell. Every time a Christian goes down the street, someone has the right to say, "There goes the Church of Jesus Christ." All they know about the Church is what they see in the Christians.

"I never walked more carefully in my life than I did for the next hundred yards," said the preacher, "knowing that the eyes of those men were upon me and that they were judging my country by me."

When a Christian spends his money, it is the Church of Jesus Christ spending. When a Christian hears an appeal for help, it is the Church hearing the cry of the suffering and the stricken. When a Christian gives to the Community Chest, the Red Cross, or a hospital drive, it is the Church in action. When a Christian goes to the dog races and wagers his money, he is the Church squandering God's money and betraying God's confidence.

The habits into which we allow ourselves to drift either honor or dishonor our Lord. Our conversation glorifies him or shames him; for when we talk, there is at least one small circle in which we are the only voice the Church has with which to speak.

⁴⁰ He testified with many other words and exhorted them, saying,
"Save yourselves from this crooked generation."

ONE CANNOT read the Acts of the Apostles or the Pauline epistles
without being impressed by the fact that those first-century Christians were expected, and attempted to be a kind of people entirely
different from the pagans among whom they lived and with whom
they were required to do business every day. If they were members
of the Christian Church, they were required to live according to an
entirely different set of standards.

In writing to the Corinthians Christians Paul said, "We are the
aroma of Christ" (II Cor. 2:15). If there were to be any of the
fragrance of Christ in the wicked metropolis, the Christians would
have to supply it. This meant that they would be, in a very
real sense, strangers in their own home town, aliens in the midst
of godlessness and lechery.

On the day of Pentecost the Old Fisherman challenged his hearers to *save themselves* from the world in which they lived. He
promised no miracle. They would have to make the supreme effort
of their lives on their own behalf. And this challenge continues
with us unto this very day.

Rare indeed is the Christian who will admit any friendliness for
Communism, but literally millions of Christians are spiritually ill
as a result of the virus of materialism that is the essence of Communism. Karl Marx's basic theory of the economic determinism of
history is universally repudiated inside the Church as a matter of
theory but widely accepted as a matter of practice. "A man has to
live, you know" is the way some of us express it, and "Your purse
is your best friend" is the language of others.

A tide of materialism is engulfing us as a nation and as a generation, so that in the widespread secularism literally millions of
disciples of the Lord Jesus are mired down. Advertisers spend huge
sums every year to convince us that life can be made out of gadgets,
possessions, cosmetics, glamor, and gin. In the face of popular
immoralities and obscenities it becomes the responsibility of the
Christian to save himself from the crooked thinking and the futile
hopes of materialism.

The Christian must shake himself loose from the sophistication,
the profanities, and the secular obsessions of this generation. We
cannot expect any miracle at this point. We must save ourselves.
We are the only ones who can do it, and God will help us.

45 They sold their possessions and goods and distributed them to all, as any had need.

WITHIN THE space of a few days following the transforming ex-experience of Pentecost, the infant Christian Church was compelled to venture into the field of economics.

The resurrection of Jesus had the effect of catching the Christians off guard. They had heard hints from Jesus concerning earth-shaking events that were to take place following his crucifixion, but they were altogether unprepared for the miracle of his reappearance among them alive. His assurances that he would return—assurances that were veiled in some obscurity—raised the hope that his second coming might be expected immediately. For men to be engrossed in property matters under such circumstances was inconceivable.

Large numbers of pilgrims, coming from the ends of the empire, had crowded into the city to participate in the Temple festivities, so that the problem of food and care was a serious one. Many of these visitors had been converted under Peter's preaching and the sub-sequent zeal of the Christians, with the result that the original band of believers suddenly found themselves under serious pressure to provide care for their new comrades.

Because of the expectation of Jesus' immediate reappearance, and the overshadowing importance of their new faith, it was easy to persuade themselves that all their resources must be thrown into the enterprise without either caution or reserve. They therefore adopted the expedient of putting everything into a common treasury with all drawing their support from the common fund.

It was a supreme act of faith quite without any philosophic or economic implications. The Church had no thought of introducing any new social system into the world's life. Their method was com-munal ownership with no communistic philosophy associated with it whatever. Those who participated in the plan did so on a purely voluntary basis (Acts 4:36-37–5:4), sharing without compulsion of any kind. The terrible fate of Ananias and his wife Sapphira befell them not because they did not enter the scheme wholeheartedly, but because they deceived the brethren with lies.

The basic doctrine of the Christians relative to property was not a social theory but an expression of profound faith. All possessions came from God, they believed, and each individual was responsible to him for the employment of any economic goods in his possession. It was that simple.

THE CHURCH IS A FELLOWSHIP Acts 2:46-47

⁴⁶ Day by day, attending the temple together and breaking bread in their homes, they partook of food with glad and generous hearts.

MINORITIES ENJOY at least one advantage: the spirit of fellowship is usually very strong among them. If it is not, they soon pass out of existence.

Some of the smaller denominations, for example, are knitted together by ties and loyalties that put the larger denominations to shame. Sometimes these loyalties are a product of the struggle the group has made to defend its peculiar doctrines; sometimes they result from oddities of dress, speech, or manner of worship. In the case of the Quakers, as well as several other bodies, this loyalty is an outgrowth of a certain aloofness from "the world."

Among all groups in which the spirit of coherence is strong, there is something that resembles very closely the ties that bound the first-century Church together. The maintenance of the fellowship was of prime importance. Every individual held himself responsible for the good name and peace of all. Among the early Methodists John Wesley had a class of minor officials whom he called "class leaders." It was their business to call upon each member committed to their spiritual care, inquire after his spiritual health, enlist the aid of the society if there were need of material assistance, and otherwise bind the individual to the group. The resulting sense of unity was very strong and explains in considerable part the phenomenal growth of the denomination.

No small part of the ineffectiveness of the modern Christian Church is due to our neglect of the fellowship. Charitable work is administered by secular agencies with the result that the chief concern for the poor, the sick, and the stricken of any community is expressed by the visiting nurse, the case workers, and the probation officer.

A profound respect for the fellowship and a concern for the spiritual nurture and growth of the individual will restore much vitality to the modern Church. Anything that tends to weaken or destroy the spirit of unity among believers is a sin in the sight of God and a crime against the cause as serious as any heresy might be.

To raise funds for the physical relief of the needy earns the gratitude of God; and when the spirit of fellowship is expressed in personal service among the poor, our Lord says, "you did it unto me."

² With his wife's knowledge he kept back some of the proceeds, and brought only a part and laid it at the apostles' feet.

IT IS HIGHLY important that we notice that the first break in the Christian fellowship came along the economic seam. Ananias and Sapphira did not suffer because of mistaken religious opinions, but because they could not be trusted in economic matters.

The infant Church in Jerusalem confidently expected the Lord's immediate return. The miracle of the Resurrection was so amazing that it was easy to believe that the second miracle of his quick return to complete his messianic work, which all agreed has been left unfinished, would soon appear. And if he were to return shortly, then quite obviously there was no point in the Christians' being absorbed in the usual economic activities to which they had been accustomed.

Jesus had been executed as a revolutionist. That is the plain meaning of the superscription on his cross. Quite naturally, as friends of a crucified pretender to the Jewish throne, the Christians were everywhere suspect both by the Jews and by the Romans. One single misstep on the part of any one of them could very easily have jeopardized the safety of all. Their very survival depended upon their ability to trust one another and to be trusted.

In anticipation of the early return of Jesus the Christians put all their possessions into a common fund, it being quite confidently expected that there was a sufficient amount in the total to provide for their material necessities during the time that would intervene between Jesus' ascension and his return. They had no thought of inaugurating any new economic order. Christianity did not teach the communal system. It was no more than a temporary expedient.

Two of the Christians, Ananias and Sapphira, could not bring themselves to trust the movement to the limit. They sold a piece of property and put a part of the proceeds into the common fund and then hid the rest away "just in case." By this act they betrayed a divided mind, a partial loyalty, a quality of character that indicated danger for the entire community. If they could not trust and be trusted in economics, then they could not be trusted to be loyal to the whole community in the event that Rome began to put on the pressure. It was not the communal system that Peter insisted upon, but an attitude of complete trustworthiness.

[1] *In these days when the disciples were increasing in number, the Hellenists murmured against the Hebrews because their widows were neglected in the daily distribution.*

IT IS MORE than a little embarrassing, but not in the least surprising, to discover that the first quarrel with which the infant Christian Church was bedeviled rooted down in an economic situation. It involved the material relief of a group of members, particularly widows.

In almost every city of importance in the Roman Empire there was at least a small colony of Jews. They were Greeks in everything except blood and religion, very few of them ever having lived in Palestine and the vast majority of them having been born outside the Promised Land in the midst of the Greek culture. To them was given the name "Hellenists."

Among them were some of the most devout and spiritually minded Jews of all the world. Their occasional visits to the Temple on the celebration of the national feasts were great spiritual adventures. Being removed from the Temple and its ritualism and ceremonialism, many of them had developed a deep spiritual interest; and to them the preaching of Peter had appealed with great power on Pentecost.

Because they usually spoke Greek, because they were actually citizens from an outside world, and because their ties to the Temple were attenuated, they were looked upon by many of the Jews as though they were aliens; and this spirit was carried over into the young Christian Church. Because those first Christians lived in a highly rarefied atmosphere, expecting the speedy return of Jesus, their physical necessities became acute very early, and the little congregation therefore set up some kind of primitive system for administering relief.

Within a short time someone objected to the way the system was working, declaring that the widows of some Hellenists were not getting their due. For a time it appeared that the dispute might have serious consequences, but in the end the matter was adjusted amicably. The secret of the settlement lay in the fact that wise and devout men were chosen, that everyone showed a willingness to concede a point, that no one fought for a principle until he wrecked the meeting, and that the supreme cause was held to its primal position. It was a very smart piece of administration, but it was also a fine exhibition of stewardship.

[21] *All who heard him were amazed, and said, "Is not this the man who made havoc in Jerusalem of those who called on this name?"*

THE DAMASCUS Christians were greatly confused. Evil reports had come to them concerning this young Pharisee named Saul. His hatred of all things Christian had earned for him a reputation for ferocity, and here he was standing in the market places and preaching the Christian message with such effectiveness that even the most convinced and stubborn-minded Jews were listening to him respectfully. It was an incredible situation.

This, however, is a part of the miracle called Christianity. There is no logic in the fact that a Man who died upon a cross has brought so large a part of the world to its knees before him, and that he set out from that cross to take all the world captive. It is impossible to fit the life and teachings of Jesus into any conventional pattern of philosophy. All patterns are too small for either Jesus or the program he proposed for the world.

The spiritual life does not conform to either physical or intellectual laws. It conforms to laws all its own. That is the reason one cannot accept reason and logic as the final measurements.

It does not make sense, for example, to say that human nature can be changed. But that is exactly what the spirit of Christ has been doing for warped and twisted human souls from the beginning. Take the transformations of Peter and Paul as illustrations. Nothing in science or philosophy can account for the changes brought about within them. They are miracles.

"It doesn't make sense," the young lawyer said to his pastor. "Nine tenths cannot possibly go as far as ten tenths will. There is nothing in economics that will justify it." And being a young man dedicated by the basic philosophy of his profession to respect facts, it seemed like proof positive. But when he accepted his pastor's proposition and tithed conscientiously and faithfully through a period of six months, he came back with a humble confession. "I do not know how it has happened. My mathematics does not seem to come out right. We have lived better on the nine tenths than we did on the ten tenths. I said it did not make sense. I still say so. But it works."

So many things God does do not make sense to us, limited as we are in our concepts and our vision. It sounds like foolishness to say that he who saves his life will lose it. But that is what is happening to people all about us. Life in the hands of God seems to be obedient to a higher logic.

STEWARDS IN MINOR MATTERS Acts 11:25-26

[25] *Barnabas went to Tarsus to look for Saul.*

THERE ARE few more interesting characters in the New Testament than Barnabas, and he owes his place in the record to his ability to play second fiddle with enthusiasm. There is no "Gospel According to Barnabas"; and so far as the evidence shows, no church ever bore his name. No letter addressed to him ever achieved the status of scripture. But the first-century Christian Church would have been vastly poorer if he had not been numbered among the brethren. He was a faithful preacher, but, unlike his friend Paul, he was never called an apostle. His greatest service was rendered because he offered himself again and again just when someone was needed to do a piece of work in some out-of-the-way place.

Lizzie Moorman began singing in the village choir at the age of sixteen. For fifty years she attended the midweek rehearsal and the morning and evening services. Much of the time she drove in alone from her little cottage a mile outside of town in order to be at her post of duty. No one knows how many dinner parties she missed, how many personal preferences she set aside, and how much inconvenience she suffered in order to be faithful. And in all those years she never sang a solo. Then, when the fiftieth anniversary of her joining the choir came around, the village proclaimed a "Lizzie Moorman Day"; and at the age of sixty-seven she sang a solo. The entire community turned out to pay her tribute, but she said when they called on her for a few remarks, "I never thought about singing the solos. I was always satisfied if the anthem went well and the people were moved." This is true greatness.

A layman with more than the average ability to give called at the pastor's office one day, left a check for a considerable amount on his desk, and said, "There is only one condition attached to this gift. I do not want to serve on the committee that spends the money. I do not want to dictate because I am able to give. God gave me the ability to make the money, and he gave some of the rest of our people the ability to spend it for him wisely and effectively. Let all of us do the thing for which we are best fitted and the cause will be set forward. That is all any of us have the right to ask or expect."

It would be a great experience in the life of any church if, once a year, a service were held and planned in honor of the anonymous workers and givers.

Acts 11:27-30   STEWARDSHIP OF THE FELLOWSHIP

²⁹ *The disciples determined, every one according to his ability, to send relief to the brethren who lived in Judea.*

THE REALITY of any Christian's churchmanship can be measured by his concern for his fellows in the faith. Word had reached the members of Paul's churches in Europe that their Jerusalem brethren were suffering dire want as a result of a famine, and under the leadership of the great Apostle they immediately organized a relief program.

Such an exhibition of concern on behalf of people who were suffering in a distant land, thought commonplace now, was unheard of in that day. As a matter of fact, a rather hurried scanning of ancient history fails to reveal anything that could be construed as a precedent. We must acclaim the infant Christian Church for having thrust its compassion across a national boundary line to include a "foreign" people.

If Christianity is ever to take this world captive, it must do this same thing on an unprecedented scale. It is of the utmost significance that the Communists have achieved results in this regard where the Christians have failed.

In the city of Chicago many years ago a boys' club was formed, having for its slogan this remarkable motto: "If there is a boy in trouble anywhere, we are in trouble." And acting on this phrase with amazing practicability, those boys sent committees to the courts, police stations, hospitals, and schools for correction to stand beside boys in trouble. It was not a clever piece of showmanship, but a desperately serious attempt to take their slogan in earnest.

It was an exalted expression of Christian stewardship when a powerful Protestant denomination, shortly after the cessation of hostilities in Europe, took $25,000 out of its missionary funds and presented the money to the leaders of the Greek Orthodox Church in Greece with the request that it be used in training young men for the priesthood of the Church as it came to life again following the war. It is true, of course, that the theologies of the two bodies differed in many respects, but the Orthodox Church was Christ's sole representative in the stricken land and its testimony and ministry were the only Christian hope the people had. If the lines were to be held in Greece, the Greeks must be equipped to do it. There was something of the spirit of the New Testament in that modern act of the apostles.

[14] *The Lord opened her heart to give heed to what was said by Paul.*

AN UNSEEN Presence is at work in every situation where a moral issue is at stake. "something" is urging, persuading, insisting, and attempting to guide the mind of man. We may use some strange words with which to describe our impressions. We may say "I had a hunch" or "Something impressed me" or "I felt as if." But these are only clumsy ways of reporting a profound spiritual experience.

One of the basic doctrines of the Christian faith is that there is an active spirit streaming from God to man. The entire history of the Christian Church bears testimony to the fact that the thing happens. There is no other way to explain the way faith has seeped into the life of the world to transform it and redeem it.

The most dangerous attitude any man can assume is one of refusal to do the thing which that inner voice urges upon us. In a hundred ways God tempts us to be good and generous every day. He exposes us to needs; he leads us alongside the suffering and the stricken; he guides us into the midst of situations that call for a cup of cold water and—sometimes—a vigorous campaign in behalf of a pure water supply for an entire city. But of one thing we can be sure. When God lays a sense of responsibility upon us, he is dealing directly with us; and nothing can be more dangerous than to close our hearts toward God and toward the cause in which he seems to be so interested.

Even the secular-minded have an instinctive fear for the man who having been "called" to the ministry refuses to become a preacher. The secularist may have little sympathy with the Church, or with religion in general, but he will be one of the first to urge the youth who is "called" to do his duty. Such is the respect in which even the money-minded hold spiritual experiences.

In equal seriousness, when any man becomes convinced that tithing would solve the financial problems of the Church, that it would issue in an exalted type of spiritual experience, and that the responsibility of Church calls for heroic measures, then the case is perfectly clear. *God is trying to open the heart of the man thus enlightened.*

When a duty becomes perfectly plain to a Christian, it is a sure sign that he has come to a crisis in his spiritual life. To refuse the guidance of God is high tragedy. *God opens hearts.*

¹⁴ *One who heard us was a woman named Lydia, from the city of Thyatira, a seller of purple goods, who was a worshiper of God.*

THERE IS something very modern about the story of the good woman who was found at the place of prayer just outside the gate to the riverside. In tens of thousands of our Christian churches it has been the piety of a little company of devout women that has saved the day. An unaccounted number of houses of worship stand today debt-free because of the patience and the devotion of the women who have worked with trifling sums until they have become adequate totals.

Lydia seems to have been a successful businesswoman who made her way in a competitive world in which men dominated the scene. That she was a business success is evident from the fact that she was the head of a considerable household, and that she was a devout woman is evident from the fact that she hunted out a humble little spot beside the river to which some faithful souls resorted in the absence of a house of worship. Her presence on the Sabbath at the place of prayer is indicative of the basic quality of her character.

In all the wide area of the work of the Protestant churches there is probably no activity better organized than that of the women's missionary societies. The broad range of the programs, the farsighted study texts used in their Bible-study courses, and the intimate organization structures—all combine to produce exceptionally well-informed companies of Christian women.

According to the statisticians of the great life insurance companies considerably more than half of the wealth of the nation is owned by women. At least 75 per cent of all insurance benefits are paid to women. More and more women are being elected to directorates of hospitals, colleges, and similar institutions.

The day of the church supper and the ice cream social as sources of support for Christian churches is fast fading, and in its place there is coming an army of women committed to tithing as a systematic method of giving. There is value, of course, in the Christian social occasion when the membership of a church sits down to break bread together; but that value is to be found in fellowship and not in finance.

It often happens, however, that a godly woman newly bereaved finds herself faced with an entirely new problem as she faces the necessity of handling the estate alone. At such a time stewardship becomes her salvation.

[32] *And they spoke the word of the Lord to him and to all that were in his house.*

THOSE WHO undertake to bring other men into a personal experience of God through Jesus Christ work a very serious injustice upon their converts if they do not require them to face up to the economic implications of their commitment at the outset. Literally millions of Christians have assumed that they have made a complete dedication of their lives and have gone on for years in a painful, and sometimes disastrous, struggle over the question of the stewardship of their possessions. The resultant spiritual losses have been staggering.

The terrified cry of the Philippian jailer, "What must I do to be saved?" imposed an obligation upon Paul and Silas that was as serious as any the apostles ever faced. The report we have in Acts cannot possibly be more than the barest outline of the actual events and the instruction given to the terrified wretch who came stumbling out of the shaken jail. Undoubtedly the exhortation "Believe in the Lord Jesus" was amplified to include its total significance. Anything less would have produced spiritual distress for the rest of his life.

As the jailer emerged from the jail he was a thoroughly awakened man, and only the awakened ever enter into the great spiritual experience of redemption. The experience he had undergone was one that would have brought even a superficial person to his senses. Realizing the desperate plight in which he stood, he was ready to make any concession to God. The situation therefore imposed an obligation upon Paul and Silas that could not be evaded if they were to save their own souls. They had to guide him through to the complete dedication of his life and his household.

We have placed so much emphasis on statistics that we have been guilty in many instances of doing a very superficial piece of evangelism. We have not insisted that the convert search his own life thoroughly. We have not required him to adjure all those interests, habits, possessions, and attitudes that might have the effect of polluting his Christian experience. As a consequence we have millions of limping Christians in our churches.

"I never leave a new convert until he has agreed to tithe," says one layman. "If he comes through on that, he has probably come through on everything."

[25] *Nor is he served by human hands, as though he needed anything, since he himself gives to all men life and breath and everything.*

THE APOSTLE Paul had a magnificent concept of God and a profound understanding of the laws that govern the human spirit. As one reads the Pauline epistles, again and again he has the feeling that he is reading a work by some modern psychologist. In preaching to the Athenians Paul used a basic idea and put his finger squarely on a fundamental defect in paganism. "As though he [God] needed anything," he said. And then, by implication, "It is man who is in need."

It is a common thing to hear those who are responsible for the promotion of good causes plead with people to make their gifts to God, and of course all giving ought to be made as though we were giving to God. But it is a mistake to suggest that God will fail if we do not give. There may be a failure, but it will not be God's.

Paul is very careful to make it plain to the Athenians that God is no beggar, pleading for alms. Rather, he is a great God who is the master and the maker of all things, the creator of the world. If he needed anything, he could have it. But in making gifts we are serving ourselves, and we are desperately in need of the grace of giving lest our own souls die from surfeiting.

It is true that God's causes must be supported, but that is not because God is poverty stricken. It is because he has loaned all his possessions to his children. If he could only get some of them back, he could do some wonderful things with them. "I would like to do this for you," the father of the family said, "but my boy has the car and I must wait until he returns it." And some Christians are extremely inconsiderate in dealing with God's property. They leave God waiting so much of the time.

Tithing is a tangible expression by which we admit God's ownership of everything. It is our confession of our dependence upon him. It is the "earnest money" we offer as evidence of our good faith— our stewardship—in handling those funds and those possessions with which we have been entrusted. It is not that God needs the tithe, but that the tither needs to give his tenth for the sake of his own spiritual integrity.

[26] He made from one every nation of men to live on all the face of the earth, having determined allotted periods and the boundaries of their habitation.

RECENT DEVELOPMENTS in the field of nuclear science, including the atom and hydrogen bombs, make it transparently clear that man cannot go on indefinitely committed to theories of race supremacy, spheres of influence, political alliances, and armed neutrality. The only hope for the survival of humanity rests on the possibility of a spiritual victory in which a common idealism and purpose capture the hearts of all men.

The only thing in this universe more powerful than atomic energy is the force of an idea and an ideal. If we can take the races of the earth captive in the name of our Christian idealism, the survival of civilization can be assured. If that cannot be accomplished, then the sun is setting on all human history.

With the Japanese in possession of Hong Kong a group of American and British missionaries were being held as internees. Because of the general scarcity of food, they suffered from malnutrition and lack of medical care. Then it was discovered by one of the imprisoned that the members of the little group were recipients of certain special favors—not conspicuous nor considerable, but very heartening. As the days passed and the considerate attentions continued, some discreet inquiries brought to light the fact that the Japanese soldiers—very humble men in the ranks—were Christians and were using the highly restricted opportunities open to them to make the imprisonment a little more tolerable. Between the soldiers and the missionaries there was something that transcended even the stern disciplines of war.

Modern science, commerce, industry, and communication continue to make brotherhood and neighborliness more and more a necessity if the world is to survive. The only institution that is formally committed to the task of increasing the spirit of brotherhood throughout the world is the Christian Church. An investment in the missionary program of the Church is an investment in that idealism which bulwarks the foundations of our entire civilization.

The only way the races of the earth can live together in peace and good will is for all men to accept the same standard of values. One race lusting for power or economic advantage can turn the whole earth into a madhouse. Missions are very practical.

⁸ *He entered the synagogue and for three months spoke boldly, arguing and pleading about the kingdom of God. . . .*

THE APOSTLE Paul never displayed greater genius than in his zeal to establish Christian churches at the centers of the great cities of his day. The cause that can capture the cities can captivate the nation. And in no instance did his strategy take on more brilliance than when he founded the Christian congregation in Ephesus.

The ancient city of Ephesus was by all standards the most influential metropolis in western Asia. Its strategic location, its culture, and its commercial importance enabled it to dominate all the eastern end of the Mediterranean. The congregation of Christians who were converted under the ministries of Paul, Peter, and John exercised an influence throughout the Church far beyond their numerical strength. It was in Ephesus, for example, that the first collection of Christian writings was made (the Pauline epistles) in anticipation of the eventual formation of the New Testament.

Practically every American Protestant denomination faces a problem at the heart of every great American city in maintaining a church that can serve adequately the throngs that mill about it in the downtown district. With rare exceptions such churches require "missionary money" if they are to survive, and the economic pressure on the suburban churches is apt to discolor their thinking on the subject. But a frank facing of denominational stewardship will result in a strong undergirding of such pulpits for the sake of the city's redemption.

On December 7, 1941—the date of the attack on Pearl Harbor—a strong church stood in the midst of the downtown district of a great Western city. With the outbreak of the war and strict rationing of gasoline the membership found it difficult to travel great distances to worship, with the result that large numbers of members transferred their allegiance to outlying congregations. Then the usual financial problem developed and strong churchmen began to ask, "Does it pay to maintain a downtown church if it is not self-supporting?"

Ten years later, one individual discovered in twelve outlying congregations key laymen—lay leaders, financial chairmen, superintendents of Sunday schools—all of whom had been young people who lived in rooming houses in the neighborhood of the downtown church a decade earlier. They were the backbone of their respective churches. The investment had paid off.

[16] Why do you wait? Rise and be baptized, and wash away your sins, calling on his name.

THERE IS something very thrilling about enthusiasm; the ancients called it "divine fire." And the man who is blessed with the power to communicate his divine inspiration quickly finds himself in a position of leadership. It is so seldom we find individuals who are genuinely enthusiastic; there seems to be some lurking fear within the souls of men.

The stewardship of enthusiasm is one of the most solemn responsibilities of life. To become enthusiastic without having examined all the facts is to play fast and loose with the truth. To be zealous for the wrong is a sin, even though the wrong is thought to be right. Good religion demands more than good intentions; it also requires that we be thoroughly informed and well reasoned in our actions.

A devout woman who had been left, by the death of her husband, with the responsibility of administering a huge estate called on her pastor and said, "I have a lawyer to advise me as to the legality of my giving, but I need your help in choosing those causes that can be supported by good reason. I propose to give rather considerable sums of money to good causes, but I want to make my contributions with the same skill as that with which my husband amassed the fortune." And from that day on her giving represented true Christian statesmanship because she did not allow her enthusiasm to betray her into foolish or ill-advised giving.

If sincerity and zeal were all that God required of men, then Saul of Tarsus would have been as acceptable in the sight of heaven as Paul the apostle. The young Pharisee was zealous to the point of fanaticism, and enthusiastic to the point of immorality. The difference between Saul and Paul was the simple matter of the stewardship of zeal.

Merely to give to what we think is a good cause is not necessarily good stewardship. To give only to those causes and organizations that are strictly managed, adequately supervised, and fully accredited is good stewardship. To pour out one's treasure without careful preliminary examination of the sponsorship of the cause is bad religion as well as poor economics.

Evil has many enthusiastic zealots promoting its causes and seeking for benefactors. Generous giving is not enough; the good giver is the informed giver.

¹⁶ *I am not ashamed of the gospel: it is the power of God for salvation to every one who has faith, to the Jew first and also to the Greek.*

ONE CANNOT read the book of Acts without getting the feeling that those early Christians were driven by some powerful inner compulsion that made them think in world terms. There was no provincialism about them. One never meets Paul that he is not hurrying on to some other city, there to raise the Christian standard and plant a church.

In this scripture from his letter to the church in Rome we have the explanation. The Apostle was a man who lived under a profound sense of obligation to every man on the face of the earth who had not yet heard the good news that the forgiveness of God was his for the asking.

There were but two classes of people in Paul's world—the Greeks and the barbarians. The great Christian missionary drew no lines of distinction between them. Both were in need of the gospel, both were in need of redemption, and to both he was under equal obligation.

In this modern day an extremely significant fact is being forced upon us to which we are strangely indifferent. In all our discussion of the problem of Communism and the threat it poses for civilization, we have been tragically indifferent to the fact that a vast amount of the world's critical materials is in the possession of those peoples and races who have not yet come under the influence of the Christian gospel. Purely as a matter of political expediency the Christian missionary enterprise should commend itself to politicians, economists, and statesmen. For if any considerable part of the world's store of uranium—to mention but a single ore—is in the possession of a non-Christian people, it constitutes a terrible threat to the world's security.

The uses to which uranium may be put will depend upon the religious convictions and the moral standards of those people who possess it. To take such people captive for Christian idealism by way of the missionary enterprise is far less expensive and infinitely more effective than to undertake a military expedition that has the same objective. As a matter of self-preservation an investment in the Christian missionary work becomes an imperative necessity in our modern civilization.

The one center about which the world can be united is a common body of idealism, and the only way in which such a unification of the world can be achieved is by the dissemination of the Christian gospel.

[14] I am under obligation both to Greeks and to barbarians, both to the wise and to the foolish.

ONE OF THE distinguishing marks of the Christian who accepts his discipleship seriously is the concern he shows for those who are his brethren, regardless of their race or nationality. In declaring that he was "debtor both to the Greeks, and to the Barbarians" (K.J.V.), Paul the Roman citizen was declaring his concern for all non-Romans.

The true measure of our Christian experience is the radius of our love. It is an easy matter to love those of our own household and a relatively easy matter to love those of our own community (at least those who agree with us), and it is only a little more difficult to love those who are of "our kind" around the world. But the Christian doctrine of love extends our obligation to all men, even the "Barbarians."

One of the elements in the success of the Communists is the fact that Communism has succeeded in leaping across so many difficult border lines. Even though it is not true, the Communists have convinced men of color around the world that communism will remove the color ban, eliminate segregation and discrimination, and usher in an era of equity and racial good will.

Unless Christianity can convince men of color that it is equally concerned with the problem of race, and unless Christians can exhibit a concern for their brethren regardless of color, the contest for the loyalty of the colored races will go to the Communists.

Never before have the interests of all the world been so inextricably mixed up and tied together. If Christians fail anywhere, the shock is felt everywhere.

That there is an enormous work to be done in both Christian and non-Christian lands is obvious. The giving of Christians to the missionary enterprise must be increased to a scale hitherto undreamed of if the victory is to be won. But at the same time the work to be done by the followers of Jesus who stay at home is equally important. Every Christian who serves on a jury where the race issue emerges, every employer who faces the problem of employing men of color, everyone who helps to form public opinion, lives under a stewardship that is exact and unrelenting. Our missionary gifts are important, but they do not exhaust the stewardship. The "Barbarians" have a larger claim upon us as Christians.

¹³ *Contribute to the needs of the saints, practice hospitality.*

It should ever be borne in mind that Jesus did not come into the world for the purpose of establishing a new economic order. His aim was to inject a new ideal and a new motive into all of life in the confidence that these would produce a new economic order, among many other blessings.

Every social system, whether it be called free enterprise, socialism, communism, or any other name, must be judged by its fruits, and the Christian endorsement—or indictment—will be rendered according to whether or not human relations are improved or corrupted.

Any system that interferes with good will among men, that arrays one man or one class against another, that exalts property rights above human rights, that drives a wedge between the producer and the consumer or between the employer and his employee, is under the condemnation of Christ. The social or economic system (or practice) that unites men in terms of good will, brotherliness, forgiveness, and Christian charity or love may be judged to have the endorsement of Christ.

The apostle Paul usually dealt with the individual as though he were a member of a group. His letters were to congregations, and only in the rarest of instances were they addressed to persons. To him it was unthinkable that Christians could be members of the Church and not be brethren. As individuals they might be the proprietors of tent shops, as in the case of Aquila and Priscilla (Acts 18:2-3); or rulers of synagogues, as in the case of Crispus (Acts 18:8); or well-to-do householders, like Justus (Acts 18:7) or Jason of Thessalonica (Acts 17:4-9). But as members of the Church they were simply brethren between whom no distinctions were to be made.

According to Jesus big business, or big labor for that matter, cannot be called Christian if it divides men into rival groups that war upon each other or upon the public, on which both depend. Neither can they be called Christian if the mad race for economic advantage is the dominating motive. To our industrial life Jesus would say, as he said to the tempter in the wilderness, "Man shall not live by bread alone." Business is responsible also for brotherhood.

[7] None of us lives to himself, and none of us dies to himself.

IT IS DOUBTFUL if any other man of the first century could as truly have been called a world citizen as Paul. Jewish by birth, Roman as a citizen, and Greek by training and culture, he was a perfect example of the cosmopolitan mind. His travels had taken him over a large section of Europe and into every city of importance in Asia Minor. It is significant that at the very hour of his martyrdom he was planning a new journey that would have taken him to Spain, at the westernmost extremity of the then known world.

His world citizenship inspired the two great texts of this scripture. "None of us lives to himself," he said; and then to complete the observation he wrote to the Roman Christians declaring that he thought of himself as "under obligation both to Greeks and to barbarians." World citizenship was, in this case, not something to be exploited for his personal advantage, but a responsibility from which he could never escape.

Whether we like it or not, we have all become world citizens since Pearl Harbor. Modern transportation and communication, transworld air traffic, two world wars and an economic depression in one generation, the cracking of the atom and the world-wide conflict of ideologies—all these have had the effect of reducing this globe to a neighborhood. And just as a slum becomes a charge against the resources of an entire city, so a backward or an ignorant people become a charge against the progress of all the race. Oil, rubber, uranium, cotton, coal, iron, and a long list of strategic metals and minerals have suddenly become the constituent elements in the lifeblood of any industrial nation. Economy, efficiency, and a healthy laboring class anywhere are of concern to men everywhere.

The Christian missionary program, with its insistence upon the doctrines of the divinity of all humanity and the sanctity of the individual, is the most effective leaven that can be thrust into a world seething with discontent. But a democracy must always rely upon an intelligent citizenry that is ready to assume responsibility; and if the retrograde peoples of the earth are ever to carry their full share of the burden of civilization, they must be inspired with a sense of their own worth. In the last analysis this is precisely what the missionary is sent out to do. By saving the backward he helps save the forward.

² Moreover it is required of stewards that they be found trustworthy.

THE YOUNG church at Corinth, composed of a body of new believers entirely without Christian experience, had been greatly disturbed by those who had divided them. Some declared that Apollos was the final authority; others said that Peter (whom they may never have met) was of superior rank; still others claimed to have some special and unique understanding of Jesus himself. But there were those who remembered their spiritual indebtedness to Paul and continued to trust him.

In an effort to clear up the confusion the apostle wrote a letter to the congregation, assuring them that none of the apostles had created any of the Christian facts or truths, but that all of them—Peter, Apollos, Paul—were only administrators, custodians, and stewards of the mysteries of God.

Throughout the Roman world of the first century a legal title was in common use by which the executor or administrator of an estate was known. He was called a "steward." He might be appointed to that responsibility by the legal owner of the property, or he might be assigned to administer it by the empire. In either case he was held responsible for the way he managed the property.

In carrying the original Greek word over into the English, the translators (both of the King James and the Revised Standard Versions) seized upon an English word that is at once both colorful and of good repute. They say he is a "steward."

In the year 1611 when the King James Version was being translated into the common speech of the English people, the word *stigu* was used for a pen in which cattle, hogs, or sheep were kept. The word *weard* was used for the man who watched, guarded, or tended the stock in the pen. In time the two words became one, *stigweard,* and later still it was contracted into "steward." But nowhere did it lose its connotation of trust, responsibility, and duty. Also in the course of time the *stigweard,* or steward, was given greater responsibility, as he demonstrated his reliability and trustworthiness; so the word came to be used to designate the executor of an estate, the manager of a business, or the custodian of valuable property, *never the owner*.

In all such assignments, however, the steward was evaluated in terms of his faithfulness, and at this point Paul makes the distinction: "It is required of stewards that they be found trustworthy."

¹⁰ *For if any one sees you, a man of knowledge, at table in an idol's temple, might he not be encouraged, if his conscience is weak, to eat food offered to idols?*

IT IS A LITTLE difficult for the modern Christian to understand the issue that confronted the Corinthian Christians in the case of meat offered to idols, because there is so little in the life of today that is precisely parallel.

According to the pagan theology and worship the finest animals were offered as sacrifices to the heathen idols. The priests at the pagan shrines took these offerings, after they had been duly presented at the altars, and put them on sale, with the result that discriminating housewives and public eating places bought all their meat at the temples. They were, in fact, the meat markets.

For a Jew to have eaten such meat would have been an absolute violation of the Law and a complete break with his conscience. This attitude had come across into the Christian Church and was very influential with some people. Others, however, taking the honorable position that an idol had no actual spiritual existence, assumed that it was foolish to allow any such superstition to influence them. Moreover, as converted Greeks with many pagan social connections they were frequently invited guests at pagan social functions where such meat was served. And they ate of it with a good conscience.

In dealing with the problem the apostle took a position that was both sensible and sensitive. He said that, so far as he was concerned, it was no sin to eat of such meat; but out of deference to the sensitive consciences of other Christians whose spiritual immaturity he could not ignore, he abstained. He did not propose that any act of his, however innocently conceived, should be the cause for another Christian's breaking up under the pressure of paganism.

A Christian woman whose name was associated with many good works was invited to attend a theatrical performance that had the reputation for being somewhat bawdy. She excused herself by saying, "I do not think my friend would want to go." When pressed to identify her friend, she replied, very simply, "Jesus Christ." The effect was almost electric. Every other Christian woman in the group suffered an immediate and sharp attack of conscience.

There is a stewardship of social behavior that requires us to ask this simple question: "What would Jesus prefer?" The application of the principle to our expenditures is obvious.

²⁴ *When he had given thanks, he broke it, and said, "This is my body which is for you. Do this in remembrance of me."*

WHEN JESUS said "Do this in remembrance of me," he placed every Christian under a stewardship that is both solemn and inescapable. No man accepting the sacred symbols of our Lord's sacrificial death is ever there after able to escape. It is a stewardship that includes all any man is, all he owns, and all he is capable of being.

Sometime during the War Between the States a young businessman in the state of Ohio, so the story goes, found himself drafted for service in the Union Army. By the provisions of the law he might be excused from military duty if he could persuade some other man to serve in his stead, and this he was able to do. On the appointed day a neighbor marched away with the regiment to discharge his duty for him and in his stead.

Some weeks later word was received that the substitute had been killed in action, and in due time his body was returned to his home town for burial. Then it was that the young businessman went through one of the most searching hours of his life. At the funeral he took his place at the head of the casket standing guard, profoundly moved. As soon thereafter as it was possible, he had erected in the little village cemetery a worthy monument on which were inscribed the words:

IN MEMORY OF THE MAN
WHO DIED FOR ME

But his tribute did not stop there. With deep humility he assumed all the financial obligations the dead man had left behind him. He paid the few outstanding bills and made whatever provision he could to care for the aged parents of the dead soldier. For many years thereafter he lived as though he were living for two men—himself and his dead substitute. Whenever a call was made for contributions to a good cause, he made two gifts, always of equal size.

The death of his substitute placed him under an obligation from which he never escaped. "I must live for him as well as for myself," he said to an intimate friend.

There is something of this in every communion service. It is a commemoration of the death of Jesus upon the cross for every man. His sacrifice, as a substitute for us, establishes a claim upon all our time, our talents, and our possessions. Who are we to refuse the stewardship or to bargain with God?

CONCERNING THE COLLECTION   I Cor. 16:1-4

[1] Concerning the contribution for the saints: as I directed the churches of Galatia, so you also are to do.

No MORE SERIOUS mistake is ever made in a religious meeting than that of apologizing for the collection, as though it were a painful necessity, an unspiritual interruption that had no actual relationship to the act of worship. In truth it would be as logical to apologize for the pulpit prayer or the reading of the Scripture.

Money is a medium of exchange. When individuals labor, they produce goods. Some part of the product is due them in the form of wages. However, instead of the worker being paid in the goods he has produced, he is paid in money that can be exchanged for other goods he may need or want. Actually the money we have in our pocket is only the symbol of the unconsumed goods in our possession—products in which we have invested some part of our effort, strength, skill, or thought. In other words, the finished product of our labor represents an investment of our personality. Since money is the symbol of goods, it also represents an investment of personality.

When we deposit money on the collection plate in a church, we are actually putting a bit of ourselves there. Because we cannot go to the ends of the earth to preach the gospel, we send ourselves in the form of money. As a matter of fact, we are sending ourselves wherever we send our money. When we spend our money for any purpose, we are lending ourselves to that purpose; when we send money to the mission field, it means that we are hiring someone else to do the work we would do if we could go in person.

If our religion means anything whatever to us, it must surely mean that we have accepted a partnership with God in the program of extending the kingdom of Heaven on earth. If a testimony is needed at our office or in our shop, then God and the Church depend upon us for that testimony. But if a testimony is needed in the mission field, our money makes it possible to send someone who will offer his testimony in our behalf.

The money we deposit on the collection plate represents the work we want done under the auspices of the Church of Jesus Christ. To treat such an element in the service with anything less than reverence is to be guilty of shaming our Lord. To apologize for the collection is a little like apologizing for him.

² *On the first day of every week, each of you is to put something aside and store it up, as he may prosper, so that contributions need not be made when I come.*

PROBABLY IT IS safe to say that more churches bring dishonor upon their Lord by disorderly and disgraceful financial methods than by any other form of immorality.

Paul was greatly concerned in behalf of the spirit of unity inside the Christian Church. Everywhere he went, he undertook to make the Christians—whether Jews, Greeks, or Romans—feel that they were his brethren and the brethren of all other believers.

A depression and a scarcity of food in Jerusalem had reduced the population of all the city to dire straits, and the Christians were suffering along with their neighbors. To the great Apostle this presented the opportunity of a lifetime to demonstrate the solidarity of the Christian brotherhood. To that end he appealed to all churches everywhere to join in a great collection to be used in purchasing food and relieving distress. In his letter to the church in Corinth he made an appeal for orderly procedure and systematic giving.

One of the great emphases in Paul's preaching was his doctrine of liberty. He believed that Christians had been released from the legalism of the Hebrew Law, and for that reason he did not mention the matter of the tithe. Instead, he assumed that loyalty had supplanted legalism and would excel it in the practical matter of generosity. He did not, therefore, ask for a tenth, but laid it upon the heart of each person to give systematically, "as he may prosper." This would mean that some of the Christians, a bit more prosperous than others, might be expected to give even more than the tithe as an expression of their sense of Christian unity.

Paul was especially anxious that his coming should not be accompanied by any fanfare or frenzy. Perhaps he did not want the false impression to go out in the pagan city that he was profiting personally by the venture. Instead, he urged that each week, on the first day of the week, when the Christians came together for their regular worship, the gathering of gifts should be a part of the service program.

Paul's program called for system as well as enthusiasm. Methodical giving was to be at least a partial identification of the Christians' loyalty to Christ. The fact that the gifts were to be brought in and deposited as a part of the worship service identified giving with worshiping.

THE AROMA OF CHRIST   II Cor. 2:14-16

> [15] For we are the aroma of Christ to God among those who are being saved and among those who are perishing.

JESUS CALLED his disciples the "salt of the earth"; Paul called the Christians in Corinth the "aroma of Christ." Both were expressing something of the same idea. The Christian is the steward of a saving element, which, when injected into society, will save it from dissolution and depravity.

There was a time when the Christian movement could be ignored by the state for the reason that it was a weak and inconspicuous affair. Its ranks were filled with nobodies. Only on the rarest of occasions was any important person allied with the Church.

The church at Corinth, for example, was begun with two displaced persons from Rome (Acts 18:2). An unemployed tentmaker who had recently been expelled from Thessalonica (Acts 17:4-15) was the preacher who got the movement under way while working at his trade in the shop operated by the refugees. There was so little about the tiny congregation even to hint that it would someday exercise a power that would shake the city.

Yet the poor, the enslaved, and the unimportant people across the empire finally created the revolution. The Christian Church eventually proved to be the one stable thing in the empire, and this it accomplished not because it enlisted the elite and the politically powerful but because the Christians outlived the pagans—they exhibited a quality of life that surpassed paganism in every respect.

The modern Church enjoys all the advantages that were lacking in the infant Church—numbers, respectability, influence, wealth, credit, learning, and trained leadership. It lacks so many of the things the first-century Church had that made it amazingly effective —faith in ideals, confidence in the transforming power of Christ, and a profound sense of stewardship.

Our weakness seems to appear in the fact that we are unable to break through our liturgy and ritual and get out into the working world. We are confined behind stained glass. Christians who are elected to office must be trained to make the Lord the master of those offices. Christians who come into possession of wealth must be taught that they are entrusted with treasure for the dear Lord Christ's sake. Wherever any Christian is, at any time, he must think of himself as the "aroma of Christ."

¹ *Now it is superfluous for me to write to you about the offering for the saints.*

EVEN A HURRIED reading of this scripture makes it plain that Paul never insisted upon generosity. He assumed it. A religious conversion that does not provoke the converted to share his abundance—whatever that abundance may be—with those who have less is of doubtful orthodoxy.

A young preacher and his wife were holding a service in one of Chicago's missions among the poor of the city. During the preaching a shabby little old lady sat down beside the preacher's wife, not knowing who she was. In the midst of the service, it being the night following Thanksgiving, she looked into the eyes of the young woman and said, "I hope you had a good Thanksgiving."

"Yes, we did," the preacher's wife replied. And with that the little old lady went on, quite oblivious to the fact that she might be disturbing the service. It was not good decorum, of course, but she was too full of good cheer to allow any formalities to interfere with her exuberance; and the Lord was probably very well pleased even with her impoliteness.

"I had a beautiful Thanksgiving," she said. "You see, I scrub the building where the Congress Cafe is; and when I got through on Wednesday night, the cook gave me a ham bone for soup, and some left-over vegetables that he would have thrown out, and half a pie he said they would never sell. And when I was getting everything ready yesterday morning, I thought about old Meg who lives down the hall, being so crippled with rheumatism she can't hardly walk at all. So I went down and got her—and what a dinner we had, and how we laughed and joked! And when old Meg went home last night, she was singing and forgetting all about her rheumatism. I expect you had a big dinner and had a lot of folks in, but I know you didn't have as good a time as me and old Meg did."

And the preacher's wife thought about the resentment with which she had faced the fact that they could not go home for Thanksgiving, and offered a prayer of penitence while the old lady added her thin voice to the singing of the last hymn.

"I hope everyone got as much out of the sermon as I did," the old lady said as they parted for the evening, not knowing how she had provoked a preacher's wife to a more generous state of mind.

¹⁰ *They would have us remember the poor, which very thing I was eager to do.*

THE BURNING issue inside the first-century Christian Church, far more serious than the clash of modernism and fundamentalism today, was the question as to whether or not a Gentile convert was to be required to submit to the ceremony of circumcision. The Jewish wing of the Church, with headquarters in Jerusalem, declared that he must be circumcised. The Gentile wing, led by Paul, was equally determined in saying circumcision was not necessary. And for a time it appeared that the differences between the two groups might result in the wrecking of the Church.

In the historic conference described in this scripture, the rift was healed on the most sensible basis that could have been devised. Paul was to go his way, the Jewish faction was to go its way, *and all were to minister to the poor!*

The spirit of generosity and helpfulness was characteristic of the Christians everywhere, regardless of their sectarian preferences. There was something about the incoming of the Spirit of Christ into the life of a pagan which, upon the occasion of his conversion, made him different. The first thing the Philippian jailer did following his realization of the character of his prisoners was to wash their wounds (Acts 16:33). The identification of a Christian was his transformation. Callous and self-centered people became new creatures.

Dorcas, one of the early Christian saints (Acts 9:36-42), made a great reputation for herself with her program of kindliness and generosity toward the poor. She was something of a personalized Community Chest in her own right, so much so that upon the occasion of her death the women of the town came exhibiting the garments she had made for the poor. She seems to have been a very unusual person, the like of whom paganism had never seen before.

Long before the Christian Church bought any land on which to erect a house of worship, the Christian congregations were taking collections for the poor. The first "crusade" ever organized by the Christians was one designed to raise funds for the relief of the hungry and cold "saints"—their fellow Christians—in Jerusalem.

Here is something the pagan mind has been able to understand in every generation. No charge of heresy has ever been leveled at any Christian because of his generous benevolence.

² Bear one another's burdens, and so fulfil the law of Christ.

GOD HAVE mercy on the Church when the poor cease knocking at its door," said an aged and beloved priest; and in so saying, he put his finger squarely on one of the tender spots in the life of the modern Church.

We assume that we have expressed our Christian concern when we have supported the Community Chest, paid the salaries of social workers, or patronized a rummage sale. All this, of course, is a part of our Christian responsibility, but the obligation of the Church of the living Christ goes far out beyond these things if it is to follow the leadership of its Master.

Nothing becomes professional more easily than helpfulness. It is so easy to become involved in case studies, techniques, procedures, reports, and surveys. The workers are always overburdened and the board of managers is statistics minded. To keep the spirit of true compassion and at the same time to defend oneself from being imposed upon is one of the finest of the spiritual arts. Here is where the service of the Church of Christ is most needed.

So very much more than technical skill and economic assistance is needed if broken souls are to be restored. It is this "something more" that the Church has to offer. No matter how much we spend for music for the worship services, and no matter how many workers we may employ on the staff, there is still an obligation that the plain member of the congregation owes to the poor, the deserted, the confused, and the suffering members. The forgotten will rise up on the Judgment Day and testify against us.

In every congregation, no matter how small, there should be an alert committee whose business is to know about the distress that is being suffered by those of the membership who are actually in need of help. That church which is really serving the people at the point of their deepest needs will never have to worry about its future. The redeemed and rehabilitated poor will take care of that. "Save the people and they will save the Church" was the slogan of an old saint who spent many hours out of every week visiting the forgotten.

It happens so many times that our stewardship does not end when we have signed the check that is intended to pay for material relief. "Do not even the publicans the same?" (K.J.V.)

THE SIN OF COVETOUSNESS   Eph. 5:3-5

⁵ *Be sure of this, that no immoral or impure man, or one who is covetous (that is, an idolator), has any inheritance in the kingdom of Christ and of God.*

THE MODERN churchman is in dire need of discovering that in both the Old and the New Testament the sin of covetousness is set down alongside licentiousness as being equally loathsome in the sight of God.

It may come as a terrible shock to some very respectable people to read that God esteems adultery and stinginess as being equally reprehensible, but that is precisely what the Scriptures teach.

John Wesley once said, "When a man becomes a true Christian, he becomes industrious, trustworthy, and prosperous. Now, if that man, whilst he gets all he can and saves all he can, does not give all he can, I have more hope of Judas Iscariot than of that man!" Again strong words, but they come from one who knew the Scriptures and human nature as few men have. It has been said that Mr. Wesley heard more than thirty thousand people tell the stories of their religious experiences in the course of his long lifetime in the ministry, and such a background gave him the right to reach moral and spiritual judgments. His opinions concerning the hazards of stinginess are therefore well worth considering.

Not the least dangerous aspect of the sin of stinginess is the fact that the stingy man seldom hears his preacher deal forthrightly about the sin. The clergy have been so often accused of "preaching about money" that they have become sensitive on the subject and afraid of stepping on rich men's toes. As though Jesus never stepped on anyone's toes!

A further sinister aspect of stinginess is that the stingy man finds it easy to maintain a good reputation in the community in spite of his stinginess. He may deal fairly with his customers and with his employees; he may be scrupulously careful to give an honest weight and a full count; he may be a respected member of the board of directors and a man whose business interests add greatly to the economic resources of the community. But if he does not learn how to share while he learns how to accumulate, his soul is in dire peril from his possessions.

The rich man, like the great man, seems insulated from the truth. Each hears so much from those who seek favors, and so little from those who are courageous enough to condemn sin when it is committed by conspicuous sinners.

⁸ Once you were darkness, but now you are light in the Lord; walk as children of light.

MAKING A GO of life depends, first of all, not upon our ability to reduce the world about us to some kind of order but upon our ability to reduce our own inner lives to system and discipline.

A certain young couple, just setting out on their great adventure together, were faced with a succession of financial difficulties. Their income was extremely modest, and it was easy to see (at least for their relatives) that, if they succeeded financially, they would have to practice the strictest economy, something to which neither of them had ever been accustomed.

Without giving too much thought to the matter, they signed a tithing covenant when the subject was presented at a young adult gathering. Then, because they were essentially honest young folk, they agreed that the pledge must be kept. That was the beginning of a complete change in their whole financial outlook and program. They literally tried to "learn what is pleasing to the Lord."

The first Saturday night when the two of them arrived at home with their pay checks, they proceeded to set aside one tenth of the total as their pastor had instructed them. It looked like a sizable amount, and the mere act of dividing had the effect of sobering both of them. Once it was done, however, they began planning their week's expenditures in the hope of keeping inside the limits of the remaining nine tenths. After some thirty minutes of figuring, anticipating, and paring their expectations down to size, they worked out their tithing plan.

The following Saturday night they went over the accounts again and discovered to their delight that they had gotten through the week on their budget. "And I did not miss a thing. Did you?" the young husband asked his wife.

Within the space of a few weeks they had become accustomed to the practice and had their habit well under way. At the end of the first year, they had actually made a small saving for themselves and astonished all their in-laws. As they became systematic, they became successful. An orderly management of our personal affairs is always the result of faithful tithing.

There is much good religion in orderly benevolence, because it represents intelligent self-discipline, and this is the beginning of victory.

YOU ARE MY NEIGHBOR   Phil. 1:27-30

²⁷ Stand firm in one spirit, with one mind striving side by side for the faith of the gospel.

IN ONE OF the amazing vegetable-growing valleys of California there lived a white farmer whose farm adjoined that of a Japanese; but between the two there was no neighborliness. It was not that the white man treated the yellow man shamefully in any way. It was only that they did not neighbor together.

In the middle of one morning when every hour was of critical importance to the growing crop, the white man's tractor bogged down and refused to run. The farmer exhausted his wit and mechanical skill with no result. The engine would not turn over. Meanwhile, he was in a good position to lose several hundred dollars' worth of growing vegetables.

At noon he saw the little Japanese farmer coming across the field, his old straw hat flopping crazily as he jumped from row to row, avoiding the tender plants. The white farmer, sore beset by the obstinacy of his tractor, was in a bad mood to greet anyone, but he did acknowledge the neighbor's greeting—though without any particular warmth.

"Is there anything I can do to help you?" the yellow man asked, very solicitously.

"No, I am afraid not," the white man replied. "I guess it will take a better mechanic than either of us to get this engine going."

"But I have my field plowed, and my tractor will be idle. If you will permit me, I will bring it over and I will get this field tended while you take your tractor into town and have it repaired."

And that is what happened, over the rather embarrassed objections of the white farmer. When evening came, the work was done and the crop was saved. Then for the first time the white man became gentle and really kind in his attitude. "How much do I owe you?" he asked the Japanese.

The little yellow man was obviously ill at ease. "Oh, nothing at all," he said. "I could not think of taking any money from you when you are in trouble. You see, you are my neighbor, and I owe you something. I cannot let you pay me. That would not be neighborly."

In Jesus' story of the good Samaritan he asked, "Which . . . proved neighbor to the man who fell among the robbers?" (Luke 10:36.) This is a bit of fine Christian discrimination.

[10] . . . *that I may know him and the power of his resurrection, and may share his sufferings, becoming like him in his death.*

It is RELATIVELY easy to persuade men to share our Lord's triumphs; it is something quite different to persuade them to share his sufferings. A shouting host of people escorted Jesus into Jerusalem on Palm Sunday, but no more than a few women and two or three obscure disciples followed him out to Calvary.

The number of those who are being imprisoned today because they believe that Jesus is the Son of God is very small. There are, of course, those brilliant examples of martyrdom who have suffered imprisonment at the hands of the Communists because of their religious convictions, but our modern persecution does not take that direction in most cases.

There is, however, an insistent call to Christians to share in their Lord's sufferings even today. There has never been a time within the memory of man when so many of our fellow Christians have been hungry, nor can any of us remember when so many of them have lain down at night with no roof over their heads and no warm blankets for their backs. Never have so many children from Christian homes been condemned to wander on the streets and beg for food. Never has it been possible to relieve so much want with so little money.

Ignorance of the world's needs may be offered as an excuse for not sharing, but to remain ignorant in such a day as this is almost impossible. "Each breeze that sweeps the ocean" brings word from the far-off places of the agonies through which our fellow Christians are passing, and every piece of such distressing news is God's call to his people to share with him in his sufferings.

He who can live in this world without a breaking heart, and without sharing in the sufferings of those whom Jesus calls his own, shares not in the spirit of Christ, no matter what his creed may be nor how loudly he may protest his devotion to Christ.

It would be a wholesome thing for the average Christian to make a list of those conditions, even in his own home town, that would make Christ weep, and then ask himself, "As a good steward what have I done to correct any of these conditions?"

No man can be a Christian, sharing in the spirit of Christ, and be a spiritual isolationist. During the war someone said, "Hitler is where Hitlerism is"; the parallel of this statement is, "Jesus is suffering wherever his children are suffering."

THE REVISED Standard Version has thrown a brilliant bit of light on this text in reporting Paul as having said to the Colossians, "In him all things hold together." There is a great tendency for life to go to pieces in the hands of modern man. Its conflicting demands are so insistent and numerous; the pressures of life are so unrelenting; the demands of life are so contradictory; the pull and the haul of life never end.

The psychologists have much to say about split personalities, divided loyalties, inner conflicts and tensions. Civilized life is so much more complex than the primitive problems of the savage in the jungle, and the disintegrating forces are so subtle.

Paul sounds like a modern psychologist when he says, "In him all things hold together." There is something about a complete dedication of life that has the effect of restoring order.

It is not true in all instances, of course, but in many cases the conflict revolves about the question of possessions. There are those who can never hope for spiritual peace until they get out of the business in which they are engaged—a business that they are convinced cannot have the endorsement of the Holy Spirit. There are others who are well aware of the fact that they will have to re-organize their entire economic program and outlook before they can hope for "the peace of God, which passes all understanding." If the lewd must seek purity of mind, and if the hate-filled must forgive, in order to know the indwelling of Christ, then it is also true that the selfish must become generous and the self-centered must have their minds turned out upon the world if they are to share in the new life that Jesus has promised to the believer.

Just as some object is needed in some solutions to start the process of crystallization—the scientist calls it a catalyst—so Christ in a man's life acts as the center about which all of life gathers.

As a spiritual antiseptic there is nothing to compare with tithing, or some form of proportional giving. Literally tens of thousands of Christians will testify to the fact that their spiritual lives settled down to order as soon as they accepted the principle and began giving their tenth faithfully. The value of the system is not in the funds it produces but in the spiritual integration that results. The evidence in the matter is conclusive.

²³ Whatever your task, work heartily, as serving the Lord and not
men.

A HOME builder who had erected nearly a thousand houses in the
city sat next to his pastor at a dinner one evening and in the course
of the conversation said, "God called you to preach the gospel, but
I think he called me to build homes. I know that I have never built
a house in this town that I have not laid the plans down and studied
them to be sure, so far as it lay within my powers, provision would be
made for the people who lived in it to be happy. Hundreds of times
I have asked my wife, 'Will this make it easier for the woman?' And
on Sunday afternoons we sometimes go out riding just to look at
some of the places we built ten or fifteen years ago, and say to
ourselves, 'The people who have lived there all these years have
been happier because we built well.'"

Up to the moment that Jesus came out of the waters of the Jordan,
having accepted John's baptism, he had never preached a sermon,
conducted a public meeting, told a parable, or performed a miracle.
He had always been a layman, a carpenter, and a plain citizen of
Nazareth. He had spent his entire time in the carpenter shop of his
home town as a workman and as an employer. But he must have
been a very splendid person in all those capacities to have earned
the high praise that was bestowed upon him from heaven.

Toward the end of his career when the authorities were combing
the record for something to allege against him, no one came forward
with the accusation that his work had not held up or that he had
been a stern employer. His craftsmanship stood every test as did also
his business management. He was a carpenter in whom God could
find no fault.

Great piety and good craftsmanship ought always to go together.
But all too often it happens that we testify to a great religious experience, though all the community knows it has made no difference in
the type we set, the bread we bake, or the signs we paint.

There was an old blacksmith who, although never able to raise
his voice in audible prayer in a public meeting, boasted inside his
family circle that he shod horses to the glory of God and that there
was not one horse in town wearing one of his shoes that was uncomfortable on it. The temptation to do shoddy work is always an
insidious one; the temptation to make money by unscrupulous
practices is never very far away.

⁷ We were not idle when we were with you.

So OFTEN we hear the employer exhorted to practice his stewardship of his workers; but rarely is the worker exhorted to practice his stewardship in relation to his employer. However, that is exactly what the apostle Paul does in this scripture.

The meaning of the passage becomes vivid in the rendering furnished us by James Moffatt: "Brothers, we charge you in the name of our Lord Jesus Christ to shun any brother who is loafing, instead of following the rule you received from us. For you know very well how to copy us; we did not loaf in your midst, we did not take free meals from anyone; no, toiling hard at our trade, we worked night and day, so as not to be a burden to any of you. Not that we have no right to such support; it was simply to give you a pattern to copy. We used to charge you, even when we were with you, 'If a man will not work, he shall not eat.'"

Really great living rests down upon a solid base of self-respect. Any man who loafs and lives off the charity of others—the plain man calls it "mooching"—degenerates as certainly as that one who despoils his body with alcohol or his mind with hate. Every individual who has ever struggled through to the heights of magnificent manhood has done so on the basis of independence and personal effort. No soul has ever been carried up to greatness; every great one has achieved true greatness for himself.

The beginning of every man's stewardship is in the work to which he is assigned. The wages he receives for his labors, the usefulness of the product of his hands, the service rendered to society by his toil, the causes to which he may dedicate his income—these are subsequent investments of one's stewardship.

The very fact that we accept employment at the hands of another implies a stewardship that requires us to give the best we have in skill and service. There is something diabolical in the system that requires a worker to loaf in order to make work for others. The whole system of "featherbedding" is as much a violation of the ethics of Jesus as the system of exploitation of the workers practiced by the antisocial employer. Stewardship is a two-way street on which employees and employers must meet in the spirit of Christian brotherhood.

¹⁸ *They are to do good, to be rich in good deeds, liberal and generous.*

THE ACID test of any doctrine is not the logic with which it is set forth, the scripture texts that may be marshaled in its support, or even its antiquity as a religious principle. Rather it is the effect it produces inside the lives of those who believe in it. On this basis tithing makes an amazing report.

The tither believes, first of all, that God is the owner of all things and that he is a steward, charged with the responsibility of managing those goods that have come into his possession so that the work and will of God may triumph among men.

The tither believes he lives every day under a sober obligation to seek first the kingdom of God and his righteousness, dedicating his strength, his life, his possessions, and his skills to the divine purposes of God.

The tither believes that, as a child of God he has a right to depend upon the love of God under every circumstance. Believing in that love and that moral concern he is able to dedicate his possessions to the accomplishment of the purposes of God without the fear that he will himself suffer want.

The tither believes that there is a sanctity about all possessions that he must respect because they are the property of God.

The tither believes that any person in need is his brother in Christ with a claim on his generosity and his concern. This has the effect of making him a guardian of all sufferers and a steward of all justice.

The tither believes that his giving makes him a comrade of all those anywhere who suffer and lack, because they, too, are children of the same Father in heaven.

The tither believes that the story of any need is an invitation from God to share in the world's redemption.

The tither believes that money was made to be invested in creative enterprises, and not to be hoarded only for the sake of interest paid semiannually.

The tither believes God honors the tithe when it is dedicated in a spirit of humility to those causes that have the approval of Christ the crucified.

The tither believes that tithing establishes a covenant between him and God not unlike the covenant that bound Israel to Jehovah in the wilderness. It is a mutually profitable and gratifying agreement trust between God and man.

Index

254